FINDING GOD IN ALL THINGS

Finding God
in All Things

Essays in Ignatian Spirituality
Selected from *Christus* (Paris)

Translated by
WILLIAM J. YOUNG, S.J.

The Library of Living Catholic Thought

CHICAGO
HENRY REGNERY COMPANY
1958

Imprimi potest

GULIELMUS J. SCHMIDT, S.J.
Praepositus Provincialis
Provinciae Chicagiensis
21 March 1958

✠ SAMUEL CARDINAL STRITCH
Archiepiscopus Chicagiensis
12 May 1958

Library of Congress Catalog Information
CHRISTUS: *(Paris)*. Finding God in all things; essays in
Ignatian spirituality selected from Christus. Translated by
William J. Young. Chicago, H. Regnery Co., 1958. 276 p.
21 cm. (The Library of living Catholic thought).

1. Spiritual life—Catholic authors. 2. Loyola, Ignacio
de, Saint, 1491–1556. I. Young, William John, 1885– tr.
II. Title. BX2350.A1C45; 248; 58–12411 ‡

18686

Contents

Introduction

The articles presented here are selected from the first twelve numbers of *Christus,* and their purpose is practically the same as that of the review from which they were selected. *Christus* is a quarterly review edited and published by the Fathers of the French Provinces of the Society of Jesus. The founders of the review felt that St. Ignatius would have loved our times and that the peculiar temper of these times would have found his message particularly opportune. They also felt that their review would be in perfect harmony with the many religious reviews already existing and that they would all serve to enlighten each other and be a source of mutual encouragement. It was not their purpose to lay out a narrower path to the great treasure of Catholic truth or to hem it up as though within the limits of a ghetto. They wished to manifest once more the unlimited variety of grace in a common fidelity to the all-embracing love of God.

But the review was to be Ignatian, in the sense that it would endeavor to portray the inspiration of one who was not only the founder of an Order, but a teacher of undeniable originality. This was to be accomplished by a threefold effort: to throw a faithful light on the spiritual events which marked the life of Ignatius and which gradually formed in his soul and in his activity, the qualities which today we call his spirituality; to trace the scriptural and traditional currents which animated this spirituality; and to state as precisely as possible the apostolic bearing which this spirituality commands. All of this was to be done apart from learned researches in the review itself; these could be carried on by others, with profit for the editors and readers of *Christus*. The review's purpose was more modest. It was to find in St. Ignatius, according to the expression of one of his first disciples, the "light which in Christ seizes, moves and directs" to help us work more fruitfully in the Church militant.

Nor was it the purpose of the editors, on the other hand, to treat Ignatian spirituality as a whole. That had already been done in innumerable books and treatises on the Spiritual Exercises and in days of recollection, which were already widely circulated, and through the influence of Institutes and Spiritual Associations which profess to be living according to his spirit. All of these influences have contributed to the wide diffusion of the fundamental ideas contributed by St. Ignatius. But there are many who are not yet acquainted with these ideas or are afraid of them, even though our Holy Father Pope Pius XII spoke of them as being "one of the most effective instruments for the spiritual regeneration of the world."

Therefore, the purpose of the editors was, in a word, to offer a synthesis of the whole of the Ignatian spirituality. For this they looked to the collaboration of those who would be willing to work with them; whether priests or laymen.

I believe that the editors of the Library of Living Catholic Thought have in general followed the same lines in the selections they have made from the numbers of *Christus* since it first appeared in January, 1954.

English readers may notice in the articles offered here some concession to modern taste. The authors themselves do not seem to be trying to reinterpret old truths to suit a changed mentality so much as to re-present these truths in a dress that will make them more acceptable to changing tastes in the ways of thought. There is nothing in them, however, that could be interpreted as a concession to a more liberal attitude in the face of familiar truths. The tone of the articles, if anything, is more intellectual, without any surrender of the spiritual content, and will therefore have, it is hoped, a wider appeal to a reading public that has become more educated in the course of a generation or two.

The translator is very happy to take this occasion to thank Father James J. Doyle, S. J., of the West Baden theological faculty, for his generous collaboration. He has subjected most of the typescript to a thorough revision and, in addition to a number of needed corrections, has made many enlightened suggestions, most of which have been adopted. Imperfections still remaining in the text must be attributed to the translator and to him alone.

WILLIAM J. YOUNG, S.J.

PART I

God, His Glory, Love, and Service

Christus, No. 6, April 1955

Finding God in All Things

Maurice Giuliani, S.J.

It is tragic to be divided between two appeals which are equally irresistible and yet contradictory. "Thou shalt love the Lord thy God with all thy heart, with all thy soul and all thy mind," says one, creating a whole procession of images—the desert, silence, the eyes closed in solitude with God. "Thou shalt love thy neighbor as thyself," answers the other, with a cry which seems to leap from the bosom of human suffering and which will bear no longer a delay to be comforted.

An actual tragedy indeed. How many Christians live through it every day, unable to choose, less able to assure their union with God along with fidelity to their activity! But it is a tragedy in which Christians must resolutely refuse to be the victim. The second commandment is "like" to the first. The dilemma is too simple to be true, and God does not wish to be served in such constraint. The saints have borne witness to it, they who have dug deep enough into their souls to reach unity. Among them it seems to have been the particular grace of St. Ignatius to recall that the spiritual life is not, first of all, a problem of prayer or a problem of activity but a fidelity to God which demands fidelity to divine tasks. This is what we should like to show in these pages in portraying the general features of his experience, his teaching, and the spiritual lines he has laid down.

St. Ignatius is never a mere theorist. What he has to tell us is not based on a teaching, but on a personal experience which finds its guarantee in the inner certainties which accompany it. We cannot here grasp what is peculiar to his teaching on the relations between prayer and action except by first going over the stages in his itinerary in the three great periods of his spiritual life.

On the road which led him to Barcelona and Jerusalem, Ignatius stopped a day or two in the town of Manresa. Unforeseen events kept him there for almost a year. Indeed, he did not lead there the life of an anchoret. He lodged at the hospital or the convent of the Dominicans or in a friendly home. He sought the company of the poor or of "spiritual persons." In the last months, he gave himself up to a real apostolate. But he remained, nonetheless, turned towards a life of penance and prayer. He prayed, he tells us, seven hours a day on his knees, and over and above this, he devoted all the time which was not taken up in "spiritual conversations" to "thinking of the things of God."

God, was, then, Ignatius' schoolmaster, and after a few months of hard and desolate prayer, He overwhelmed him with mystical favors. Prayer was the privileged time of a union with God which was made manifest in fruits of "devotion" and "consolation."

If we can easily distinguish a progression in the course of the varied experiences through which Ignatius was then led, if the dawning of his zeal modified more and more not only his life of penance, to mitigate it, but his prayer as well, to burden it with all the appeals of the Kingdom of Christ, it is nonetheless clear that at Manresa, the pilgrim knew no other prayer than that which he practiced alone with God in the grotto, on the banks of the Cardoner, to which he liked to retire every day, in the liturgical offices and especially the Mass, or at the foot of crucifixes which marked the waysides. Prayer, in forms already varied and sown, moreover, with temptations and illusions, grew rich on its own joys and left in Ignatius "no other desire than to have God alone for refuge."

A new period began when Ignatius decided, "in order to be able to help souls," to enter on a long course of studies. From the first lessons in Latin grammar he met, almost habitually, with "a new understanding of spiritual things and new consolations" which flooded his soul but which were an unmistakable obstacle to the effort demanded by his task. Already on the way to the "discernment of spirits," he soon recognized and overcame the temptation. But he will have to go much further still, submit to the demands laid upon him by his studies—the frequent omission of his prayers and a postponement of his apostolate. When, on the ship which brought him back from the Holy Land, he matured in God's presence his "intention of studying," did Ignatius imagine that he was going to enter a period in which, to obtain the "knowledge acquired" by natural effort, he would have to make the dread sacrifice of the gifts which God was communicating to him in prayer? It does not seem so. For him, this discovery was gradual. It was experience that taught him what he later taught his sons, that "study demands in a certain sense the whole man,"[1] body and soul, and that it absorbs, under pain of failure, all the powers of the mind. Polanco, one of Ignatius' most faithful biographers, notes the fact as follows:

"It was his habit, when he had no other occupations undertaken for God's greater glory, such as for example, to travel on the roads, etc., to give himself for longer periods to devotion and mortification. And when he was busy teaching Christian Doctrine and at other important works for the help of the neighbor which required a great deal of time, or at studies likewise, he greatly shortened the time for prayer, and was satisfied with Mass, the examens of conscience, and about an hour for meditation. He thought it would be more acceptable to God our Lord for him to give more time and effort to the activities which he undertook solely for His service and glory. The result was that despite the numerous difficulties he there met with, he was during his studies one of the most zealous and hardest workers."[2]

Father Nadal, recalling later the three principal difficulties encountered by Ignatius during his studies, remarks that the most serious was "his tendency to devotion and his habit of spiritual absorption."[3]

To lessen prayer in order to avoid feeling its fatigue or its too encroaching joys—was this not for one who had already so fully tasted of them a strange sacrifice carried out in faith? Polanco notes again that Ignatius "studied with a wonderful constancy ... *doing himself great violence,* so as to be able to train under earthly masters a mind grown accustomed to a better Master, the Holy Spirit."[4] Great violence which a decisive conviction inspired: God is not served by love, but by works which love causes to be undertaken and in which it loses itself to be at once purified and transfigured.

It seems that God himself concurred in this violenec of love. Not only did Ignatius have to reduce his hours of prayer, but he also had to offer himself to what he called "the dryness of studies" dryness born of labor, always a bit painful, but still more so because God no longer made Himself felt in the soul with the same abundance of consolation. Ignatius recalled in a word the contrast between the graces which preceded and followed his ordination and, on the other hand, those which marked the time of his studies. He had many spiritual visions and many *quasi* ordinary consolations, *the exact opposite of what happened in Paris.*[5] After the dryness, it seemed to him that it was the springtime of Manresa that had returned.

This is not to say, of course, that during this life of study Ignatius did not continue to apply himself to prayer and did not feel in his soul at times its extraordinary effects. But the "great violence" which he had to do himself to limit his prayer and the practice of "spiritual things," in order to give himself entirely to the happy issue of the human work undertaken "for the love and service of the Lord," caused him the better to discover the spiritual way which was his own. The consolations which came upon him after his years of study were a divine confirmation assuring him that the faithful effort pursued for more than ten years, from Barcelona to Paris and Venice, had its source in a very pure love of God. They were like the blossoming in his soul of an inner liberty long matured by effort. From then on, "consolations" were granted him as a ceaseless grace, an answer to the servant who, in order to love his Master better, serves Him faithfully with the "human means," even in his aching trudging through things and works.

We must thus, it seems, understand the last stage of Ignatius' itinerary. Cut off from his immediate communication with God, he reached, by a fidelity that was almost heroic to works undertaken in His service, that special liberty which enabled him "to find God in all things."

Such is, in fact, the formula by which Ignatius characterized the spiritual life of his last years: He always grew in devotion, that is to say, in the ease with which he found God, and more so now than ever in his whole life. Every time he wished to find Him he found Him.[6] This admission was made in October, 1555, less than a year before his death. Even before 1547 he had already confided to Laynez that "what he had had at Manresa (and what, at the time of his distracting studies, he exalted and called "his primitive church"), was little enough in comparison with what he then had."[7]

This spiritual progress was very clear to those who came near him. Not only did they remark "his ease in uniting himself with God in prayer," but more still, "the devotion he so easily felt in all things and in all places," being "turned towards God even when he seemed at the time to be doing something else. He raised himself to God in any circumstances."[8] The seven hours of prayer at Manresa became the continuous and spontaneous prayer of a life in which activity, far from disturbing his union with God, was the privileged means of maintaining it.

We must summarily recall three stages, for they ask us the important question: How did the solitary of Manresa become an apostle who nourished his contemplation on all "created things"? These stages, by their very unfolding, furnish us with the answer: Love is borne towards God, not so much by prayer as by fidelity to works, which makes use of everything according to the mystery of the Divine Will.

St. Ignatius often had to explain himself in order to help his sons "follow the same spirit." We might say, I think, that the essence of his teachings revolves about what he called "continual prayer" in the midst of activity.

It was all the more necessary in that the essential idea of his work was to recruit men who were capable of finding the perfection of their interior life in their apostolate at a time when the manner of thought of the sixteenth century hardly permitted a separation between holiness and contemplation. Thus while he spoke unceasingly of the necessity of a union with God that admits of no limits or obstacles, he showed himself very reserved in the matter of long prayers, which to him seem to offer serious danger of complacence and illusion. Speaking to apostles for whom alone the unreserved gift of their strength for the present needs of the Church and of souls has any value, he urged them preferably to "find God" at the very time of their activity. Far beyond all private "prayer," their activity should slowly turn into a spiritual grasp of every thing, so that their zeal will never be a theft from God, but the very breathing of their love.

In his name and under his eye, Polanco wrote to the new rector of the scholasticate at Coimbra:

"As to prayer or meditation, unless there is a special need arising from troublesome and dangerous temptations, of which I have spoken, I see that our Father prefers that one try to find God in all that one does, rather than devote a long time to it. And this is the spirit which he desires to see in the members of the Society; that if possible they do not find less devotion in any work of charity and obedience than in prayer or meditation. For they should do nothing except for the love and service of God our Lord. Acting thus, each should find more satisfaction if the thing is commanded him, for then he can never doubt that he is conformed to the will of God our Lord."[9]

To a father who asked him "on what things to meditate most in order to be more faithful to our vocation," he answered:

"Considering the end of study, the scholastics can hardly give themselves to prolonged meditations. Over and above the spiritual exercises assigned for their perfection, namely, daily Mass, an hour for vocal prayer and examen of conscience, weekly confession and communion, they should exercise themselves in seeking our Lord's presence in all things, in their conversations, their walks, in all that they see, taste, hear, understand, in everything they do, since it is true that His Divine Majesty is in all things by His presence, power and essence. And this kind of meditation which finds God our Lord in all things is easier than raising oneself to the consideration of divine truths which are more abstract and demand something of an effort, if we are to keep our attention on them. But this method is an excellent exercise to prepare us for great visitations of our Lord even in prayers that are rather short."[10]

We have the same teaching again in this letter in which we catch the echo of the times when Ignatius, at Paris, suffered, so to speak, from being deprived of divine consolations:

"It is not surprising that not all our scholastics experience that relish for devotion which is desirable. For He Who dispenses this grace does so when and where He thinks fit. During the time of studies, which require no little spiritual effort, it is to be thought that the Divine Wisdom often suspends such sensible visitations. For although the mind can take great delight in them, they sometimes have a weakening effect on the body beyond measure. Besides, the occupation of the understanding with scholastic pursuits usually brings on a certain interior dryness. But when the study is directed purely to God's service, this is very good devotion. Finally, if one does nothing to endanger the solid virtues and gives the time to prayer demanded by the Constitution, with few or many consolations, he should in no way be disturbed, but accept from God's hand what He disposes in this matter, always making more account of what is really important, that is, patience, humility, obedience, charity, and other virtues."[11]

The instance of the scholastics furnished him with a welcome occasion of making his thought understood, not only because what is said of study can easily be applied to every human effort employed by the apostle, but also because it was supremely important not to run the risk of directing the young religious, under pretext of their spiritual inexperience, towards a form of prayer which later on would leave them unskillful in activity. For the rest, the saint harps upon the same theme, using almost identical expressions when he writes to men who are burdened with heavy responsibilities. Thus, to a father who was in charge of the material direction of an important and difficult house:

"Although the care of temporal affairs seems to be, and is, distracting, I have no doubt that by your good and right intention, you make something spiritual of everything you do to God's glory, and thus very pleasing to His Divine Goodness. For the distracting occupations undertaken for His greater service, in conformity with His Divine Will, interpreted to you by obedience, can only be, not the equivalent of the union and recollection of uninterrupted contemplation, but even more acceptable, proceeding as they do from a more active and vigorous charity. May God our Creator and Lord deign to preserve and increase this love in your soul and in the souls of all. We will be right in holding that any operation whatever in which charity is exercised to God's glory is very holy and suitable for us, and those more so in which the infallible rule of obedience to our superiors has placed us." [12]

Let us quote again a few sentences from a letter to a superior. The "great reward" which Ignatius had him envisage recalls the "great visits of the Lord," for which the scholastics who seek God in all things are "prepared":

"We need not feel surprised at finding ourselves at times without devotion and distracted by the burden of government. But this absence of devotion and this distraction patiently borne when it is caused by the holy obligations imposed by obedience and fraternal charity, with the intention of God's greater service, are not without their reward, and a great reward, in the presence of God our Lord." [13]

These texts denote an exact steadfastness of teaching. St. Ignatius insists on a kind of union with God which seems to him "easier" and of higher spiritual value than prayer properly so called because it is "more acceptable to the Divine Majesty." This last formula is one of those which he uses most readily. Drawing up the *Constitutions,* he wrote first that the scholastics "ought to find in their studies . . . a true prayer and one more acceptable to His Divine Majesty." A few years later, he added, in his own handwriting, one of those marginal annotations, where we become strikingly aware of his insistence, "*much* more acceptable." [14]

But now and then there is a vagueness in his expressions which comes close to concealing his exact thought. The word "prayer" means now a disinterested prayer which is established in the solitude of the heart and then the spiritual attitude which causes us to "find God" in the thick of activity, even the most absorbing. On the one hand, prayer is considered as a particular and definite "exercise" and, on the other, the continuous union with God in activity.

"In activity and in study, the mind can be turned towards God; and when we direct everything to the service of God, *everything is prayer.* Hence, all the members of the Society should be persuaded that when exercises of charity very often take from them *the time of prayer,* they are not for that reason any the less acceptable to God than during prayer."[15]

This twofold value of the word "prayer" is found in more than one text in which Ignatius' disciples pass on to us his teaching:

"He did not wish the members of the Society to find God only *in prayer,* but in all their actions, and he wished these *to be prayers.* And he approved this method rather than prolonged meditations."[16]

"Someone understood that Father Ignatius said that there was no need of being urgent in prayer, but that in this matter one advanced gradually, and acquired the faculty of *finding prayer* in anything, *without having to depend on prayer and the feeling that went before.* But he understood that one could not attain to it unless he gave himself with fervor to interior purification and the works of the Society, and unless one embraced prayer with calmness, humility and fidelity."[17]

"Finding prayer without depending on prayer and the feelings that went before"—there is question here, therefore, of uniting oneself to God in activity by an inner attitude which, distinct from every exercise of prayer, is also in a certain way independent of it.

Doubtless (and Nadel himself points this out at the end of the passage we have just quoted), the faithful practice of prayer at a given
time is an indispensable condition for remaining united with God and
"finding" Him in all things. But he who would act as a spiritual man
has no need of referring, even implicitly, to a *preceding* grace. His
action at the moment becomes for him a veritable prayer which
unites him with God and causes him to taste all the friuts of this
union. This is a spiritual plenitude which supposes a soul already
advanced in the ways of God:

"I also understand that Ignatius himself found God every time that
he gave himself to prayer in an any way at all, and that he did not
have to follow any determined rule or method, but that he had to
exercise himself in various ways in prayer, and seek God in every
kind of meditation. But if someone began (to seek God) under the
effects of the last grace received in prayer, he did not condemn him,
but he said that it was the way of beginners."[18]

The beginner, in fact, "by means of determined rules and methods,"
first exercises himself at prayer. He tries thereafter to preserve in activity, and almost in spite of it, the union with God which had been
granted to him in the peace and silence of his prayer. But the spiritual
man finds God in his atcivity without "depending" on this previous
time of prayer or any other methodical preparation:

"As someone said that he repeated the points of the evening before,
to place himself in prayer and union with God, he said in his turn:
'For myself, I find devotion where I wish and as I wish.' "[19]

It is in this kind of prayer that the beginner should already exercise himself in the midst of an activity which will have been adapted
to the fragiltiy of the spiritual means at his disposal. If he is to make
progress in this way,[20] he will not have recourse to prayer, as a ship-
wrecked man turns to the shore, but, surrendering himself to "a more
violent and stronger love," he will learn from the activity itself, and
from the virtues he must practice in it, ceaselessly to purify that love
which unendingly carries him to activity. It is unquestionable that

St. Ignatius did not wait for the extraordinary ways of grace to bring about this purification. Recommending with so much insistence this manner of prayer to the scholastics, he made it clear, on the contrary, that the very beginner should confidently exercise himself in it almost habitually. Even now one learns to find God by finding Him.

If we must therefore conceive of a privileged period for prayer, it can not be after the manner of "a spiritual capital" which, acquired in the morning, for example, will be slowly spent throughout the course of the day under the corrosive and disintegrating effect of the manifold tasks which duty imposes. Far from destroying the work of prayer, activity ought to awaken a fresh prayer suitable to the very conditions in which it unfolds, which causes us "to find God" in all things. "In all things he found God," said Nadal of St. Ignatius, "in business, in conversation."[21]

No longer should we hesitate before activity and the wide range of its demands by dwelling with longing on the time which, while it lasted, at least united us with God. Such a pining for prayer runs the close risk of making impossible that "devotion" which accompanies activity generously undertaken "for the love and service of God our Lord." There is danger, at the same time, of actually attributing to activity that dissolving effect against which we are trying to protect ourselves, thus creating a difficulty that becomes insoluble.

If, nevertheless, the apostle feels as a sacrifice the situation which obliges him to forego the joy of prolonged prayer—and we have insisted on the "great violence" St. Ignatius had to do himself to accept such a situation—this can be only in a higher flowering of his spiritual life. St. Ignatius writes to Borgia:

"It is certainly a higher virtue of the soul, and a greater grace, to be able to enjoy the Lord in different duties and places than in one only. And we should make a great effort to attain this, in the Divine Goodness."[22]

Our own inexperience and our own weakness could momentarily prevent us from "enjoying" God both in prayer and in activity. Borgia was a man of lofty virtue and was already favored with exceptional graces. Thus St. Ignatius could at the time place no restriction on the the advice he gave him to cut down on the time of his prayer. But knowing men only too well, he was aware that there were spiritual states or situations which made more necessary the time for prayer properly so called, and which would consequently withdraw the apostle from giving himself to an activity which had become fatal for him. We have already seen, in the passages quoted the limits laid down for this attitude of soul, which nonetheless remains the best: "Unless there is a special need arising from troublesome or dangerous temptations. . . . Provided that the solidity of virtue suffers no harm, and that the time prescribed by the *Constitution* is given to prayer . . . ." Elsewhere he leaves to the superior the liberty to "increase or lessen the time for prayer"[23] for the scholastics. For the mature religious, he leaves it to a "discreet charity" to regulate prayer and all the other exercises of the spiritual life, "it being supposed that they are spiritual persons . . . one should only be watchful lest the spirit grow cold, or human and low passions be rekindled."[24]

There is also a pedagogical necessity. At certain times we are all beginners with divided hearts, forced to insist on longer prayer because activity, instead of awakening a union with God, is an obstacle to it, But the principle remains firm:

"It will be good to reflect that man does not serve God only when he prays; for then those prayers would be short which did not last for twenty-four hours a day (if that were possible!), since every man ought to give himself to God as completely as possible. But what is true is that God is served at certain moments by other things more than by prayer, to such a point that He is pleased that for them one omits prayer, and *a fortiori,* shortens it. Thus, *oportet semper orare et non deficere,* but this must be properly understood after the manner of the saints and the doctors."[25]

Is this to say that the love that carries us to works, there to "find God," has definitely overcome in us the desire of a "fixed" prayer? Is the longing for this prayer, which we recalled a moment ago, mere weakness in the presence of activity? The example of St. Ignatius himself would warn us of the contrary, were there any need. In the years in which he declared that "he found God more than ever," we still see him giving himself to long hours of prayer. And our own experience is always there to make us feel that the more love carries us to activity, the more we feel the irresistible drawing to God alone, even to spending in prayer "twenty-four hours a day, if that were possible!"

To return to prayer, therefore, is not to retire from activity, like the fighter from combat, but it is to elevate our activity even now to the level it wishes to attain—the repose of all things in God. In fact, if the soul has first enjoyed God in prayer, it was only a passing anticipation of the Kingdom. It is dragged away by "violence," withdrawing from the goal which it thought it had reached in order to build up by its activity the Temple to which God will come to repose with His own. The soul returns to prayer in order to experience anew its desire to see the work finished at last and to cherish the hope of God's coming.

"I hope in God our Creator and Lord that, far from diminishing it, you will from day to day give more reasons for increasing my joy, and that you will be among those of whom the Wise Man speaks in Proverbs: 'The path of the just man is like the light of the dawn until it grows unto the brightness of the perfect day.' And I ask of Him Who is the Author of this perfect day, as the Sun of Wisdom and of Justice, that by His Mercy, He will carry to perfection the work He has begun in you, until He allows you to find Him and learn 'where He feeds His flock, where he reposes at the hour of mid-day,' glorifying Himself in you, and manifesting the riches of His all-powerful hand, and the infinite magnificence of His spiritual gifts in your souls, and through you in the souls of many others."[26]

But St. Ignatius recognizes that activity is at once the happiness and the torment of love: happiness, in finding God; torment, in not being able to repose finally in God. The violence which love imposes upon itself to give itself to works is a kind of crucifixion.

"Thus the enlightened soul, its understanding clarified by dew from heaven, when it suffers contradictions, places its nest on high, and desires nothing but Christ and Him crucified, so that if crucified in this life, it will rise in the next."[27]

While waiting for this tension to be released in the contemplation of the heavenly Jerusalem, love will not cease to be carried to works "undertaken for the service of God."[28] For St. Ignatius, as for all those who live with this violence of love, mystical graces will not be given in the ultimate degrees of a prayer indefinitely refined, but they will accompany or follow the effort of active charity carried to heroism in all the virtues.

He, therefore, who has lost his fidelity to prayer must not delude himself that he will replace it with activity. Deprived of this ever necessary tension, his activity will be carried on in dissipation and the diversion of the figures of this world without revealing their divine mystery. Only the taste for prayer keeps alive the meaning of the mystery and keeps the soul attentive to the needs of the Kingdom and the ever imminent coming of God.

From the center of all the Ignatian formulas which we have found so far, two words shine forth: finding God. Is it not possible to clarify their mysterious meaning somewhat further?

St. Ignatius, we have said, does not ask the mind to distract itself from the present activity to become aware of God by a sort of division which would eventually be intolerable and a source of countless anxieties. At every moment we have but one thought which cannot at one and the same time provide for prayer and activity, if prayer and activity are two distinct occupations.

We must recall the long cry of joy, which in the absolute destitution of the ruined convent at Vivarolo, Ignatius, just ordained, caused his friends to hear, to celebrate the return to his soul of his divine consolations:

"Now if everything will be added to them who seek first the Kingdom of God and His justice, can they be lacking anything who seek nothing but the justice of the Kingdom and the Kingdom itself, they whose blessing is not so much "of the dew of heaven and the fatness of earth," but of the dew of heaven alone? I mean those who are not divided, those who have both their eyes fixed on heaven."[29]

This unity of view is not the term of a contemplation in which "by an effort to make oneself present to divine things" the apostle would be absorbed in God in an adoration more and more alien to the world of sense. But it is the fruit of a union finally realized between his will and the will of the living God Who is always at work in history.

"When men leave themselves to belong to their Creator, they gain an inner knowledge that is full of consolation of how our eternal good is spread through all creatures, giving them existence, and preserving them in His own infinite Being and Presence."[30]

The spiritual movement peculiar to St. Ignatius does not go from created things to the Creator, but always from the Creator, Father, Son, and Holy Spirit, to created things through which shine the glory and the majesty of Him without Whom they are nothing. This implies that one has "entered" into God by a conversion of heart and has never left Him, not even in an activity which through the natural means it uses should continue to be adherence and submission of the whole being to the sole action of God, Who is leading the world towards its fulfillment.

St. Ignatius expresses in words that are familiar to him: The apostle is "God's instrument" a living instrument which makes itself more and more docile to Him Who makes use of it and more and more intelligent in the apostle's activity. The more intelligent he is, the more effective he will be; the more docile, the more he will enter into the mystery of God, Who is working in him and through him in every created thing. His love itself, fixed in God, grows through the "things known and loved for God."

"For we know that all creatures are at the service of those who love God entirely, to help them to even greater merit and joy and union through an intense charity of the Creator and Lord."[31]

We must love the Lord "entirely," and then everything makes us love Him more by revealing His work to us, by a kind of "ease in finding God," which St. Ignatius expresses in a word we have met often already: devotion.

This devotion consists in a certain "familiarity with God" which develops in the work undertaken "for His love." There is here an inner dialogue in which the soul questions God on the meaning of an activity which it perceives is always shot through with impulses which are beyond its control. Adherence, again and again renewed by love, to the events of a history which finds its origin, its middle, and its end in God alone. It is fidelity at every moment to the most humble demands of duty in order to grasp in it the confident movement of the Kingdom of God which is being accomplished.

There is question, therefore, of a gradual revelation of the "glory of God, for which all creatures have been made and ordered by His Eternal Wisdom."[32] Recognizing the activity of God is co-operating with Him and "glorifying Him with that which He gives as Creator, nature, and with what He gives as the Author of grace, which is supernature."[33] It is "to give glory to Him for that which He accomplishes" in souls.[34] It is a supernatural view of the world in God, to grasp, more and more, men and things in the splendor of "creation" altogether. "And all the other things on the face of the earth . . . " runs the text of the *Exercises;*[35] no scorn, of course, no suspicion, no reserve, but the certainty that all things are given to render to God the service and glory that He expects of us.

"The soul, watchful, contented and consoled . . . our thoughts, our words, our works . . . warm, clear and just, for the greater service of God . . . the soul, tranquil, at peace and ready for whatever our Lord might wish to do in it";[36] the effects of devotion are multiplied in the soul, but one word seems to summarize them all: thanksgiving.

For the apostle united with God, devotion is nourished by the ever growing and ever relished certainty that everything is the gift of God and that it is proper for him to refer all back to God:

"For my part, I am convinced that I am nothing but obstacle at any time both before and after. And I find this a source of great satisfaction and spiritual consolation in our Lord, because I can thus attribute nothing to myself which has any appearance of good."[37]

Ignatius thus expresses himself confidentially to Borgia. But was it not already a hymn of thanksgiving sung by the retreatant at the end of the "contemplation for obtaining love?" "Behold how all blessings and all gifts come down from on high ... as the rays from the sun and the waters from the spring."[38] A simple sentence, the echo of which is heard countless times throughout the correspondence of St. Ignatius:

"I rejoice very much in the Lord at seeing the zeal and the desire He gives you to employ yourself in the service and help of souls. ... We must never cease giving thanks and praise to their Author Who is the Author of all good.

"I rejoice very much in the Lord Whom you are serving and Whom you desire to serve even more, Him to Whom we must attribute all the good that we see in creatures."[39]

This feeling of gratitude could develop fully only on the occasion of activity and through it, since it is activity, in fact, that reveals how "God acts in His creature." It is the privilege of the "perfect," who, "by a continual contemplation and illumination of the spirit, consider, meditate, and contemplate more the presence of God our Lord in every creature."[40] It is, however, the good fortune of every apostle, even the "imperfect," to be nourished on this presence.

We understand, therefore, to what extent the feeling of "devotion" was, for St. Ignatius, rooted in the reality of the Eucharist. It led to it; it was nourished on it by the thanksgiving of Christ; it opened the heart for a fresh thanksgiving by a new gift to the service of the neighbor. His spiritual life, which we know was closely centered on the Eucharistic Christ (to be convinced, it is enough to read at random a few lines of the *Journal*), finds for that very reason in the apostolate the most trustworthy of expansions.

It was a continual devotion, the most radical demand of which we must make known at once—mortification, which was also "continual."[41] They are like the two surfaces of the same reality, at once death and resurrection, sacrifice, and liberty in God.

Activity, as a matter of fact, because of a dynamism which causes sin to proliferate in us spontaneously, attaches us to ourselves all the more strongly as it permits our personality to set itself up and to develop in a movement which of itself closes again on its own riches. Even more, it offers as a prey to be conquered and won from God,

the earth "and all the things that are on the face of the earth." Even
if it is undertaken "for the love of God," no work can ever be followed up without being the occasion, more or less confusedly entertained, of selfish enjoyments of the flesh and the mind.

To pretend to disengage oneself *before* the selfishness which is
joined with it becomes active is gullibility, perhaps madness. St.
Ignatius is at once wiser and more spiritual. For him, the radical
abnegation of himself is a fruit which ripens slowly, to the rhythm
of successive abnegations which the activity determines. Placing the
apostle in a path that is dangerous, where each "created thing" may
be for him the occasion of an interior struggle, he asks him not to
evade any of them, but to follow up by purification of heart and by
a heroic burst of confidence in God, the development of the activity
begun for "the love and service of His Divine Majesty." "It is not
for you that I began, and it is not for you that I will stop."[42]

Therefore, union with God through activity, while a devotion, is
at the same time an inexhausible source of mortification. And if the
work undertaken further demands that "the whole man" be consecrated to it, we must rejoice because of a more radical interior immolation. Thus, far from attaining the ideal purity, he who is afraid
of activity shows that he refuses to lose himself and that he mistrusts
God, since our sole fidelity in this domain consists in a ceaseless conversion of our entire faculties to help us at one and the same time to
find God and to die to ourselves:

"They should frequently be encouraged to seek God our Lord in
all things, setting aside, as far as it is possible, all love of created things,
placing it in their Creator, loving Him in all things and all things in
Him, according to His most holy and divine will."[43]

It is in this effort to have a conversion of love in the very thick of
activity that there resides for St. Ignatius "the mortification and
abnegation of the will" which he considers the "foundation" of spiritual progress,[44] an effort to be pursued unweariedly

"until all our wickedness shall be entirely consumed in the furnace of
the eternal love of God our Creator and Lord, when our souls shall

be completely penetrated and possessed by Him, and our wills thus perfectly conformed, or rather transformed into His will, which is itself essential rectitude and Infinite Goodness."[45]

While awaiting this hour when our mortification will be consummated by death and when at last we shall find God fully by the complete transformation of our will into His, it is in our works that our love stands revealed, more and more relieved of all human impurity:

"I do not know what I can do to return such remembrances and affection except to correspond with an increased remembrance and affection, praying that God the Author of all good will increase in you those desires for His honor and service, with the continual increase of His grace, to carry them into effect, and that He may be pleased to relieve you of those burdens which in your letter you rightly judge to be a great embarrassment for one who has to ascend to so high a throne as Paradise.

"And although we should not abandon offices which we have received and fulfill for God's honor, the weight of the soul, which is love, can find relief when even in the midst of things that are earthly and base one does nothing that is earthly or base, but loves them all for God our Lord, in so far as they are directed to His glory and service. This is a duty towards Him Who is our last end, Who in Himself is perfect and infinite goodness, Who must be loved in all other things, and to Whom alone should be directed the whole weight of our love. And indeed He is entirely deserving of that love, since He created us all, redeemed us all, thus giving Himself without reserve. It is right that He will not have us withhold a part of ourselves, since He has so completely given Himself to us, and desires continually to give Himself."[46]

That is quite the last word: If "everything is prayer," it is because activity and love grow together.

The love, the fruit of which is the possession of all things in God and the dispossession of self, is nothing other than the Spirit of God. "I have no doubt," we read in a letter of St. Ignatius, "that your holy intention and direction will make *spiritual* and very acceptable to His Infinite Goodness all that is keeping you busy to God's glory." Making everything spiritual through the Spirit is the devotion which surrounds and consecrates the work accomplished for the sole love of God.

In the last period of his life, such as we have tried to particularize it at the beginning of this article, St. Ignatius seemed to find God spontaneously in all things. Was it not also the period in which the Person of the Holy Spirit was more revealed in him?

"He told me various other things concerning the visitations he had had dealing with the mysteries of the faith, on the Eucharist, for example, on the Person of the Father in a special manner, and sometime later, I think, on the Person of the Word, and *finally on the Person of the Holy Spirit.*"[47]

Laynez's testimony is confirmed by that of Nadal:

"I myself learned later from Father Ignatius that he lived in the Divine Persons, and that he found all kinds of gifts, distinct, according to the Persons, but that in this contemplation, he found the *greater gifts in the Person of the Holy Spirit.*"[48]

It is thus that the gaze of the apostle achieves its clarification to discern in all things the presence and the "work" of God. "All should endeavor to have the Spirit of the Lord, or devotion, to raise themselves to God in all their actions."[49]

We have come at the same time to the very heart of the life of Ignatius, to that marvelously living center where his prayer, ceasing to be "multiple,"[50] remains definitely fixed in God and where the whole world appears to him "in its beginning, its middle and its end": the life of the Most Holy Trinity. All that we have said up to this would be incomprehensible if we did not have this luminous source of prayer, love, and activity to clarify it.

"We know that Father Ignatius had received from God the exceptional grace of being able without effort to pray and to repose in the contemplation of the Most Holy Trinity . . . a contemplation which was often given him, but especially, and then almost continually, in the last years of his pilgrimage. By a great privilege, Father Ignatius was acquainted with this manner of prayer to an eminent degree. To this was added, that in all things, actions, conversations, he felt and contemplated the presence of God and the attraction of spiritual things. He was a contemplative in action, something he expressed habitually in the words: we must find God in all things.

"Filled with admiration and consolation, we saw this grace and this light of his soul glowing in some way upon his countenance, manifesting itself in the clearness and certainty with which he acted in Christ. And somehow we felt some influx of this grace spread even to ourselves. That is why we think that this privilege granted to Father Ignatius has also been granted to the whole Society. We are confident that the grace of such a prayer and such a contemplation is offered to all of us in the Society, and we assert that it is bound up with our vocation."[51]

We do not think that there are two privileges here—contemplating the Trinity and finding God in all things—But these two graces, which can only be understood one by the other, form in reality but one single grace. Nadal's conclusion is without ambiguity:

"Since this is so, we must place the perfection of our prayer in the contemplation of the Trinity (with love and the union of charity) extending to the neighbor through the works of our vocation; works which without difficulty we prefer to the relish and sweetness of prayer."[52]

Thus it is affirmed that the same divine charity nourishes our prayer and commands our activity. Our works "extend" to the neighbor the love which unites us to the Most Holy Trinity.

A mysticism of God purely transcendent would lead us, perhaps, to prayer as to an absolute. But when, carried along ourselves with this broad movement, we feel in faith that the Creator wishes to be glorified by His creature in the place and in the time of his creation, that He has sent His Son to take possession of His Kingdom in His

Name, that He sends daily His Spirit to extend His Kingdom among His own, that the redemptive work of Christ follows the creative work of the Word of God, that both are a history in which the Three Persons work in concert and in which They ask us to collaborate, it is then that we find God in activity, for the history which we build with our hands is nothing more than this divine history, apart from which there is nothing but hell.

In this light, which is also a condition, activity and prayer tend to fuse into one single activity. We should not separate them as if, in the labor of the day, we kept the longing memory of the rest upon the mountainside. This would mean a desertion of activity. Or, as though in prayer, if we remained uniquely stretched towards the abyss of divine grandeurs, this, too, would be to misconceive the mystery of God, Who reveals Himself continually in history.

When man, in an adherence ever more clear and deliberate to the divine plan of creation, of redemption and sanctification, is absorbed in the work charity commands him, that is to say, the love of God living in him, he is at the same time lost in the current of his love which flows through the world. With his eyes clarified by his faith, he goes to the "vineyard of the Lord" as to a divine meeting-place. He labors there all the day in religious reverence because he knows that the Master will remain with him until the evening.

Sweetness, clearness, certainty, constancy—all are Ignatian words which deserve an individual study. They express the inner attitude of him who can no longer doubt that his activity is associated with the activity of God, that it is God's activity itself through him, and that in carrying it out, he is bringing to perfection the prayer which, in the Holy Spirit, causes him to aim at the glory of the Father.

Christus, No. 11, July 1956

St. Ignatius and the Greater Glory of God

FRANÇOIS COUREL, S.J.

IN THE FABRIC of our Christian life, woven of acts of heroism and of treachery, faith alone is able to recognize the progress of the Kingdom and the victory of Him Who fights in us and triumphs even in our weakness. But our weakness is not the sole contributing factor in the dulling and paralyzing of our activity. It happens that even when completely generous, we hesitate before assuming an obligation, not knowing how to discern with certainty the call of the Spirit. It is here that the Exercises propose a valid criterion for every decision: choosing that which will assure "greater service and greater glory to God."

No Ignatian text develops what we must understand by this "greater glory of God," for before being a vision to be contemplated, it is an end to be promoted. We know it only by entering into the mystery which reveals it to us, which is also the movement by which God saves the world. It is this movement of glory which we shall try to follow through the Exercises,[1] first in the order of *creation,* then in the history of our *redemption,* which, making us enter into the glory of the Father, brings us at the same time to the duties of the *Christian life,* there to assume our responsibilities as men under the light of the Spirit.

Creation, Reflection of Glory

He who makes the Exercises is not invited with Moses to Mount Sinai, there to contemplate face to face the glory of the living God. It is the whole world which is first offered to his regard, not to have him pause at Creation, but for him to become aware of the position of the creature as it is ordered for the service and praise of the Creator. [23] Such is the "Foundation" of the edifice which he is going to have to build. Such will also be its summit in the "contemplation for obtaining love." There, Creation will be placed before us again, radiant and transformed by the glory of the risen Christ. It will not then be a question of our repose, but of a thanksgiving offering for all the benefits received, to the service and praise of the Divine Majesty. Between these two poles, the Exercises are going to unfold, "leaving the creature with his Creator." [15]

That is why St. Ignatius, in the Foundation, does not yet speak of glory. He wishes only to lead us to define our attitudes in the presence of "things" which are given us. This attitude he summarizes in a word—indifference. It is not yet a standard of action; it is an inner preparation, a preliminary balance to be achieved. The soul that is indifferent to every other entreaty but the divine call turns its eyes toward the Lord and allows itself already to be drawn by the weight of love. It discovers that everything on earth is for the good of man. But man himself is dependent. He comes from the Creator, and he must return to Him. Not only does indifference place us in the presence of things in order to detach us from them and to set limits to the reasonable use we should make of them, it draws us much farther, to recognize in a dynamic view of the universe the place where man ought to take his stand. "The central idea of the Foundation," writes Father Leturia, "is the descent of creatures as they come from God, and their necessary ascent and their redintegration in their last end which is God Himself."[2]

There is present an essential rhythm of the Exercises. The man who is able to recognize himself as a creature in the presence of his Creator, coming from Him and returning to Him, is drawn by an irresistible love, after he has become indifferent, through the stripping of "real poverty," of "the third degree of humility," to the total oblation of the "contemplation for obtaining love." The attitude which is asked of him at this summit remains fundamentally the same as at the starting point; it is a matter of comtemplating how "all things come from on high." [237] For St. Augustine, in the progressive flight of the ecstasy at Ostia, the soul rose step by step from the beauty of the visible universe to the inaccessible glory of the Creator. With St. Ignatius, on the contrary, the soul contemplates a descending movement which radiates from the creative Trinity towards created things through which shines the Majesty of Him in Whom all things subsist.

The glory, at the level of creation, is the reflection of God in the mirror of the world and in man created in the image of God and filled by Him with blessings. [235] It is already the progressive glorification and resurrection of nature by the action of God, "Who works and labors for me in all creatures on the face of the earth." [236] It is, finally, the life-giving current of divine light which descends from the Creator, "as the rays of light descend from the sun, and as the waters flow from their fountains." [237]

But this descent is immediately perfected in an upward movement which is inseparable from it. If the glory is revealed to us in the existence and in the harmony of the universe, it is that we should recognize the active presence of God in the world and collaborate with His action. It is for us to make use of creatures for God's glory and to glorify Him with the gifts He has made us. In proportion, as we behold the discovered splendor of creation which comes down from God, we are called upon to make it ascend to Him. It is on this note of a universal return to the Father that the Exercises end. And this supposes that love, the fruit of the final contemplation, is not yet enjoyment and repose but service offered by "reason and justice." [237] Our activity is, then, in the strongest sense of the word, "a thanksgiving" which should be fulfilled on the level of our daily life. Far from carrying us off to heaven before the time, the "contemplation for obtaining love" casts us into the thick of the apostolic conflict. It places us in the presence of a creation that is taking place and a glory that has yet to be given. That is why one of the equivalents which St. Ignatius prefers in defining God's glory is "the service and praise of the Divine Majesty."

In his own personal life, St. Ignatius shows us that the radiance of the glory in creation has struck him from the first moments of his spiritual awakening. Having renounced the world and being fixed in indifference, he felt "free of all personal concern" to be "closely bound to the glory of Jesus Christ our Lord."[3] His gaze thus purified, he contemplates, even at Manresa, how all things come from God. In the fundamental mystical experience which opened his eyes and gave him a new understanding of creation, his gaze was turned first upon God. It was in God that he found, as in the hundredfold promises to his friends, the wealth and the beauty of sensible images:

"One day while he was reciting the Hours of Our Lady on the steps of the same monastery, his understanding began to be elevated as though he saw the Holy Trinity under the figure of three keys. This was accompanied with so many tears and so much sobbing that he could not control himself."[4]

He then sees the creation in a dynamic movement which passes from God to things:

"Another time there was represented to his understanding with great spiritual delight the manner in which God had created the world. It had the appearance of something white out of which rays were coming, and it was out of this that God made light."[5]

As in the Exercises, St. Ignatius' personal mysticism sees immediately in this radiance of the Glory the necessary return to God by service and praise. The reflection each time it is contemplated in things is a spur to service. Already during his convalescence at Loyola, the relish for the beauty of the creature was only a stimulus to give himself all the more:

"It was his greatest consolation to gaze upon the heavens and the stars, which he often did, and for long stretches at a time, because when doing so he felt within himself a powerful urge to be serving our Lord."[6]

Until the end of his life, he remained sensitive to this beauty of the "heavens which sang the glory of God" which at the same time led him to the summits of praise. One can still see in his tiny room at Rome the window on which he went to lean while admiring the sky at night. Ribadeneira reports for us a scene from his life which has come down to us, thanks to the patient observations of Laynez:

"He went up to a terrace or belvedere, where one could get a good view of the sky. He stood there, head uncovered, a long moment, without moving, his eyes fixed on the heavens. Then kneeling, he humbled himself before God, and finally sat down upon a small stool, because his weakness did not permit him to do more. He remained there, head uncovered, weeping softly. The tears flowed so silently that not a sob or a groan, not a sound could be heard, or a single movement of his body."[7]

The ecstasy at the end of his praise enables us to get a glimpse of the power of emotion which these simple words had for him: "the Divine Majesty." We shall never find in St. Ignatius the great frescoes of glory such as Isaias comtemplates in the inaugural vision of his ministry: "Holy, holy, holy, is the Lord God of armies; all the earth is filled with His glory." (Is. 6:3) The word "glory" itself, which is one of the most characteristic of the Ignatian idiom, is practically absent from the extant fragments of his *Spiritual Journal.*[8] It is there, however, that we find most of his inner experience. When he wishes to put into words what he has contemplated, he speaks of the "Majesty" of the Most Holy Trinity. But under this disconcerting sobriety, we feel the splendor of Isaias and at the same time the tenderness of Jeremias. They are visions of light and heat, "a devotion, very clear, luminous and warm."[9]

"Appearing rather to be united more to His Divine Majesty, I felt the unique essence as in a luminous clearness. It drew me wholly to His love . . . with the full confidence of finding more grace, love, and a deeper satiety in His Divine Majesty."[10]

But at the sweetest point of the consolation, the return to the world, to service, to action, is never far off. It is quite contrary to a selfish enjoyment. He asks, on March 16, "that the visits and the tears be not given me, if it be equal service to the Divine Majesty."[11] As in the Exercises, the very sweetness of the divine visit is entirely orientated towards combat. It is the intimacy of the creature with the Creator, Who communicates Himself to the soul, "inflaming it with love of Himself, and disposing it for a better service of God in the future." [15]

This zest of a militant soul in whom the beauty of creation is a constant summons to the service of glory is found in the advice he gives to the young students of Coimbra in 1547. They, too, before "God our Lord, from Whom descends every blessing," have assumed in return "the common obligation which we all have for loving the glory, the honor, and the praise of God our Creator and Lord."[12] The whole world lies open before them, and in the world, man is the most beautiful of its creatures, and they should recognize the glory in him: "Look upon your neighbor as the image of the Most Holy Trinity and as the receptacle of its glory Whom the whole universe serves."[13] Since God Himself is at work in the world, they should be, in their turn, "the jealous servants of His glory and increase and preserve continually in His holy service, for the great honor and glory of God and the help of His holy Church . . . to satisfy God and to serve Him in a thousand ways for His divine honor and glory."[14] Creation is the place of His glory because it is the place of an exchange, the meeting-place between the glory which radiates from the Divine Majesty and the glory which returns to its source in the service and praise of God.

Christ, Mediator of Glory

The movement of creation which in the Foundation and through the Exercises appears as coming from God and returning to God is such only because it is first the movement of the Creative Word Himself. It is He Whom the prologue of St. John describes. It is at one and the same time the movement of Christ the Redeemer, Who, from the glory which He had with the Father from the beginning, wished to humble Himself to the death of the Cross, to reascend to the Father in the glory of the Resurrection. This movement of glory, an essential relation between the Son and the Father, is also the movement of the Exercises, in particular the contemplation of the Kingdom.

The Kingdom is above all the meeting of the soul with its Creator and Lord.[15] What aspect of Christ is there presented? More than the

Christ of the Synoptic Gospels traveling throughout His public life in the villages and synagogues of Palestine, it is the Lord of the entire universe Who stands erect before us in His full stature. More than the meek and humble Christ of the Sermon on the Mount, it is the image of the invisible God of the letter to the Colossians (1:15): "the firstborn of every creature, in Whom all has been created in heaven and on earth." From everlasting to everlasting, He is "Eternal Lord of all things" [98], and He comes into the world, "that in all things He may have the first place." (Col. 1:18) His will is "to conquer the whole world." [95] It is the Christ in glory of the portals of Vézelay, around Whom is gravitating the redeemed universe. If He comes to His own, it is in fact to invite all men, His brethren, to a vast enterprise. [96] His will, which is not His own, but the will of Him Who sent Him (John 5:30, 6:20), is to "conquer all my enemies, and thus to enter into the glory of My Father." [95]

Here, for the first time in the Exercises, St. Ignatius speaks explicitly of glory.[16] And we now understand why it leaps in advance over all created things. It is the very movement of the Word passing through creation to transfigure it and to cause it to mount again to God. That is why glory, the term of the work accomplished by the Redeemer, will also be the term of the praise and service of all those who have judgment and reason, and who, wishing to give proof of greater love, pledge themselves entirely to work after Him in the achieving of the Redemption. Glory is also the last meaning of the "Reign," or the "Kingdom," where each one works according to his rank, with Christ at the head as Prince, and then those who will belong to Him following when He restores the Kingdom to His Father. (1 Cor. 15:23–25) In offering ourselves to follow Him, we do not begin a new personal enterprise, but we inscribe ourselves humbly and proudly in the ranks of all those champions and conquerors who, with "the glorious Mother of God," have their eyes upon us and await us in the triumph of the "heavenly court." [98] In a word, we enter into the movement of glory.

What follows in the Exercises only develops this movement of which the Kingdom has given the general outline. The road to glory, for Christ, passes through the secret of the divinity, which hides itself in the desert by the mysterious hazard of the temptation, through the struggles of the public life, through suffering finally, and the ignominious death on the Cross, to triumph in the glorious Resurrection and Ascension. For us also will it pass through the struggle against the demon and against ourselves, under the Standard of Christ, by "perfect humility" in union with Christ outraged, by the crucifying choice of the election, to end in the joy of the return to the Father with the risen Christ, when our faces shall be resplendent with "the glory of God shining on the face of Christ Jesus." (2 Cor. 4:6)

But before the definitive glorification of the apostle, the way that is open to him is that of the imitation of Jesus Christ in the mystery of the Passion. Here again St. Ignatius has gone through the experience in his own life. After the first discovery of Christ at Loyola and the visions of light at Manresa, in which God taught him the discernment of spirits, he felt himself called to put his feet in the footsteps of Jesus and take the road to Jerusalem. In the first half of the sixteenth century this was a choice means of sharing in the sufferings and the humiliations of Christ, in the dangers of the voyage, and in the holy places occupied by the Turk. Indeed, sufferings and humiliations are not lacking for the "pilgrim" without provisions or money. Some of his adventures irresistibly evoked the memory of Christ brought before the judges, keeping silence, of Christ stripped of his clothing, derided by Herod, and delivered to the soldiers. On his return journey, St. Ignatius was arrested as a spy and treated as a fool:

"But at sunset he came to a walled town where the sentries took him into custody, thinking that he was a spy. They put him in a hut close to the gate, and began to examine him, as they usually do with suspects. To all their questions he answered that he knew nothing. They stripped him and searched him even to his shoes, overlooking no part of his person, to see whether he was carrying any letters. But as they could in no wise learn anything from him, they were angry with him and led him to their captain. 'He would make him speak.' When he told them that they had taken away all his covering with his clothes, they would not return it to him, and led him away, clad only in his breeches and jacket, as above described.

"While they were on their way, the pilgrim remembered how

Christ was led away, although there was no vision here as on other occasions. He was led through three main streets. He went without any sadness, rather with joy and satisfaction."[17]

A few years later, the same joy laid hold of him when with his first companions he still walked in the footsteps of Christ. Then it was no longer the literal imitation of the wayfaring in Palestine, but imitation, nonetheless, of the poverty and obedience of Christ. Together, the companions relived the movement of abasement and exaltation of the Lord, such as is gathered together in the second chapter of the Letter to the Philippians (2:5–11). Christ Jesus, Who was equal to the Father, becomes poor and obedient unto death, and that is why God exalts Him and causes him to ascend to the glory of God the Father. In 1536 and 1537, fatihful to the call of the Kingdom, the companions relived the same mystery in the joyous poverty of Venice and Vicenza:

"Up to now, by the goodness of God we are doing wonderfully well. Every day we experience more the truth of the words: 'having nothing, we possess all.' I mean 'all' that the Lord has promised to grant in abundance to those who seek first the kingdom of God and His justice. . . .

"May He deign to hear us Who when He was rich in all good, stripped Himself of all for our instruction; He Who lived in the glory of His Omnipotence, of His Supreme Wisdom, of His immeasurable goodness, nevertheless submitted to the power, to the judgment and to the will of the least of men."[18]

The glory of God did not then appear to the companions as a future compensation for present poverty and contradictions. It is in the poverty and the lowliness already present because they are then united in the glorious passion of Christ. Le Jay writes from Bassano on September 5, 1537:

"May God grant, according to the richness of His glory, that we be fortified by His Spirit in the inner man. Amen. . . .

"Blessed be Jesus Christ for Whose name we must suffer all the adversities and disappointments of this present life. Better still, we must be glorified in our adversity, because adversity produces constancy, constancy produces tried virtue, and tried virtue, hope, and hope does not deceive (Rom. 5:3–5). The world seeks and amasses gold and silver and glories in them. But the servant of Christ delights in poverty and glories in it. Happy is he who does not run after gold, or place his confidence in treasures of silver. The world rejoices in the praise of men; the servant rejoices in suffering humiliations for the name of Jesus. The cross of Christ seems folly to the world, and it treats as fools those who carry the cross after Christ. St. Paul, on the contrary, said: 'May it please God that I am glorified only in the Cross.' That is why he who is poor with Christ is sufficiently rich."[19]

With poverty, it is obedience that appears to the companions as the privileged means of joining the glory of Christ, hidden in His Passion, and of arriving at perfect humility, "supposing that the praise and glory of His Divine Majesty is equal, the better to imitate Christ our Lord and to be in reality more like him." [167] The very expressions of the Exercises, the desire "to be regarded as nothing worth and a fool for Christ" are found in the "Deliberations of the First Fathers," of 1539. It is understood that

"each one will endeavor to find joy and peace in the Holy Spirit in the matter of obedience by endeavoring as much as he can to incline his will to obey rather than to command, should an equal glory of God follow or an equal praise of His Majesty."[20]

At the end of the election, the companions chose obedience to one of their number, through conformity with Christ "obedient unto death," which thus mounts to the glory of the Father. From this decision was born the structure of the Society, such as it was later approved by the Church. This is what St. Ignatius had already recognized the preceding year in the chapel at La Storta. He was certain from then on that the Father "had placed him with the Son"[21] and that with his companions he was henceforth always to be associated with Christ bearing His cross. Commenting on this incident in 1557, Nadal re-

minded the young Jesuits of the Roman College of it in a very striking summary:

"And now, let us say a few words on the purpose of the Society,
ad majorem Dei Gloriam. . . .

"The foundation of our Society is Jesus Christ crucified. As He has
redeemed the human race by His cross, and as today He undergoes
the greatest pains and crosses in His mystical body, which is the
Church, so, he who belongs to our Society should have no other aim
than to follow Christ through persecutions without number, to procure the salvation of souls along with and in company with Christ."[22]

For every companion henceforth and with him for every Christian, the Cross is therefore the privileged place of glory. "Our cross is
very sweet because it has already the splendor and the glory of the
victory of Jesus over death."[23] It is, according to the word of Father
Richeome, "the source of our good, the foundation of our salvation,
the treasures of immortal glory."[24] God's glory at the level of the history of redemption is the glory of Christ in His combat, of Christ leaving the Father and returning to the Father. All creation is associated
with this going out and coming back. It is Christ alone who reveals
its downward movement by the abasement of the Word and the
redintegrating movement by the resurrection of all things in Him.
The glory of God becomes, then, for us the relation between Father
and Son and Son and Father in the Redemption. For the Eternal
Word is nothing outside the Father, from Whom He proceeds. His
mission coincides with His Being, which is to reveal the Person of the
Father to all that is under the heavens. We might say, then, that the
glory of God and the movement of the Redemption are one and the
same thing and that for us, the glory of God is Jesus Christ the
Savior. "Mediator" of the glory between God and us (Rom. 15:3–14),
it is He Who glorifies us, thereby laying the foundation of our Christian life, which is assimilation to the life of the Trinity.

The Christian in the Service of Glory

In the universal return to the Father summarized in the Exercises,
the glory acquired in the Death and Resurrection of the Son becomes

the very rhythm of our Christian life: "Those whom he has justified, them he has also glorified." (Rom. 8:30) God is glorified in the apostle by the ceaseless exchange of the trinitarian current, the luminous source and the ultimate term of all love and of all service. A mysticism of the glory of God is necessarily a trinitarian mysticism and a mysticism of return to the Father.

But it is at the same time a mysticism of return to the world and to apostolic activity. The servant of glory is carried into a movement of the service of God which leads him to the love of the neighbor and in a movement of the service of the neighbor which leads him back to the love of God. He builds the Kingdom, which the Son finally places in the hands of the Father by a lucid adherence to the plan of Creation and Redemption, that is to say, to the plan of the divine activity in the world.

The Election, the center and aim of the Exercises, is nothing more than the fundamental choice which freely associates us with this economy. That is why it demands the spirit of the Third Degree of Humility, not as a concrete choosing, but as an interior disposition of conformity with the movement of Jesus the Savior.

But in its turn, this essential choice, which pledges our life as Christians, implies all kinds of particular choices along the stream of our daily lives. For these detailed choices, which await our coming out of the Exercises, St. Ignatius coins, so to speak, the spirit of the Election in a series of practical rules—Rules for Scruples, Rules for the Distribution of Alms, Rules for Thinking with the Church, and so on. Fragmentary documents which do not in any way pretend to furnish a manual of conduct but merely to show how, on some occasions, to search for God's greater glory ought to clarify our activity.

The greater glory of God is, in fact, the standard proposed to judge the quality of our service. If it is a matter, for example, "of the way of distributing alms," the first thing to consider is that "the love which leads me to make these donations finds its principles on high in my love for God our Lord." Just as in the contemplation for obtaining love, all glory descends from God and ought to shine through our countenance by the charity which we have for others "so that God is manifestly the cause which makes us love them more." [338][25]

In a similar way in the Rules for Scruples, it is our inner life which is going to be directed towards the same objective. In the struggle against the demon, such as Christ undertook in the Kingdom and the Two Standards, we should, after Him, in peace, carry on the combat, despite the obstacles set up by the enemy: "I did not undertake this because of you, and I am not going to relinquish it because of you." [351] To deliver us from all of the enemy's snares, the tests are always the same; they are the service and the glory of God which will be the principles of our inner liberation.

These two aspects of our effort, peace of soul within and radiant charity without, are joined in the most well-known practical application of the spirit of the Exercises, the Rules for Thinking with the Church. More than ever, it is concern for the praise and service, for the glory, such as the Kingdom defined them, which makes a unity of these prescriptions, the details of which might otherwise seem to be lost in an underbrush of unimportant rubrics. But everything counts here, for it is concerned with the glory of the Spouse. It is in the Church, in fact, that the glory of her head shines forth, the Eternal Lord of the Kingdom. Glory frequently hidden, glory "all interior" (Ps. 44:14), which calls on pure faith to believe, if need be, against the evidence that what appears black is white, that which seems to me to be sordid bears the reflection of glory. [365] *Nigra sum sed formosa.* (Cant. 1:5)

Praise or service through love finally aims at making us adhere more closely to the visible structures of the Church. The "rules" offered by St. Ignatius touch on every area of our interior life, on our relations with others, on our prayer and our activity. They are trifling only in appearance, for there is nothing small in the order of a mysticism of the present moment, in which are offered grace and God's will. Their greatness is to help us feel in the Spirit the particular choices which will make us enter into the movement of glory, that is, into the history of our salvation.

Each page of the Constitutions later remained animated by the same ardent desire of collaborating with the work of creation and redemption. The apostle, conscious that the total weight of the responsibility of the Gospel rests on his shoulders, finds in this divine union the strongest stimulant to his "zeal for souls, for the glory of Him Who has created and redeemed them."[26] From his tiny cell in Rome,

St. Ignatius contemplated, as he wept, the beauty of creation, which had become transparent for him. Raised frequently "beyond the heavens,"[27] he saw how "the light which illumined the decisions he had to make had to descend from the Supreme Wisdom."[28] But from these summits of ecstasy, he is also, more than ever, present at his daily tasks, busying himself, when called to do so, with the important business of rectors of the university, or professors in their official proceedings,[29] "for a greater glory and a greater service to God and for a universal good, for such is the one and only aim that is followed here as in all other points." He was concerned, even to deetails, about the "better" choice to be made.

We find here a characteristic aspect of his spirituality which can be defined in one word: *magis*. Present throughout the Constitutions, this seeking of the "better" is indeed anterior to them. Nadal pointed it out as a constantly recurring feature of the conversion at Loyola:

"Our Father was a magnanimous, noble and generous soul. He began to be disturbed by various thoughts and movements. At one time it was vanity and the desire to achieve great things in the service of a king at war, just as he had done before; at another time, it was the desire to imitate Christ, and to achieve great things in the service of God our Lord, as did St. Francis and St. Dominic. In the ceaseless return of these opposed thoughts, he felt that the first, which were vain, left him dry, weary and ill disposed. The second, which were good and spiritual, gave him devotion, peace and consolation. Thus he thought of giving up the world with its vanity to follow our Lord as best he could, and to do all things for His greater glory. At the beginning of his religious life, there is, therefore, the renouncing of the world to follow and serve Christ, and in this always to aim at and achieve the best."[30]

More than to the fervor of a character always tending to surpass itself, the "magis" therefore corresponds to a desire and a spiritual attitude. More must be done for the praise and the service of the Lord, and the more one does, the better it will be.[31] But it is not a question of cracking one's head in a self-confident effort. Paradoxically, our

Lord wishes to assure in us the meeting "between His greater service and our greater repose":[32]

"The Lord does not ask you to do things which are tormenting and to the detriment of your person. What He wants is that you live in Him in joy, allowing to the body what it needs. You should be much more eager to surfeit yourself with His gifts."[33]

"To be always eager to receive His gifts" is indeed the perfect expression of our collaboration in the creative and redemptive work of Christ. It is thus one of the best definitions of *magis,* in which, according to Nadal, the whole Ignatian theology is summarized:

"This is the whole theology of our Father: his desire was always to seek how to employ himself more in the service of the Lord, and to do always the best."[34]

St. Ignatius' warmest desire was to see this spirit live in his successors. Again Nadal concludes the portrait of his "Father" which we quoted earlier:

"This was why in our Constitutions, in each chapter, each paragraph, you will find: 'For the greater glory and the greater service of God our Lord.' "[35]

And he notes elsewhere:

"In the service of God [our Father] has set down as a first principle which must always be followed, that which tends to the honor and the glory of God. This became as it were the unique foundation and the unique rule of the whole Society, in the light of which all the Constitutions and all the works of the Society are examined and always ought to be.[36]

"The Society is founded on the principle: seek in all things God's greater service and His greater glory. That is the end to which it tends, and its members ought to tend to it in everything, for it is the highest possible end.[37]

"The Society is therefore the communication of this grace, the Pope granting the exercise of all ministries to members of the Society, so that it might the more cooperate with God's plan, for His greater glory.[38]

"*Ad gloriam Dei.* It must always be understood 'for a greater glory,' even though the word happens not to be there."[39]

That the *magis* can, therefore, be understood through the Constitutions does not mean that it adds a nuance which is more or less superfluous. Present and active as a prime essential to give direction to the least decision, it is, more than a simple standard, the spiritual atmosphere in which the whole apostolic activity is bathed. Thus it is explained that St. Ignatius, when he wishes to define the end of his new Society, speaks of a *unique end* which is identically the glory of God and the salvation of souls. The salvation of souls, in fact, is not numbered in the order of ends with God's glory. It is interior to it. God's glory is transcendent and immanent to all the partial ends, the ultimate significance of which it assures by placing them in relation to the unique end, which is the redemption to be achieved.

Such is the final sense of the *magis* and of the *major gloria*. God must be glorified by a more beautiful praise, by a more intense apostolic service, and finally by an evangelization more total and more universal, "which will be more divine as it is more universal."[40] God's greater glory is thus the very vocation of the Christian. A desire which renews ever more its thirst for God, it carries him ceaselessly to new tasks. He well knows in this effort that the whole of creation which he is trying to uplift has not definitively entered into the bosom of the Father. Even today Christ dies and rises in His mystical body. The *major gloria* is the time of the Church militant, which is preparing and building the *maxima gloria* of the heavenly Jerusalem.

Conclusion

The last stage of the Exercises was a prayer, not to "contemplate the glory," but "to obtain love" such as is expressed in a greater service. If in St. Ignatius there is no imaginative representation of glory, it is because everything is offered us in Christ, in Whom "the Divinity hides itself" [196] and in Whom "the divinity is revealed." [223] There is given us for the moment no other Sinai.

But in Christ we possess all. The glory we pursue is not an inaccessible transcendence situated beyond all images, but the very mystery of His love manifested and offered in the divine activity, which at every instant creates, redeems, and sanctifies the world.

Mystery of the continuous *creation,* glory is, at the heart of the visible universe, the presence and trace of the Creator. To Him we should refer all things by placing ourselves in the perfect balance of indifference, which is already love and service. It is this total adherence of our will to the divine plan which makes us "capable of glory," that is to say, which causes us to enter into the movement of the creative liberality by which God gives Himself to the world. To participate in this movement is to recognize in creation the reflection of Him Who has clothed everything with the beauty of the Creator; it is to open our hearts "to the knowledge of the glory of God shining upon the face of Christ." (2 Cor. 4:6)

Mystery of *redemption* which is finished, glory is still always the actual Work of Him Who, Creator of the World, is also the Lord of history. The Majesty of the Creator is concretely revealed to us in the Work of Christ the Redeemer, Who, already glorified upon the Cross, perfects His work of glorification in the final mystery of His resurrection and His ascension to the Father. The apostle, in turn, pursues the historical realization of this mystery of glory by attaching himself to the Person of Christ, seeking His glory in the Passion of Jesus and in the daily suffering of the Church: *Mihi absit gloriari nisi in cruce Domini.* (Gal. 6:14)

Mystery of universal *sanctification,* the service of glory is, finally, our vocation itself in the Church militant. For if we are already risen in Christ, it is only to labor without respite for His final triumph over the powers of evil. The promised glory does not excuse us from the daily battle for the progress of the Gospel, even to the most faraway horizons of the earth, even to the most secret corners of the human heart. All our energy, all our talents we should place at the service of glory for the building up of the Kingdom, which the Son, at the end of time, will hand over to the Father. Having entered with Christ in the movement of glory, we contemplate in Him the history of our own sanctification, we become co-operators today in His work of creation and redemption. Companions of His suffering and companions of His glory, we do not have to leave Him to descend again into the plane of commonplace tasks. It is He Who raises us to the summits of apostolic activity. In this vocation to His service we are already glorified. And yet it is never enough; glory calls to glory as abyss calls to abyss. Such is the *magis,* the desire of the human heart, gushing fountain of divine grace, which transforms us from glory to glory by inserting us ever more closely in the history of salvation, by bringing us ever more intimately into the profundities of the Trinity.

To know, then, that glory is in us a vivifying current which causes us to ascend with the Son to the Father may not be of immediate help to us in choosing the paths of activity. But this luminous certainty prepares and enlightens our future obligations by opening our eyes and our hearts to the fountain from which descends all light. The rest will be given us from day to day. We know, in fact, that a mysterious presence perfects in our soul the movement of the life of the Trinity and causes us to mount to the Father. It is finally to the Spirit in us that is due, in certain concrete instances, the "discernment" of glory.

Christus, No. 2, April, 1954

The Service and Love of God

Andrè Lefèvre, S.J.

"The zealous service of God our Lord out of pure love should be esteemed above all." [370] In this assertion, which is found almost by accident on the last page of the *Exercises,* an expert like Father Joseph de Guibert sees the substance of the spirituality of St. Ignatius. Concerning this spirituality, we can now refer to the study by Father de Guibert, which has at last appeared. Here our purpose will be simply to seek in Scripture the roots of the formula "love and serve God." This expression, which constant use has made a little dull, will thus, we think, take on some of its rightful brilliance.

The word "serve" has in our language a meaning that is noble, and we can speak of serving God. Accustomed as we are to this language, we forget its origin. For the Latins and the Greeks, who are at the very sources of our culture, the word "serve" could not be used in a religious sense. Among the Romans, slavery was too hard, and the Hellenes were too much in love with liberty for such a word to awaken in them anything other than an instinctive repulsion. Moreover, the practical Roman was more inclined to have his gods serve him rather than he serve them. For the educated Greeks, the gods were nothing but supermen. The Greeks bowed only before a nameless and inexorable power, Destiny, to which the gods, as well as they, were subject. We do not serve a blind force like Fate. We submit to it.

The religious attitude of the Semite was altogether different. God is for him a Lord before Whom he prostrates with great reverence and proclaims himself His servant. It was on this basis that the religion of Israel was built, the religion which we have inherited. If our language speaks of service in the sense of noble devotion, it is due to the influence of Christianity upon it.

The language of religion only transfers to a different area the daily usage of our common speech. A glance at this usage is indispensable if we are to understand the nuances of the words "to serve." First of all, to serve is to work. The same word has two meanings. Thus, in the Decalogue, "Thou shalt *serve* God alone" and "Thou shalt *work* only six days" are expressed in Hebrew by the one verb. Service is not a condition, it is an activity, a work that is paid for, one that usually has some result; but it is also an activity that is dependent on the orders and, at least in part, one that is done for the profit of another.

Slavery indeed existed in Israel. But it did not entail, as it did in Roman society, that inhuman alienation by which a person became the property of his master. The oldest legislation, in spite of its harshness, recalls that the slave is a man. Not only should he work only six days a week, but he should not be forced to serve his master more than six years. (Ex. 21:2–11, 23:12) At the end of this period he could remain in the service of his master for good, but on condition of making a declaration before God in legal form that this service was voluntary on his part. Legislation on the point became milder in the course of ages. (Cf. Deut. 15:12–18) But from the beginning, the principle of voluntary service is unquestionable. Thus in the mind of an Israelite service is not a synonym for coercion. Dependence is compatible with liberty and is normally a free submission.

The components of service, work and submission, are two ideas that are full of nobility. To obey, as to work, is to give proof of liberty. Thus the Bible mentions with honor the "servants of the king," those whom we would call his officers or his ministers. The quality and the number of his servants increased the glory of their lord, and, inversely, the glory of their lord reflected on his servants. "Blessed are thy men, and blessed are thy servants, who stand before thee always," exclaimed the Queen of Saba in her enthusiasm. (3 Kings 10:8) Moreover, the Israelite king does not correspond to the fanciful idea one forms of the oriental potentate. Every subject is called servant of the king; but the king is chosen by his subjects, and their relations are regulated by a covenant. (2 Kings 5:1 *et passim*) Here, too, we find the character of submission to be free and humane.

The noble meaning which a Hebrew attaches to the word "service" also appears in his formulas of politeness. We might be tempted to see in them only a base kind of obsequiousness. They are, on the contrary, the expression of a lofty nobility of soul. What is more noble than the manner in which Abraham received his guests? He ran to meet them and greeted them by bowing to the earth: "Lord, if I have found grace in thy eyes, do not pass by without stopping with thy servant." It is not an empty phrase. Abraham placed himself at the disposal of his guests. He had water brought to wash their feet. He had bread and meat prepared, and he served them himself, remaining on his feet near them throughout the repast. (Gen. 8:1–8) Even today a sheik is thus honored to receive a guest in his tent. Service, consisting of work and submission, realizes its ideal perfection only because of this shade of reverence, which does as much honor to the servant as to the lord.

Nobility of reverence, liberty in dependence, active and useful work —these are the elements of service for an Israelite. We understand that on so lofty a notion we can graft the idea of the service of God.

To serve God, then, will be to recognize Him as Lord, to give Him the marks of honor which this title supposes, to admit freely the submission which is due Him, to labor effectively at His work, and thus to procure His glory. When God created man, He placed him in a garden which He Himself had planted and turned this garden over to him to be cultivated. Man is called to the honor of finishing the work undertaken by the Creator, and by doing it according to the orders he has received from Him, he will do honor to his Lord.

Sin destroyed the original harmonious ease of this service, and the service of God became difficult. But it is nonetheless the law of the creature—for the creature's own honor and for the glory of Him Who created it. "Fear the Lord, and serve Him, and hearken to His voice, and do not provoke the mouth of the Lord." (1 Kings 12:14) We should not forget that this "fear" is less fear of His punishments than reverence for His Divine Majesty. Fear and obedience make a service of the work of man.

Worship occupies the first place in the service of God. It expresses itself, first of all, in adoration, the posture of the servant prostrate before his lord: "The Lord Thy God shalt thou worship and Him only shalt thou serve." (Matt. 4:10) So the first commandment is summarised. Worship with its sacrifices, its songs of praise, its feasts; this is the official expression of the service of God. Worship is the first of the divine demands. Pharaoh learned this to his sorrow, he who aimed at opposing it, in order to keep the Hebrews at his own service.

An outward worship, however, is not enough: "Therefore, serve the Lord in truth and with your whole heart." (1 Kings 12:24) The heart is not, in the language of the Bible, the seat of the affections. This role is assigned to the bowels. The heart is the mover of the free, voluntary, conscious life. In its depths it fashions the counsels which direct man towards good or evil, and it is in the heart that impulses from on high will be perceived, the spirit which God sends to man to permit him to realize great accomplishments. To serve God with all one's heart is, therefore, to turn all one's conscious and free activity to giving God the honor and the obedience which are due Him. It means giving this homage deliberately and willingly. Thus God repelled the people who aspired to approach Him, honoring Him with their lips while their hearts contradicted their words, and their outward signs of reverence became merely practiced gestures. (Is. 29:13)

It was many centuries before the mountains of Ephraim heard like an echo the words of Jesus to the woman of Samaria: "True adorers adore the Father in spirit and truth." These long centuries have served to teach us that the spirit of God is necessary to the heart of man to permit him truly to serve God; for, of itself, the heart is incapable of such a service. Through all its history Israel experienced this difficulty.

From the beginning the people had been warned, from the covenant at Sichem in the days of Josue. (Jos. 24) It was in virtue of a free alliance that the Israelites chose to serve their Lord: "But if it seem evil to you to serve the Lord, you have your choice. Choose this day that which pleases you, whom you would rather serve, whether the gods whom your fathers served in Mesopotamia, or the gods of the Amorrhites, in whose land you dwell. But as for me and my house, we will serve the Lord." "We also, we will serve the Lord," answered the people, "for He is our God." Josue did not conceal the difficulties which such a promise entails: "You will not be able to serve the Lord: for He is a holy God and mighty and jealous, and will not tolerate your wickedness and sins." "No," cried the people, "but we will serve the Lord." "You are witnesses against yourselves," answered Josue, "that you yourselves have chosen the Lord to serve Him." "We are witnesses.... We will serve the Lord our God, and we will be obedient to His commandments."

The enthusiasm of the people is sincere. It had its source in their gratitude to Him Who has drawn them from their harsh servitude in Egypt, where they were subject to back-breaking labor by the pitiless Pharaoh. By freeing them from this slavery, God acquired a right to their voluntary service, and the power which He manifested in this circumstance helps us to understand what kind of protection could be expected from such a Lord. The whole history of Israel, however, is there to show how well founded were the fears of Josue. The children of Israel were no more able than their fathers to serve their only Lord. They did not cease to have recourse to all the Baals in the land of Canaan, hoping to obtain from them the fruits of the land. Their conduct was just the reverse of the commandments they had received: "For there is no truth, and there is no mercy, and there is no knowledge of God in the land. Cursing and lying and killing and theft and adultery have overflowed, and blood hath touched blood." (Osee 4:1–2) "Israel has become a wanton heifer: she has broken my yoke, she has burst my bands, and has said, 'I will not serve.'" (Osee 4:16, Jer. 2:20) History confirms the gloomy outlook of Josue: The service of God is above the capacity of the human heart, of its good will.

Prophets like Osee and Jeremias, who reproached Israel for her infidelities, also had the mission of applying the remedy. Right reason, that is, the heart, demands that man serve God. The creature should serve the Creator, those whom the Lord has freed from servitude should pledge themselves to the service of their Liberator. Their duty is clear. It is inevitable. But the distance from God to the creature is too great; man is too close to his immediate needs and his instinctive desires for his rational will to be sufficient to keep him faithful to the service of God. The profound vital thrust, which the language of the

Bible calls the soul, is irresistibly borne to tangible goods, and it draws the heart along in its disorderly pursuit of its ravenous appetites. To quell this tumult in the soul, to direct its desires, Osee and Jeremias insist on an aspect of God which until then had passed almost unnoticed. God is not only the Lord Who has created Israel and Who has freed it by the strength of His arm, He is for His people a father with a mother's tenderness, a spouse passionately in love with Israel. Therefore the service of God ceases to be merely a debt of gratitude, a duty in conscience, a rational attitude. It becomes a spontaneous need of the soul, which, sensing the love with which it is surrounded, clings as though with an instinctive yearning to Him Who loves it: "For Thee my soul hath thirsted, in a desert land where there is no way and no water. And I will rejoice under the covert of Thy wings. My soul hath stuck close to Thee." (Ps. 62) This adherence is the answer which the kind attentions of God's love commanded: "I have loved thee with an everlasting love: therefore, have I drawn thee, taking pity on thee." (Jer. 31:3)

The expected formula will come to light from the pen of the preacher in Deuteronomy: "And now, Israel, what doth the Lord thy God require of thee, but that thou fear the Lord thy God, and walk in His ways and love Him, and serve thy Lord and thy God with all thy heart, and with all thy soul: And keep the commandments of the Lord, and His ceremonies which I command thee this day, that it may be well with thee? Behold, heaven is the Lord's thy God, and the heaven of heaven, the earth and all things that are therein. And yet the Lord hath been closely joined to thy fathers, and loved them and chose their seed after them: that is to say, you, out of all the nations, as this day it is proved." (Deut. 10:13–15) Service through love in answer to the divine predilection becomes a work of the whole man, heart and soul. It ceases to be an impossibility.

God has taken the first step in this love. "The Lord thy God hath chosen thee to be His peculiar people of all the peoples that are upon the earth. Not because you surpass all nations in number, is the Lord joined with you, and hath chosen you: for you are the fewest of any people. But because the Lord hath loved you." (Deut. 7:6–8) He has a right to expect the attachment of His people in return: "The Lord your God trieth you, that it may appear whether you love Him with all your heart, and with all your soul, or not. Follow the Lord your God and fear Him, and keep His commandments and hear His voice. Him you shall serve and to Him you shall cleave." (Deut. 13:3–4)

Summarizing the teaching of the Prophets, Deuteronomy is careful not to forget that the service of God does not consist merely in giving Him worship. The love which God has shown for His people by giving them positive services demands in return that His servants show the same kindness towards their neighbor: "Because the Lord your God, He is the God of gods and the Lord of lords, a great God and mighty and terrible, Who accepteth no person, nor taketh bribes. He doth judgment to the fatherless and the widow, loveth the stranger, and giveth him food and raiment. And do you therefore love strangers: because you also were strangers in the land of Egypt. Thou shalt fear the Lord thy God and serve Him only. To Him thou shalt adhere." (Deut. 10:17–20) To serve God by following Him is therefore to imitate Him, that is to say, to take Him not only as a Model in one's manner of acting, but also to co-operate with the work which He Himself is doing. The servant who loves his lord should earnestly work with him for the realization of the plans he holds dear. "He that oppresseth the poor upbraideth his Maker; but he that hath pity on the poor honoreth Him." (Prov. 14:31) The service of God thus understood is not mere submission to His orders; it becomes a glad and practical co-operation with Him Who attaches His servants to Himself because He loves them and because He wishes to associate them with the glory of His works.

The revelation of the love of God helps us to see the possibility of the service of God. At the same time are brought into detail the means, the end, the task that lies ahead, and the glorious issue. "But thou, Israel, are My servant, Jacob whom I have chosen, the seed of Abraham my friend. I have taken thee from the ends of the earth, and from the remote parts thereof have called thee, and said to thee: Thou art My servant, I have chosen Thee, and have not cast thee away. Fear not, for I am with thee; turn not aside, for I am thy God. I have strengthened thee and I have helped thee; and the right hand of My just one hath upheld thee." (Is. 41:8–10) "You are My witnesses,

saith the Lord: and I am God. I am the Lord, your holy One, the
Creator of Israel, your King. They who hear My Name, I have created them for My glory." (Is. 43:7, 10, 15)

Created for the service and glory of its King, Israel was crushed
under the weight of such honor. It had abandoned its God to run
after idols. Neglecting its Lord, it allowed itself to be led astray by its
disordered appetites. Sin drew it far from its God and far from happiness. "But this is a people that is robbed and wasted. They are all
the snare of young men, and they are hid in the houses of prisons.
They are made a prey and there is none to deliver them; a spoil, and
there is none that saith: Restore." (Is. 42:12) God's love, however, is
bound to prevail. Sin itself can set no insurmountable obstacle to its
victorious march: "And now saith the Lord that created thee, O
Jacob, and formed thee, O Israel: Fear not, for I have redeemed thee
and called thee by thy name. Thou art mine." (Is. 41:3) "I have blot-
ted out thy iniquities as a cloud and thy sins as a mist: return to me,
for I have redeemed thee. Give praise, O ye heavens, for the Lord
hath shown mercy: shout with joy, ye ends of the earth. Ye mountains, resound with praise, thou, O forest and every tree therein: for
the Lord hath redeemed Jacob, and Israel shall be glorified." (Is.
44:22–23)

To manifest His glory in the creation, the formation, the assem-
bling, the deliverance, the redemption of His people, God chose, in
the course of the centuries, certain privileged men who were His
friends and servants in the highest sense of the word. To bring about
the birth of His people, He chose the Patriarchs, His friend Abraham,
Jacob His servant. "To feed Jacob His servant, and Israel His inheri-
tance, He chose David, and took him from the flocks of sheep." (Ps.
77:70–71) To transmit His word, to seal His alliance, to tighten it
when it showed a tendency to relax, He first sent Moses His servant
and then, through the course of the ages, His servants and prophets.
Despite many weaknesses, the founders, the builders of the people and
of the kingdom, truly played their roles as servants, cleaving to God
and to the realization of His work, faithfully carrying out His will,
supported in all their toil by the Lord, Who had chosen them and
Who was always with them. God called them His servants and His
friends, and they responded to that love of choice by placing all their

energy at the service of the work to be accomplished for the glory of their Lord.

God's supreme glorification is to be found in His triumph over sin. It will also be the glory of His Servant. The Redemption, which in spite of sin brings the work of Creation to perfection, is the most glorious of the works of God. In this work also God wished to associate His free creature, man His servant. At the culminating point of the Old Testament's revelation, God glories in the triumph of this Servant: "Behold My Servant shall understand: He shall be exalted and extolled, and He shall be exceeding high." (Is. 52:13) We know the description that follows. The Servant, the Elect, the Friend of God, has taken upon Himself the sin of the multitude, He is humbled even to the bearing of chastisement for the crimes of His people, He carries His devotion even to the sacrifice of His life. He thus accomplishes to the very end the divine good pleasure. Conqueror by this total immolation of Himself in the service of God and of His brethren, He now shares the fruits of His victory with them for whom He suffered. The triumphant Servant makes just the multitude whose sin He bore. The ritual sacrifice was the highest expression of the service of God in worship, the act of adoration, in the fullest sense of the word. By sacrificing His will and His life for the good of His brethren, the Servant accomplished the greatest of the works of God, the Redemption.

In the course of the centuries which followed this prophecy, there were not wanting good Israelites who endeavored to serve their Lord with all their heart and all their soul. There are even found such servants who belong to Israel only in spirit, without being of the race of Abraham according to the flesh: "And the children of the stranger that adhere to the Lord, to worship Him and to love His name, to be His servants. . . . I will bring them into My holy mountain and will make them joyful in My house of prayer . . . for My house shall be called the house of prayer, for all nations." (Is. 56:6-7) But not so much the people as a whole, as the best of its sons, attained the summits of the service and the love described by the prophet of the Exile. The triumph of the suffering Servant remains for Judaism an ideal and a mystery. How, in fact, are we to reconcile the assertions of the prophet? The Lord is the sole Redeemer of His people fallen into the slavery of sin, and it is His Servant Who, taking upon Himself this sin, removes it and obtains the victory. Logic at once demands and rejects the identity of the Servant and of the Lord.

The fulfillment has come to set at rest the demands of logic by the revelation of a fresh mystery. He Who was the servant, obedient even to the death of the cross, was truly the equal of God. And God has glorified Him by bestowing on Him a name that is above every name in heaven, on earth, and under the earth. Thus every tongue proclaims that Jesus—the Servant—is Lord, to the glory of God the Father. (Phil. 2:6–11)

The Christian revelation does not renounce the truths that were given to Israel. But in revealing the point at which they should converge, it gives direction to all the lines of research into the Old Testament. Who would have suspected at what point the work of the Servant and His victory were going to become identified with the work and the glory of God? The illumination of the Christian revelation casts a new light on the notion of the service of God.

In every servant it is love that reconciles the contradictory aspects of service, liberty and dependence. But in the Word Incarnate this reconciliation goes beyond all limits. It is rooted in the mysterious Unity of the Trinity. The work of the Son and the work of the Father is all one. (John 5:17) "The Son can do nothing of Himself, but only what He sees the Father doing. For whatever He does, this the Son does also, in like manner." (John 5:19) Jesus does not seek His own glory, but only the glory of Him Who sent Him. It is the Father Who is concerned in glorifying Him. (John 7:18, 8:50) The world will be obliged to recognize that He loves the Father when it sees Him carry out His orders. (John 14:31) "The Father is greater than I. I also have kept My Father's commandments, and abide in His love." (John 14:28, 15:10) The love of the Father and the Son, the unity of the Father and the Son in this love, such is the mystery, the revelation of which throws a light on the role of the Servant. The Love of the Father awakens in the Son an equal and identical Love, which causes Him to accomplish with a liberty and a dependence, each as total as the other, what the Father does. This mystery, hidden in God, our eyes have beheld in the Humanity of Jesus.

For Jesus, as for all men, the service of God through love is expressed in the love with which He places Himself at the service of His brethren. "I am in your midst as he who serves." (Luke 22:27) He serves them at table better than Abraham served his guests. He washes their feet, He gives Himself to them as food. These outward demonstrations are only a sign of His total service. Savior, He has taken upon Himself all their sorrows. Lamb of God, He has taken upon Himself all their sins, and thus He fulfills all justice. "I have not come to be served, but to serve, and to give my life as a ransom for many." (Mark 10:45)

After such an achievement, Christian service knows no limits. Its possibilities, like its demands, become infinite.

The service of worship has been carried to its perfection since Christ's coming into this world; as He said to His Father: "You are not pleased with holocausts and sacrifices; behold Me here to do Your will." This sacrifice of His will the one Priest has offered in a humanity identical with ours. He has learned through suffering what obedience means. When we ourselves enter into His obedience, we become capable of giving the Savior a perfect worship. The death of the Savior has freed us from the slavery in which he who holds sway over death has held us in fear. It has purified our hearts of the works of death, and we are henceforth able to offer to God a living and true worship which is pleasing to Him, the homage of our submission and our thanksgiving, the sacrifice of ourselves in the service of our brethren. (Heb. 2:14–18, 5:7–10, 9, 14, 10:5–10, 12, 28, 13:15–16)

By adoring and serving the creature instead of the Creator, the lie instead of the true God, we had become slaves of vanity. (Rom. 1:25) Sin reigning in our bodies made us subject to its lusts. (Rom. 6:12) Christ's death delivered us; delivered from sin, we have become servants of God. We are able to bear fruits of holiness; we labor for eternal life. (Rom. 6:22) The spirit of Christ dwells in us and spreads in our hearts the love which comes from God. (Rom. 5:6) The Christian is moved to serve God by the same love which inspired Christ in the service of His Father. To serve God in Christ is to be drawn into the eternal movement which unites the Son with the Father. The Christion can henceforth love and serve God with all his heart and all his soul.

He who is seized by this Spirit becomes the friend, the brother of

Christ, and, at the same time, the beloved son of the Father. If he is capable of serving God, it is because he has become the servant of Christ. The Spirit which makes us cry "Abba" (Father) is the same which makes us proclaim, "Jesus is Lord." (1 Cor. 12:3) This profession of faith is the sign of the Christian. All his glory is to call himself the servant of Christ. For the Christian, freedom and slavery are indifferent things. The service of Christ makes him free in slavery, just as it holds him back from abusing his liberty. (1 Cor. 7:21–22; Gal. 3:28, *passim*) Free, St. Paul becomes the servant of all in order to win all to Christ. (1 Cor. 9:19)

This service of Christ cannot be better expressed than by the service of others, in a gift of self to the work which Christ began upon earth. The servant begins to follow his Lord, to continue His work by the same means: "If I were still trying to please men I should not be a servant of Christ." (Gal. 1:10) "For we preached not ourselves, but Christ Jesus, and ourselves merely as your servants in Jesus." (2 Cor. 4:5) Seeing His apostles continuing His work, the Lord called them His servants and His friends. The love which they had for Him could only be manifested by submission to His instructions and by the actual and very humble service of their brethren. "Abide in My love. . . . If you keep My commandments you will abide in My love, as I also have kept My Father's commandments. . . . These things I command you, that you may love one another." (John 15:9–11, 15, 17) "You call Me Master and Lord, and you say well, for so I am. If, therefore, I, the Lord and Master, have washed your feet, you ought to wash the feet of one another. . . . My commandment is that you love one another as I have loved you." (John 13:13–15, 34)

This service is founded on the love which makes the presence of the Savior constant. As the Father is always with the Son, Christ will always be with His servants. Attached as they are by this love, everything is common among them. "If anyone serve Me, let him follow Me; and where I am, there also shall my servant be. If anyone serve Me, My Father will honor him." (John 12:26) Woe to the servant who in the Lord's absence mistreats his companions. (Luke 12:45) "But blessed are those servants whom the Master, on His return, shall find watching. He will gird Himself and make them recline at table and come and serve them." (Luke 12:37) For those who, after His example, will become the servants of their brethren, He prepares a table at which He will treat them as kings. "But to you who have continued with Me in my trials, I appoint a kingdom, even as My Father has appointed to Me." (Luke 22:28–30) To serve God is to reign.

Revelation progresses from service to love. Men spontaneously become aware of their duty to serve God, but for them to be able to answer with deeds to this demand, God must reveal His love. Even this knowledge is not enough. God Himself must place His love in the heart of man in order to draw him effectively to His service. In Christ and through His Spirit, the service of God is in us the activity of this life by which we enter into the vital current uniting the Father and the Son.

By unveiling the mysterious splendor of the service of God, the Christian revelation emphasizes its demands. But this is not the place to go into detail. We can see from this general view whether the life of the Christian ought to be active, personal, and how, at the same time, this activity is necessarily dependent. Here abnegation and obedience play an essential role, the necessity and depth of which St. John has especially emphasized. The apostolic mission, which is the highest form of the service of God, is also that which requires the most complete sacrifice of all personal interest and all self-will.

Love is exacting. But, happily, it is a gift of God, the gift in the truest sense of the word or, rather, God giving Himself. Everything is grace in the service of God, through love. The love that urges a man to give himself more to the service of God and to choose the best means for this purpose should be considered as a love which comes from on high. (*Exercises,* 184, 338) The Creator and Lord, communicating Himself to His creature, embraces him in His love and praise[1] and places him also in the disposition of choosing the best way for advancing in His service. (*Exercises,* 15) To serve the Divine Majesty will always be a grace to be asked without ceasing. (*Exercises,* 46, 104, 233)

Christus, No. 11, July 1956

God's Glory and Apostolic Activity

YVES RAGUIN, S.J.

AT THE END of the history of salvation, the heavenly Jerusalem will rise in the clouds to welcome the elect. In the midst of the City, the Lamb shall be enthroned. Woe, weakness, honor, and power will be absorbed in His glory. In this light, the elect will discover the grandeur of God in Himself and in all creation. This glory was hidden in the world of men and they knew it not. . . . God, present in creation, allowed a few rays of His splendor to escape, to draw the attention of men, but men saw nothing in their brightness but a reflection of the things that pass and not a sign given them by God to invite them to seek, beyond the glitter, the fullness of His glory.

To see the divine glory, one must seek it passionately. Before Christ, men were afraid to look upon it, for it was not then possible to "see God and not die." The too brilliant reflection of this glory must inflict a terrible blow on the hearts of man, like that of a blazing arrow. Was it not for this reason that Moses, coming down from Sinai, had to cover his face? But in the New Law there is no longer need to shade one's eyes with one's hands to be able to look upon the divine glory. It appeared in Jesus, the Son of God. Looking upon Him, we can contemplate with wide-open eyes the very glory of God. That is why St. John exclaims: "And we have seen His glory—glory as of the only-begotten of the Father." (John 1:14) That is also why St. Peter found it so good on Thabor; it is so pleasant to live in the reflection of God's glory!

Men are ignorant of this glory. They seem to be more ignorant still of the fact that the only task truly worthy of man is the glorification of God. We have, however, the example of Christ, Who refers all His activity to this glory. He wishes this glory for His Father; He wishes it also for Himself, for being Son; He knows that His own glory and that of His Father are one and the same glory. He comes into the world, He lives, He dies, He rises, He ascends to heaven, always and only for this glory and to draw all humanity in His wake. All those who shall have followed Him shall one day be "absorbed in glory." From the present, according to the word of St. Paul, "with faces unveiled, reflecting as in a mirror the glory of the Lord, we are being transformed into His very image from glory to glory, as through the Spirit of the Lord." (2 Cor. 3:18)

We see the glory of the Lord illumine us, but what can we do to make it spread farther over the face of the earth and to make it penetrate a greater number of souls? What can we do for this glory?

The Torments of Glory

In the way of love there are many degrees—from the love that is still too taken up with personal enjoyment to the love of complete forgetfulness and of loss beyond hope of return in Him Who is loved. No human love can produce so profound an effect of detachment and dispossession as this perfect love of God. Without living outside this world or outside its senses, the soul lives in an ecstasy. With wide-open eyes it contemplates the divine glory and lives only for it. The glory which envelops it transforms it from light to light and the soul is overcome by a strange ailment, the "ailment of the glory of God."

All who draw near to God know this ailment, those in the active life as well as those in the contemplative. It was this ailment which was devouring little Therese Martin as she wrote the eleventh chapter of her *History of a Soul*. "I would like to enlighten souls as did the prophets, the doctors. I would like to travel over the earth, preaching Your Name, and planting Your glorious cross, O my dearly Beloved, in the land of the infidel. But a single mission would not be enough for me. I should want to be a missionary, not only for a few years, but I would want to have been one from the creation of the world, and to continue to be one to the consummation of the ages." Before her, it was the ailment of St. Francis Xavier. There is no denying that this love of the glory of God led him into follies. But God often allowed him, in the thick of the greatest dangers, to feel the effects of this divine glory and this power which filled the whole universe. Where our eyes are blind, he saw. He saw all the miseries of this world and his own bathed in this same glory. Perhaps it was for that reason that he, Xavier, dared to present himself, miserably garbed, before the powerful as the herald of the King of Glory. Before these two modern apostles, it was the torment of John the Baptist. He saw the divine glory soaring above the head of Jesus. He had conceived such respect for it, he found himself caught by such a desire to see himself seized and wholly enveloped by it that he was able to say nothing other than, "I am not worthy to loosen the latchet of His sandal," and, "He must increase, I decrease."

Before all, it was the ailment of Jesus Himself. All through the Gospel there is question of this glory. There is, however, one passage which strikes me as being more significant than the others. At the moment of the triumphal entry into Jerusalem, some pagans asked to see Jesus. For the Jews this little triumph had a messianic meaning, and one can say that in paying homage to the Messias, they were conscious of giving glory to Him Who sent Him. But what were these non-Jews to think, even if in their hearts they adhered to Judaism? What is certain is that Jesus wished to put them into contact with His Father and to turn their eyes towards Him. This modest triumph is merely symbolic. Jesus called upon His Father: "Father, glorify thy name!" Then came a voice from heaven: "I have both glorified it, and I will glorify it again." (John 12:28) "Father glorify Thyself!" Jesus had no other cry throughout His life. And when, from the height of the cross, He cried, "Father, why hast Thou abandoned Me?" was it not because He knew that this time, truly, His Father had "drained" Him of His divine prerogatives in order to give His own glory all its brightness? Which glory He will return to His Son on the day of the Resurrection.

Since that time, there have been no apostles who are not devoured by the same desire of being reduced to nothing for the glory of God. The apostle dreams the wonderful visions of the Apocalypse, where he sees the Lamb surrounded by the elect. He dreams of a humanity of which the Church will be the form. Seeing the end and the means taken by Jesus Himself, he yearns to throw himself into the experience of a crucifying love. It is for this reason that Therese of the Infant Jesus desired all martyrdoms together. "I should like to die, stripped like St. Bartholemew; like St. John I should like to be plunged into boiling oil." St. Francis Xavier wanted to run the danger of death from the hands of the inhabitants of the island of Moro to make trial of this word of the Savior: "He who wishes to save his soul shall lose it, and he who loses it shall save it." If Xavier had a clear, unhesitating confidence, it was because he knew the divine omnipotence and because he sought in all things only the glorification of his God. To those who accuse him of rashness, he can make but one answer: He has had the experience of the divine power, and the assistance of this power has been promised him.

Xavier passed over the sky of human history like a brilliant comet. His trail of fire still shines there. But other men whose flame has burned more obscurely have been consumed in a fire just as devouring. The example of St. Ignatius is striking. Was it not this hidden fire which set the soul of Xavier aflame? Then both of them, in their very different spheres of activity, have burned for the glory of God with a fire, the source of which was that which they wished to glorify. So true it is that there are many ways of being an apostle of God's glory. The field makes little difference, little difference its width. If the field of activity is too vast, the apostle runs the risk even of losing his head and thinking that he is doing much when he is making something of a stir. The first few easy casts may lead to illusion, but when the human dough becomes hard, the test of zeal for God's glory begins. If the exterior spaces close up, there remain at least some immense possibilities of activity in the interior spaces of the mystical Body of Christ. What a wonderful field for the torment of God's glory.

But time kills zeal, trial does also, and disillusion even more. These, however, are only stages which mark the road of glory. It is useless to go back to the history of the disciples of Emmaus. . . . It is more worth while to consider Christ Himself directly. The closer His Passion approaches, the more the torment of the glory of the Father consumes Him. But He knew that when all would be lost, all would be saved. We, too, ought to know this in the experience which He has left us.

The Illusions and the Mirages of Glory

When the love of God passes over a soul, it arouses it to its innermost recesses, and the whole man trembles with it. Many human feelings combine to harmonize the impacts of divine love. The same thing happens with zeal for the divine glory. It is the charity of Christ, of course, which urges the apostles to do great things for God's glory, but it happens often enough that self-love raises itself in them. Who has not dreamed of being surrounded and, as it were, of being clothed by the divine glory for which he is expending himself? A pursuit innocent and naïve, for the most part. God, instead of being offended, is amused.

The old temptation to power and rule always remains. The apostle does not want any glory for himself, but he wants it for his religious congregation, or, since that form of pursuit is sometimes a little ridiculous, he wants it for the Church. A more subtle temptation. The Church is not a purely spiritual society. Present in the world with the powers Christ has given her over men, she has received from this same Christ the mission of becoming, as it were, the form of the perfect humanity. Far indeed from reducing herself to a vision more or less inconsistent, under pretext of detachment and purity, the Church is an active reality in the world. God has placed her there to play a role, and this role cannot be of secondary importance. The Church has a keen consciousness of her rights, her privileges, her powers, and her ambitions. She also knows that Christ her Spouse wishes her to be beautiful and resplendent.

Now it is when we come into possession of these prerogatives and wish to glorify the Church by every means that seems good to us that the tragedy begins. Along this road there are plenty of illusions. Even while we wish for God's glory alone, we run the risk of satisfying our own inclination for a human glory with which neither the Church nor God has anything to do. We know all the value of prestige among pagans, and when we can, we never fail to display before their eyes the signs of a too human power. We repeat the saying of Tertullian,

"The blood of martyrs is the seed of Christians," but we know well that persecutions, when they continue, end by destroying the life of the churches. Was it not, after all, the favor of Constantine that allowed this seed to germinate and give a hundredfold harvest? Or rather, the seed being already broken from the earth, was it not the support given by the emperor that allowed it to become a mighty tree? Since then, the Church has not ceased to develop the point that in the Western world, nothing really great was done without her. But the blessing of prosperity given by God to His Church became for her the source of a terrible danger. She had enjoyed power too much and had taken too much delight in glory.

At every epoch some country can be found in which the Church enjoyed a privileged position. We should be glad of that, for it is normal for God to show that His work is not a failure but a real success. The recent inquiry made by American specialists on the efficiency of the Church shows that as an organization, the Church has nothing to fear, even from the best managed enterprises. But it is indeed quite difficult for some to see just where to stop in the pursuit of success. They are in danger of getting the Church into one of these impasses from which God can draw her only by persecution and the brutal loss of all her power and accumulated riches. We must not play with power or run after glory. When God gives them, we should use them discreetly, keeping in mind only the good of men and God's true glory.

At the other extreme, we see others with a desire to remove from the Church every kind of human incarnation. The dream of a purely divine glory is an illusion in this world. God wishes for her a glory which finds its expression in the whole of creation and especially in His Church. If the Word is made Flesh, if He has founded a Church, the members of which are men living in a human society, it was not to claim a glory that was purely spiritual. We must not forget that God has accepted and desired that everything be offered to Him, the precious stone and the ore that surrounds it. We must not be afraid of what is human; it will be found mingling always with the purest actions of man. In whatever we offer to God for His Glory, He Himself knows how to discern the pure from the impure, and even if what we offer is not without some human self-interest, He knows that the intention was good, and it is that which gladdens His heart.

For God's glory, the apostle should mobilize all his powers and all the riches of creation, and he should do it with a generous heart. If he keeps before his eyes the image of Christ crucified, he will never forget what price the Son of God has paid to redeem creation and on what conditions He is glorified today in the glory of His Church.

The True Glory of the Church and of God

We have said that the apostle ought to be burning with the desire for the glory of God and His Church. Some would wish to separate these two glories, making God's glory the object of long-term research and the other the end of an immediate and concrete research in which one could have fewer scruples. The fact of the matter is that these two glories are only one glory perceived from two different points of view.

The essential glory of the Church is that which she has from God Himself through the intermediary of the most sacred Humanity of Christ. It is of this beauty that the Holy Spirit speaks when He tells us that it is all interior, for the beauty of the bride is all for the joy of the bridegroom. This glory of the Church is a reflection of the Glory of God; more than a reflection, it is a sharing of this glory, since the Church has it because of her union with the Word of God.

The apostle sees this glory grow in the Church in the proportion that souls give their adherence to Revelation. He sees this glory, which God possessed before all time, become manifest in the soul that has just received the divine life in baptism. It is a great thing for the apostle that this glory shine in one soul more. He knows from then on that "God's glory" is not in the wealth of the churches, nor in the majesty of their buildings, schools, and ultramodern hospitals, but in the total adherence of souls to the divine life. The rest has its greatness and its value, of course, since it allows of a deeper rooting in human society, striking the imagination, drawing the eyes, sheltering the faithful, assuring the development of needed works. But what is essential remains the fruit of grace, hidden with Christ in God.

Around the glory which His kingdom in souls procures for God, the purest glory of the Church, are organized all the splendors, which are the gilded fringes of His vesture, such as the body of teaching and the practices which produce such wonderment in converts. One often hears it said in the midst of pagans that Christianity is poor in comparison with Buddhism, for example. A pardonable illusion, for these pagans have so few means of knowing the splendors of the Church. Her doctrinal splendors are never exposed in all their riches except in books written in foreign tongues. The splendors of her worship are even more inaccessible, and those which reveal to souls prayer and sacramental practices are even unsuspected. We who live the life of the Church know, however, that the body of teaching, that of the liturgy, that of religious practice, and that of discipline are wonderful collections which draw all their harmony, their grandeur, their savor, and their mystery from their union with the life of Christ in His Church.

The Word of God took a body to become the center of the new humanity while being the heart and soul of His Church. The latter, always guided by the Holy Spirit, is given all the exterior forms of worship and discipline. She is, for all her members, buried in the mass of humanity, like a tree thrusting its roots more deeply into the soil. She wishes to draw from man all the riches capable of being turned to the greater glory of God. What has she not changed into glory by the simple contact of her hand! She has blessings for everything, and by means of them she spreads something of the fragrance which He, the dearly Beloved of the Canticle of Canticles, left on what He touched. For this touch, all creation gives glory to God, for it recognizes the passing of the dearly Beloved.

The apostle who has come to grips with the mass of paganism must have a singular "view of faith" to believe that from the moral "misery" of these souls he can make glory gush forth. He understands that the cross alone can make of this misery a "glorifiable paste." If Christ did not lose heart before the Samaritan woman, before the adulteress, before Magdalen, or before Peter who denied Him, neither should the apostle, knowing as he does that the Savior has paid for all and that from the height of the cross He sees millions of souls, wretched before their meeting, become resplendent with His divine glory in the flood of water and blood of His great pardon.

The Apostle and the Stigmata of Weakness and Misery

In his second epistle to the Corinthians, St. Paul calls the ministry of the New Law the ministry "of the Spirit." If, he adds, the "ministry of death," that is, that of the Old Law, was surrounded with so much glory "that the sons of Israel could not fix their eyes upon the face of Moses because of the brightness of his countenance" (2 Cor. 3:7 ff.), what glory will not surround the activity of the apostles of Christ?

As we said at the beginning, this glory does not blind any longer, and to look upon the Savior we need not veil our eyes. The apostle knows himself to be bathed in the reflection of divine glory in virtue of his election to the apostolate. The message which he bears is not his own. His words have a weight given them by a power coming from elsewhere. He pronounces the words, and in them, the power of the Word goes into action. When he consecrates the bread and wine, he sees the Almighty give body to the words he pronounces. When he absolves, he knows that the same power washes souls. Seeing Paul and Barnabas perform miracles, the pagans wished to offer them sacrifices, as to gods traveling upon the earth, so great was the glory that blazed in their works.

Bathed in the reflection of the divine power, the apostle bears also the marks of the Passion. Ever since Christ saved the world by the cross, God's glory gushes forth in still greater paradoxes. The more the apostle resembles, in his soul at least, Christ humiliated and despised, the more glory will he give to God. When St. Paul shows his misery, when he lets his anguish appear, he knows, nevertheless, that this misery is an exaltation of the divine power. "For we the living are constantly being handed over to death for Jesus' sake, that the life also of Jesus may be made manifest in our bodily frame." (2 Cor. 4:11)

Participation in the death of Christ makes of the apostle a man crucified. The world knows this. Emancipated from religious prejudices, it casts upon the apostle a look of superiority. And the apostle seeks, if I may say so, to excuse himself from the consequences of his faith and of his adherence to the crucified Savior. That which is worth all the contempt are these stigmata which have not yet allowed their glory to escape. The faithful already perceive it, by faith. But the rest . . .

St. Ignatius, who was so smitten by the divine glory, has some marvelous pages on Christ humiliated and derided which seem at first to contradict what we know of his apostolic spirit and his sense of human realities. We must believe him on the point, just as we must believe St. Paul and St. Francis of Assisi: Apostles, we are men who are crucified, and we ought to clothe ourselves with the robe of contempt and humiliation with which the Savior Himself was clothed. This is not a wild dream, an anachronism. Contemporary history furnishes us, in the Communist countries especially, examples of terrible and humiliating treatment meted out to apostles and to Christ's faithful. These humiliations, which were inflicted in a prison or before a mad crowd, are the source of an infinite glory for God. God takes his glory and guards it jealously in His heart while waiting to return it to earth and clothe with it the Church of tomorrow.

Misery and failure united to the misery and failure of our Lord produce an incommensurable weight of glory. Xavier, hurrying along the coasts of India under a burning sun or stammering incomprehensible words before stupefied Japanese, is a good example. What kind of man was Francis of Assisi, with his pierced hands and feet, which caused him pain? But since it was Love that had reduced him to that condition, Love would draw from it an infinite glory.

If we only knew what glory God finds in the continual redemption of his apostles, we should be amazed. God is always there, bending over them to give them courage after their falls and nursing their wounds. But this glory is so hidden that the angels alone can rejoice over it with God and with him whom God treats with so much tenderness.

The apostle almost always feels a movement of interior revolt when, for the first time, he is presented to the way of glory through the Passion. He was ready to allow himself to be carried by the powerful wind of the charity of Christ and to allow himself to be devoured by the fire of Pentecost. One is so fortunate in the wind and in the fire. . . . But the way of the cross. It is easy to love it at one's *prie-Dieu,* more difficult to accept it in the concrete. God doesn't ask everybody to glorify Him in trial and failure. Those whom He asks should thank Him, and others, who seem to go from success to success, should not forget that someone is paying for them in secret. I believe that there must always be in the Church an equal weight of misery and failure which Christ unites to His own Passion to make the true, divine glory spring from it. Whether God bestows success on us or not, we should all, in activity or mystically, in the secret life of the soul, share in the sufferings and failures of the Savior and offer our poor person to the glorifying power of the Passion and the cross. Our stigmata are glorious, at least in the hopes they offer.

As St. Paul understood it, the mission of the apostle is a paradox, the key to which is the mystery of the Redemption. If we remember that He Whom we preach is the Crucified and that the cross is a madness, then everything becomes clear. It is impossible for us to escape the straining arms of the cross. We are crucified with Christ. That is why we carry a weight of miseries, promise of glory in Christ's resurrection. That which sends us forth on this way is love, the love of Christ which urges us. Love ineffable, but in the fruits of glory which it will one day produce, we shall see that it was this eternal love which God bears Himself and in which He allows us to participate.

PART II

Christ and His Mother

Christus, 1 January 1954

Christ in the Spiritual Experience of St. Ignatius

Donatien Mollat, S.J.

In these pages we should like to show the stages by which grace led St. Ignatius ever forward in the concrete and lifelike knowledge of the mystery of the Christ and how it caused him to pass from a generosity which in its beginning was somewhat showy to the highest supernatural wisdom. At the same time, we should like to throw some light on the powerful unity of this spiritual journey. It is the unity of the flame which from beginning to end consumed the life of Ignatius, a passionate devotion to the glory of our Creator, King, and Eternal Lord, Jesus Christ.

Loyola and Montserrat

The first spiritual experience of Ignatius of Loyola was the reading of the *Vita Christi* of Ludolph the Carthusian and the *Flos Sanctorum,* or *Golden Legend,* of Jacobus de Voragine. It was reading which, for lack of a better pastime, was done by a bedridden convalescent. The autobiography of Ignatius still betrays the surprise he felt. We see him taking up these books, putting them down, then taking them up again, "drawn by what he found written there." [6][1]

What, then, did he find there? What a noble Basque needed: deeds of prowess, exploits, "things that were difficult and arduous" [7], accomplished by the saints for our Lord. These lofty deeds enchanted him. Soon he was burning to equal them. "He paused to think and to reason with himself, 'Suppose that I should do what St. Francis did, what St. Dominic did?'" "All his thought was to tell himself, 'St. Dominic did this; therefore, I must do it. St. Francis did this; therefore, I must do it.'" In their footsteps he would go barefooted as far as Jerusalem, eating only herbs and undertaking all the hardships, "disciplines and abstinences which a generous soul on fire with the love of God is wont to desire." [9]

Through all the first hours of his conversion, therefore, Christ reveals Himself to this competent critic as the Teacher of the heroic, to this liegeman as his Lord. Ignatius was in a hurry to be cured so that he would lose no time in going on to distinguish himself by following Him. Meanwhile, with the respect of a disciple, he began to summarize in a copybook "the most important passages from His life." [11] In his fine handwriting he transcribed the words of Christ in red ink and the words of our Lady, His Mother, in blue. Already the noble formula "to serve our Lord" begins to appear in the *Autobiography*.

This first experience is a genuine spiritual experience. There is no mistaking the expressions of Ignatius. It is even now the vocabulary of the discernment of spirits: "Things seemed to him easy to accomplish." [7] This "ease" was not a mere impulse or a natural animation. Ignatius speaks of it with a calm, inward assurance which does not come entirely from himself. It is the first touch of the "good spirit," the function of which the *Exercises* will tell us is to give "courage and strength."[2] Already Ignatius notes the "consolation," the "contentment," the "joy," the "relish" [8] which he found in his reading. He sets up a contrast with the sadness in which his worldly dreams left him. He also received the grace of purity. At the sight of an image of our Lady and the infant Jesus, he felt himself cleansed and had from then on nothing but distaste for his carnal past. He prayed. The contemplative who was at the very heart of this soldier manifests himself: "It was his greatest consolation to gaze upon the heavens and the stars, which he often did, and for long stretches at a time, because when doing so he felt within himself a powerful urge to be serving our Lord." [11] A rare confession. In the depths of the night, John of the Cross discovered the mystery of faith; before the silence of the "infinite spaces," Pascal experienced a holy fear. In the starry heavens, which Ignatius was then reading, what was it that gave him so much courage to serve, if not the "glory" of his Lord. For him, Christ is more than a teacher of heroism and a noble lord. He is the Creator, Whose divine glory urges him on. From the days at Loyola, Ignatius had a knowledge of Christ that has an undeniable religious value. Already the essence of his Christology is preparing—our Creator and Lord. In the soul of this soldier, whose honesty is complete, there is already a great deal of love.

He presents himself, however, as a soul that "is still blind." [14] As his mule bears him slowly to Montserrat, "he does indeed think of the great deeds he was going to do for the love of God." [17] What draws him on over the roads of Spain towards distant Jerusalem is the attraction of the difficult, the relish for the rare deed, the famous exploit: "When he remembered to do some penance which the saints had performed, he resolved to do the same and even more. All his consolation was in these thoughts. He never took a spiritual view of anything, nor even knew the meaning of humility, or charity, or patience, or discretion as a rule and measure of these virtues. His whole purpose was to perform these great external works, for so had acted the saints for God's glory, without any thought of more particular circumstance." [14] Ignatius judged that he was then "without any knowledge of the interior things of the soul." [2] He was unable to solve for himself the case of conscience occasioned by the Moor whom he met on the road and who had spoken ill of our Lady. Should he "defend" at the dagger's point the "honor" of the Blessed Virgin against this Saracen? Like a modern Balaam, he had to refer this question to his mule. [15–16] His code was a code of honor and greatness with very little of intelligence in it. Amadis of Gaul still haunted his spirit. It was to his influence that Ignatius attributed the staging of the knightly watch of arms at Montserrat. It was then a spiritual man, very imperfect and still much of the novice, who "clothed" himself the night of March 24–25 at the foot of the altar of our Lady at Montserrat "in the arms of Jesus Christ." [17]

Manresa

At Manresa Ignatius began his meditations on the mysteries of the life of Christ: seven hours of prayer daily [26], besides High Mass, during which, "as a rule, he read the Passion." [20]

One day an elderly woman, well known throughout Spain for her piety, meeting "with this new soldier of Christ, said to him, 'May it please our Lord Jesus Christ to appear to you some day!'" Ignatius, "taking her words at their literal meaning, was surprised" at them "and asked, 'And how would Jesus Christ appear to me?'" [21] As far as apparitions went, this was indeed the dark night. The approach of Christ took place amid tortures. For months, scruples brought Ignatius to the brink of despair. "Help me, O Lord," he groaned. "Do you, Lord, show me where I can find it, and even though I should have to follow a little dog to find it, I would do so." Obsessed by the thought of suicide, he protested, "Lord, I will do nothing to offend You." [23–24] He who from the time of his conversion admitted "that he had continued in this same interior state of great and undisturbed joy" [20] went through the agonizing experience of ceaselessly repeating the confession of his sins, to which he had devoted three whole days at Montserrat. At last, "by the mercy of our Lord, he awoke as from a dream." Christ was not slow in showing Himself.

Concerning the new period which was beginning, Ignatius kept the conviction that he had been dealt with by God as a boy is dealt with by a schoolmaster. [27] He thought that five points summarized the lessons he then received.

God enlightened him on the Trinity. "One day while reciting the Hours of our Lady on the steps of some monastery . . . he saw the Holy Trinity under the figure of three [organ] keys," [28] giving forth a chord, the perfection, the harmony, and the fullness of which drew him outside himself. For the first time he speaks of tears and sobs. They were so strong that all his strength could not restrain them. Throughout the procession that morning he did not succeed in doing so, nor until dinner time. "Even afterwards he could not stop talking about the Blessed Trinity. He made use of many different comparisons and experienced great joy and consolation."

God also enlightened him about the creation: "With great spiritual delight" there was represented to his understanding "the manner in which God had created the world. It had the appearance of something white out of which rays were coming, and it was out of this that God made light." [29]

Once again, after having received the Body of Christ, "he saw with the eyes of his interior something like white rays which came from on high." This vision was accompanied with a high intellectual illumination, and "he saw clearly in the spirit how Jesus Christ our Lord was present in the Most Blessed Sacrament."

Many visions likewise showed him the glorious luminosity of the humanity of Christ: "When he was at prayer, he often and for a long time saw with the inner eye the humanity of Christ. The shape which appeared to him was like a white body . . . but he saw no distinction of members."

There was finally the dazzling experience of the Cardoner. On this point, one scholar has spoken of a "complete spiritual regeneration,"[3] of a kind of re-creation of the very function of knowing."[4] That is, in fact, what Ignatius suggests: "The eyes of his understanding began to open. He beheld no vision, but he saw and understood many things . . . with so great an illumination that all these things appeared to be something altogether new. . . . He thought he was another man with another understanding than before." [30–31] Concerning the object of this illumination, Polanco is satisfied with saying "all things divine and human."[5] More exactly, Ignatius declares that he "saw and understood many things, spiritual as well as those concerning faith and learning." [30] In the saint's language, "spiritual things" are God's ways in the guidance of souls and the principles of spiritual discernment; "things of faith" are what Polanco calls "divine mysteries," the Trinity, the mystery of Christ. It is strange, and yet characteristic, to find here "things of learning." Ignatius must doubtless place this light in relation to the vision of the creative act, with the contemplation of the starry heavens at Loyola, with "the other things on the face of the earth" of the *Exercises*.[6] Ignatius beholds the universe with new eyes, in a new light. "The fundamental grace" of this illumination has been characterized as "a synthetic view (according to the expression of Father Leturia) of the connection between all revealed truth and of the relations of all with the Majesty of the Most Holy Trinity: and this in Christ and in the Church."[7] On the subject of this grace, Nadal has pronounced the most profound judgment. According to him, Ignatius had then "received all from the Lord in a kind of spirit of architectonic wisdom."[8] Thus Ignatius came from it transfigured, as though he had come from Sinai.

Beginning with this day," writes Nadal, "some indescribable air of joyousness or of spiritual light radiated from his face."[9] This illumination of the Cardoner unified all earlier lights and visions. It made known their meaning. It developed their consequences in all directions. A solid tradition attached to this mystical vision the whole substance of the *Exercises* and even of the *Constitutions* of the future Society. Right up to the end of his life, Ignatius "refers"[10] to this grace for all kinds of decisions.

We are now able to draw the axes of the spiritual world of Ignatius and to reconstitute the interior vision which, little by little, was sketched in him. At the heart of everything is the Holy Trinity in its ineffable unity. On the first level is Its creative work, filled with light. Shining in the center of this bursting universe is the radiant Humanity of Christ, invisibly present to the world in the mystery of the Eucharist. It summons to the service of this work this soldier, cleansed by a purifying trial. Following the divine "consolations," Ignatius becomes human, tempers his austerities, trims his nails and his hair, takes an interest in the "fruit" which his words produce in souls. By means of the Humanity of Christ, the knightly deed is integrated with the deed that is cosmic and creative. The horizon upon which the Person of Jesus stands out is broadened. It has retreated to the infinity of the divine mystery. The glory that sits upon his brow is no longer merely the heroic glory of the leader or the aureole of the teacher. It is the glory of the Eternal Lord of all things. The "eyes of his interior"[29][11] are open. The great deeds of penance are now subordinated to the works of the apostolate.

In the Footsteps of the Savior

Meanwhile, Ignatius remained faithful to his first plan, Jerusalem. "The time was drawing near that he had set for his departure."[34] But the voyage conceived in the beginning as an exploit of penance became, after "his inner eyes" were opened, a theological act. "He desired, he said, to practice three virtues charity [which he names first], faith and hope." He was then a pilgrim, thirsting for "God alone," who ventured out upon his journey. He refused the companions that were offered him. He would travel alone, with "God for his sole refuge," with his three beloved virtues. "If he had a companion," he explained, "he would expect help from him when he was hungry"; if he fell, he would look to him for help in getting up, and he would thus trust him and place his confidence in him for these services and would place his affection in him, "when he wanted to place all this confidence and affection and hope in God alone." [35] He wanted no "other provision than the hope he had in God." [44] At the moment of embarking at Barcelona, "finding five or six *blancas* [small pieces of silver] in his pockets, all that was left of what he had begged from door to door ... he left them on a bench there on the seashore." [36] It was thus he left Spain, "penniless with only God."[12]

At the heart of his poverty, the Christ of Manresa was still radiant in the hours of dereliction. Ignatius was on his way to Venice, where he was to embark. As he neared Padua, he was so exhausted that a man catching sight of him, pale as death, thought him plague stricken and took to his heels. A few men, however, joined him, but they walked so fast that he could not keep up with them. They left him there alone that night "on a great plain." In the midst of this distress, "Christ appeared to him as He was accustomed to ... and strengthened him considerably." [41] During the crossing, "our Lord often appeared to him and gave him great consolation and great courage." [44]

The stay in the Holy Land was nothing but an act of love. He thought he was at the end of his vocation and planned on establishing himself in Jerusalem, "perpetually visiting the holy places." [45] Under the discretion of this formula, we recognize the confidence of love. To live in poverty in the land of his Lord, perpetually visiting the places sanctified by His presence, kissing and venerating His footsteps, impressing on his heart even His least movements, finally pursuing at great risk at this advanced post of Christendom the works of the Savior by "helping souls," the souls of the Turks about whom no one bothered, such was now for Ignatius, as it was later for Charles of Jesus, his whole "devotion." But the Franciscan guardians of the holy places could not countenance this .

Ignatius' dream lasted only about a fortnight. The final episode gives expression to the candor of his love. Before departing he was "seized with a great desire of again visiting Mount Olivet, since," he observed sadly, "it was not our Lord's will that he remain there in those holy places. On Mount Olivet there was a stone from which our Lord ascended into heaven, and the print of His footstep is still to be seen. It was this he wished to see again. Without a word to anyone, therefore, or without taking a guide (for those who go without a Turk as guide run great risk), he slipped away from the others and went alone to Mount Olivet. The guards did not want to let him in, but he gave them a desk-knife which he carried with him. After having prayed with deep devotion, he wanted to go to Beth-phage, and while he was there, he recalled that he had not noticed on Mount Olivet in what direction the right foot was turned, or in what direction the left. Returning, he gave his scissors, I think, to the guards for permission to enter." [47] Father Brodrick, commenting on this scene, writes: "Somehow one feels that few evidences of love could be greater than that little anxiety of Ignatius."[13] Such, it seems, was the thought of Christ Himself. In fact, "when they learned at the monastery that he had left without a guide, the friars made every effort to find him. As he was coming down from Mount Olivet, a 'belted Christian'[14] who worked for the monastery came upon him. The man had a large staff and, showing signs of great anger, made as though he were going to beat him with it. When he came up to him, he grabbed him roughly by the arm, the pilgrim easily allowing himself to be led away. The good man never let go of him. Coming thus in the grasp of the 'belted Christian,' he had great consolation from our Lord, Whom he thought he saw above him all along the way." All the meaning of the Jerusalem pilgrimage is in this wordless dialogue of love.

What Is to be Done?

It is significant that the last place venerated by Ignatius was the scene of the Ascension; again significant that Ignatius, thoughtful as he was, wished to impress on his memory the direction in which Christ faced as He took leave of earth and enjoined His Apostles to be His witnesses to the very ends of the world. The *Exercises* also end with a contemplation on this mystery. Ignatius, therefore, left the Holy Land, like the Apostles after the Ascension. In his turn, he heard the "Why do you stand here looking up?" Thus as he leaves Jerusalem, the Gospel pursues its course. To the very end of the universe, if necessary, Ignatius will still be the pilgrim of Christ. And yet, "after the pilgrim understood that it was not God's will that he remain in Jerusalem, he kept thinking on what he ought to be doing." [50] No more for him than for the Apostles was the future an open book which he had only to consult. It was a book to be written in tears, in sweat, and in blood. Ignatius knew only one thing: that he must "help souls." This expression, which occurs ceaselessly in the *Autobiography,* is that of the meditation of the *Two Standards;* there it designates the mission of Christ's envoys. The envoys of the wicked chieftain have the purpose of putting men in chains and fetters; those of Christ have the purpose of "helping" them.[15] The idea which Ignatius had of this task is as yet limited to this.

After an appalling passage of two and one-half months, Ignatius was again in Europe. It was the depth of winter; the cold was severe, and there was much snow. "The pilgrim had no more clothes than some breeches made of coarse cloth which reached to the knee, leaving the rest of the leg bare, a jacket of black cloth, much slashed at the shoulders, and a short vest of light hair." [49] At Venice, he received "a large piece of cloth which he folded several times over his stomach because of the severe cold." [50] Such was the poor wretch on his return from the tomb of Christ, who wanted to "help souls" in that brilliant and explosive Europe of the sixteenth century. The Kingdom of God does not come with much show. But what was he to do? Finally, the pilgrim "felt more inclined to study so as to be able to help souls."

Then began the long period of his studies. With heroic determination, this soldier, with no previous preparation for such an adventure, slowly won, after conquering the rudiments of learning, his university degrees. A forbidding undertaking and, in one sense, foolish. After his experience with poverty, Ignatius now lived more strictly the mystery of the humility of Christ, the second step in the programme of the *Two Standards.* All this period is under the sign of the shame of Jesus. From the first hour, one scene designates it clearly. Without giving an ear to human prudence, Ignatius takes to the highway, which is infested by the warring armies. Arrested, stripped of his miserable rags, and taken for a fool, he is led through "three main streets." It was then that he had the "representation of Christ led away," and he continued with his usual conciseness of speech; "he went without any sadness, rather with joy and satisfaction." He simply notes that "it was not a vision, as on other occasions." [52] Doubtless, he no longer perceived the luminous halo of Manresa. Now it is the humble "led away" Christ he is to follow. For Him he has revised his code of honor and courtesy. The noble Spaniard no longer says "Your Lordship" to anyone. "He had acquired the habit of saying simply 'You' to anyone at all, out of devotion, for it was so that Christ and the Apostles spoke." This, whether it was the Archbishop at Valladolid [63] or the captain whose soldiers had arrested him and to whom, in order to overcome all human respect, he not only did not say "Your Lordship," but also showed him no sign of reverence, not even removing his cap in his presence. The captain thought he was a fool and said so to those who brought him in: "This fellow has no brains. Give him his things and throw him out." [52]

In this period of his life occur scenes of derision and insults of every kind. One day at Alcalá an ecclesiastic and some laymen roared with laughter as they saw him begging. They leveled such insults at him as they do at beggars who are hale and hearty. At Salamanca he was jailed, calumniated, and suspected of heresy. At Paris everything is contained in the phrase, "He studied with young boys." [73] In order to earn his living, he was thinking of becoming a servant to one of the professors. The thought of Christ is ever guiding him: "I will imagine that the teacher is Christ. . . . If the teacher tells me to do something, I will fancy that it is Christ Who tells me." [75] A Spaniard whom he trusted stole his meager means. Ignatius abased himself to the extent of going barefoot the eighty miles between Paris and Rouen, without eating or drinking, to hurry to the care of this swindler and win him back to God. [75–79] He is not above that modest form of humility, humor. He is not afraid to tell Father Gonzales, with a smile we are sure, of an adventure which befell him towards the end of his life of study. On his way from Genoa to Bologna, he lost the road and ended by finding himself along the banks of a river on a path that was so narrow that he had to crawl on all fours for a very long time for fear of falling into the water at any moment. "But he reached the end at last. Just as he was about to enter

Bologna he slipped from a little wooden bridge and found himself as he rose covered with mud and filth. The bystanders, of whom there were many, had a good laugh at him." [91] Where is the headstrong gentleman who in the streets of Pamplona rushed, sword in hand, upon the handful of rustics who ventured to take liberties with him? The Lord to Whom he is pledged is a King Who is "led away" through the streets. To work in His kingdom and to "help souls," Ignatius became a child again and the most simple of men.

La Storta

His long novitiate is over. In order to "help souls," Ignatius must now be a priest. He enters into the mystery of the priesthood of Christ with this grace of the Gospel, this deliberate thought, this noble seriousness which clothed all his deeds with greatness. Ordained on June 24, 1537, with five of his six companions, he postponed his first Mass until Christmas of 1538. He needed these eighteen months to get ready. With his companions, he devoted himself to the life of the Gospel. One speaks of "a wonderful idyl at the beginnings of the history of the Order,"[16] an idyl of poverty and love. Ignatius was with Faber and Laynez in the countryside of Vicenza. They lived in a half-ruined monastery without doors or windows. Ignatius did the cooking, a kind of soup in which they soaked pieces of bread received in alms. All three slept on straw. It was Bethlehem all over again. They were overjoyed at living to the letter the life of Jesus. Ignatius wrote to a friend: "Every day we feel more the truth of the words, 'Having nothing, we possess all things.' "[17] At the end of this retreat, when they started off for Rome in little groups, they decided to tell any who asked them who they were: "We are companions of Jesus."[18]

During his studies at Paris, Ignatius had fewer "spiritual visions" and fewer "consolations" than before. Since his ordination at Vicenza, heaven seemed once more to bestir itself. "While he was . . . getting ready to say his first Mass," the pilgrim, as he continues to call himself, had these consolations, especially of the kind he used to have when he was at Manresa. [95] We know what reality these words conceal, the all-radiant Humanity of Christ. We feel that a new supernatural favor is in preparation. The year slipped by like a sacerdotal watch of arms, such as that he made during his knightly watch of arms at Montserrat. He asked our Lady "to place him with her Son." [96] The formula will flow a number of times from his pen; heavy with mystical intimations, it defies analysis.

Heaven's answer came in the chapel of La Storta, a few miles from Rome, with a fullness and a majesty that Ignatius would never have suspected. We have several accounts of it. They all coincide on the essential point, mentioned by Ignatius himself in his *Spiritual Journal*: "The Father placed me with the Son."[19] As at the Cardoner, he had the certainty that a profound change was taking place in his soul. God united him to Christ in a singular manner. According to Laynez's account,[20] which is supported by Ignatius himself, certain words confirmed this grace of true transforming union: "I will be propitius to you at Rome," or, according to St. Peter Canisius: "I will be with you at Rome."[21] Ignatius did not understand these words, and he asked whether he and his companions would not be crucified. According to Laynez, he added that he thought he saw Jesus Christ our Lord with a heavy cross on His shoulders and near Him the Eternal Father, Who said: "I wish, My Son, that You take him for Your servant." And Jesus, pressing Ignatius to Himself and to His cross, said to him: "Yes, I wish to have you serve Us."

In the life of Ignatius, this vision plays something of the same role as the stigmatization in the life of the Poverello. It is taking total possession, the conformity with Christ on the cross. The watch at Montserrat was brought to perfection by the marvels of the Cardoner; the watch of arms of the old student, now a priest hungering to help souls, is perfected in the close embrace of the Crucified. But, just as at Manresa, the vision of Christ was Ignatius' introduction to the Trinitarian life. The Father gives Ignatius to Jesus, He "places him with His Son," and Jesus, in accepting him from the hands of the Father, offers him to the Father in turn: "I wish to have you serve Us." Is not this an echo of the most profound revelations of the Gospel of St. John? "Father, You have given them to Me . . . because they are Thine, and all that is Mine is Thine, and all that is Thine is Mine." By this union with the Redeemer, Ignatius beheld himself admitted to intimacy with Father and Son in the secret of their mutual love. He is mystically pledged and consecrated to the service of divine charity. High and profound "sacerdotal mysticism,"[22] which will grow deeper from Mass to Mass and end only with death.

He who, on Christmas night of 1538, mounts the altar of St. Mary Major, *ad praesepe Domini,* is another man. We may be permitted to ask what this altar meant to Ignatius in the contemplation of the Christmas mystery in the *Exercises,* one of the rare texts in which he allows us to pierce somewhat the veil of his emotion and his tenderness. In a few words, he recalls the destitution and the love of our Savior, "the extreme poverty" to which Jesus reduced Himself "that after many labors, after hunger, thirst, heat and cold, after insults and outrages, He might die on the cross, *and all this for me."*[23] At the crib, Ignatius is already contemplating the Passion. In the same way, at his first Mass in St. Mary Major, he relived again, *ad praesepe Domini,* the scene at La Storta, where, at the prayer of the Blessed Virgin, "the Father placed him with the Son," and Jesus pressed him to His cross.

Rome

Christ trained Ignatius slowly. He brought him into His secret mystery. At Loyola and at Montserrat, the Master had won over Ignatius' chivalrous imagination, had inflamed his will. At Manresa, the Word, Creator and Light of the world, had dazzled and, as it were, recast his mind. At Jerusalem, at Salamanca, at Paris, the poor and humble Savior had marked out the way for him, step by step. At La Storta, the Crucified, in pressing him against Himself, had admitted him to the sacerdotal mystery of redeeming love. He had captured his heart forever. Ignatius was matured for the last stage, towards which an irresistible power had been urging him, ever since Manresa, "to help souls." [98] From now until the end of his life he is going to be closely associated at Rome with the mystery of Christ and of the Church.

The newborn Society was thinking of taking up the first plan of Ignatius. Its eyes were still fixed on Jerusalem. It was there that the first Jesuits were thinking of living out their poverty in "helping souls." But the journey was admitted to be impossible. They then did what they had forseen. They went to "offer themselves to the Vicar of

Christ, asking him to make use of them wherever he thought it would be more to God's glory." [85] A letter of Ignatius emphasizes the spirit of this step:

"We who have come together in the Society have offered ourselves to the Supreme Pontiff, as he is the lord of the harvest, which is Christ's. In this offering we made it known that we are ready for any task which he may think it good to give us in Christ. . . . We have subjected ourselves to his wish and judgment, because we felt he has a broader understanding of the worldwide needs of the Church. . . . May only that be done which is more pleasing to Christ! . . . Pray, therefore, for us that he make us his ministers in the Word of Life."[24]

To co-operate with the Church in the work of Christ, to wear oneself out in the Church in the service of souls redeemed by Christ, to be at the disposal of the Vicar of Christ, no longer to live or breathe, except to procure in the Church and through the Church "the honor and praise of Jesus Christ our Redeemer,"[25] such is now the whole ideal of Ignatius. So it is that in legislative texts, in letters of direction, in acts of government, we find traces of Christ in his life. The rather dry objectivity of these documents should not deceive us. For him who has understood the spiritual journey of Ignatius, it is an expression of his love; the highest, perhaps, is that of the love which is consummated in humble service. For him, the Church is Christ.

How did Ignatius represent to himself this unity between Christ and the Church? Hardly at all, it would seem, under the form of a spiritual organism of which Christ is the vital principle. He happens, it is true, to recall to the young religious of Coimbra that the neighbor is "a member of Jesus Christ."[26] His only thought is to be "deeply rooted in God our Lord."[27] Several times he proposes Christ to the sick as "He Who is eternal health."[28] But these images of the biological order and these allusions to the resurrection of Christ, principle of life, are rare. Most often Ignatius expresses the relation of Christ with the Church in the terms of lordship. Christ is "the head of the Church,"[29] the Church being His "harvest,"[30] His "vineyard,"[31] His "spouse."[32] If once or twice Ignatius calls it a "body," he is thinking of it as a social body of which Christ is the Leader rather than an organism of which He is the Head. "We should," he said, "love the whole body of the Church in its Leader, Jesus Christ."[33] In the meditation of the *Two Standards,* Christ is the Captain Who gathers his men into His army.[34]

And yet we should not be mistaken about this lordship of Christ. Although it is not connected with biological images, it does not go any the less beyond the juridical and moral level. In the thought of Ignatius, the universe and the Church are bound to Christ in their very being by the twofold title of creation and redemption. Being the work of His love and His grace, they owe Him their existence and have no other end but Him. He is the "common Master and God of all creation,"[35] the "Lord of the world,[36] Whose sovereign name ought to be praised and exalted by all creatures . . . created and ordained to so just and so worthy an end."[37] He is the center of history. Men have their place in relation to Him,[38] "our Eternal Savior"[39] [95], "He who is going to judge us"[40] [96], "Eternal King,"[41] "God all-powerful."[42] "He has created us all, redeemed all. He has given Himself entirely and wishes to give Himself to all forever."[43] "The weight of our love ought to draw us towards Him alone,"[44] Who, "Creator, has regarded His creature with an infinite love; being infinite, He has become, to to speak, finite, in order to die for it."[45] Of all these formulas slipping from the pen, there is composed an Ignatian hymn to the Lordship of Christ which recalls and sometimes borrows the accents of Paul: "All has been created by Him and for Him; He is before all things, and all things subsist in Him." (Col. 1:16)

To this lordship of Christ is joined His glory. It is the end of all creation and of the Order founded by Ignatius, which has no other purpose than to work for it. "We are pledged,"[46] "we are strictly bound to the glory of Jesus Christ our Lord,"[47] "glory and service," "service and praise," all these terms crowd upon each other in the the writings of the founder. But we are too quick to limit their meaning to an increase of honor given to God and to Christ. There is question, it seems, of something quite different, of a profound biblical reality. The divine glory is, in a more objective sense, that power of radiance belonging to the Divine Essence which causes all creation to be, envelops it, and manifests Itself through it. Creatures are only a reflection, a receiving point, a passageway for this powerful radiance of the Lord, "capable of receiving His divine and eternal glory."[48] Did not the creative act appear to Ignatius as something dazzling, out of which rays were leaping and out of which God produced light? [29] God had no other purpose in creating than "to draw His creature to Himself, embracing it in His love and praise."[49] The human soul is "an image of the Holy Trinity, capable of enjoying its Glory, at the service of which is the whole universe."[50] A vision of glory sustains and enlivens the entire course of the *Spiritual Exercises,* that Christ drawing after Him men of good will unto the glory of His Father.[51] This divine glory transfigures His humanity. It invisibly crowns the Eucharist with a halo. After Manresa, Ignatius often contemplated its brilliance. At the time he dictated his autobiography to Father Gonzales de Cámara, "he still had these visions often . . . in which he saw Christ as a sun." It is worth noting that this often happened when he was engaged on important matters, and it confirmed him in his decision. [99] This last characteristic is connected, perhaps, with an older notation. From the days at Loyola did not Ignatius draw from the sight of the starry heavens "a great courage to serve our Lord"? [11] It seems that here we reach a constant attitude of his soul. This great active saint lived with his eyes fixed on the glory of His Lord, reflected in the universe or mysteriously radiating from His Person. In this contemplation he found spirit and light. It was his food. He drew at the very source the strength to spend himself in the service of this glory. Thenceforth the Ignatian apostolate was first of all a collaboration in an "epiphany." A note to St. Peter Canisius seems to indicate this. It is an outburst of "joy in Christ Jesus" at the announcement of the fruit obtained by the apostle of Germany. "Joy," writes Ignatius, "to see the name of the Savior, to see Jesus Christ manifest Himself to all those of His Church through the virtue of His blood."[52] We come back here to the very thought of Jesus at the Last Supper: "And I am glorified in them." (John 17:10) For St. Ignatius, as for St. Paul and St. John, the Church is therefore the place where all the power of the divine radiance which Christ holds from His Father and which unites Him with the Father is unfolded.

No less interior and no less vast for Ignatius is the "service" of

Christ. It was for him, first of all, the devotion of the soldier and the knight for his Leader and Lord; hence the important role of the images taken from chivalry in the origin and formulation of his spirituality. But the reality they express overflows them. Christ "governs and rules"[53] the interior man by His grace, transforming him little by little into His "perfect instrument"[54] No one ever recongnized the meaning of this intimate action better than Ignatius. He is a master in the art of discerning these "visitations," these "movements," these "lights," these "spiritual relishes"[55] by means of which the Lord endeavors "to unite souls to Himself in intense charity,"[56] to make them "leave themselves" to "enter into their Creator,"[57] to travel towards the day when, "in the furnace of the eternal love of God our Creator and Lord, all our malice will be consumed. Our souls will then be penetrated with Him alone, our wills completely conformed to His and transformed into Him Who is essential rectitude and perfect goodness."[58] Then the soul will be "united to the charity and the infinite power of its Creator and Lord."[59] Such is the union envisaged by St. Ignatius when he asks his sons to be, in their apostolate, "instruments united to God"[60] and when, concerning the vow of poverty of his Order, he himself begs Jesus, in his *Spiritual Journal,* to conform him to taking the way willed by the Most Holy Trinity.[61] "Service" thus understood becomes an interior fidelity to grace and a kind of fusion of the human will with the divine will in love. We come back to the Augustinian teaching of God being more intimate to us than we ourselves are. The soul burning with divine charity and freed from its self-love finds itself again in God. "Ruled and governed" by Him, free and pliant in His hands, sharing in His infinite love and power, it sings the canticle of John of the Cross: "All is mine."

And yet it is in the Church that this transformation of our wills takes place. In the eyes of Ignatius, only the Church assures and guarantees this perfect union of man with God because, completely given to the service of God and His glory, she is uniquely ruled by the Spirit of her Lord. "Between Christ, the Spouse, and the Church, His Bride, there is one same Spirit, which governs and rules us for the salvation of our souls."[62] This unique Spirit inspires the Church from within and works in the innermost part of its soul. The Ignatian spirituality of service presupposes this objective and mystical reality, this nuptial union between Christ and the Church. It is not understood except in this perspective. To consume one's life and to surrender all one's will to the service of the glory of Christ in the Church is for St. Ignatius nothing other than to live, in fidelity to the Spirit, this mystery of love.[63]

The Spiritual Journal

A precious document permits us to enter still further into the spiritual experience of Ignatius. It is the fragment of his *Spiritual Journal,* of which we have already made use several times in the course of this article. It covers a part of the years 1544–1545. The devotion of Ignatius to the Man-God there appears constantly bound to the Eucharist and reveals itself in this period of his full spiritual maturity in all its mystical depth.

Accent is often placed on the Humanity of Christ, Whom Ignatius there calls Jesus. He beholds Jesus with His Mother. "He sees the Mother and the Son favorable to intercede with the Father." He calls them the two "Mediators" or "Intercessors." He sees at the consecration that "the flesh of the Blessed Virgin is [in] that of her Son," with such understanding that he cannot write about it. In reciting the *Confiteor* at the beginning of Mass, he unites himself with the *Confitebor tibi, Pater* of the Gospel, and he beholds Jesus in His sacerdotal function, "presenting the prayers to the Father, or accompanying what he says in the presence of the Father." He is flooded with tears "at the thought of Jesus . . . seeing Him disposed to intercede." The name of Jesus fills him with sweetness. Before the Mass, he thinks of it "with much love," and during the Mass, "all his devotion and thoughts end in Jesus." He repeats the name of Jesus with a tenderness that recalls St. Bernard. He feels as though "he were in the shadow" of Jesus. Recalling La Storta, "he feels bound forever to Jesus." He clings to Him as to his guide. "Following You, I can never be lost." On February 27, reciting the prayer *Domine Jesu Christe* before communion, he beholds Jesus, "white, that is His humanity." At the same time, he feels that "it is not the Humanity alone, but that He is all my God." And there is a gushing of tears and great devotion.[64]

We are struck by the affective character of this devotion. The shedding of tears, in the *Spiritual Journal* of Ignatius, occupies a place "truly extraordinary ... without precedent," thinks Father de Guibert, "in Catholic spiritual literature."[65] And with the tears there are sobs and sighs. The adjectives, "fervent," "warm," "intense," recur ceaselessly: "warmth and intense love," "love for Jesus," "very intense love, warmth and great relish for divine things," "increasing love for His Divine Majesty," "great and excessive love," "all in love for Jesus . . . and desiring rather to die with Him than to live with another."[66]

But in this mysticism one characteristic prevails; it is "essentially Trinitarian."[67] Ignatius beholds Jesus "at the feet of the Trinity"[68] and Jesus "in the shadow" of Whom he beholds himself, leads him to and unites him with the Trinity. He thinks that "it is from the Most Holy Trinity that he has just beheld and seen Jesus." When "all his devotions end in Jesus," he sees "how the first Person" was the Father of this Son, and he took hold of this thought: "What a Father and what a Son!" He received the highest lights about the Divine Persons, on their operations their procession, their circumincession, on the Divine Essence in its Unity. He "knows or sees, *Dominus scit,*" how each one of the Three Persons is "essentially in each of the others," particularly, and at different times how the two other Persons are "in the Father" and how all ends in the Father "as in a circle." At the begining of his Mass on February 16, Ignatius felt himself "drawn to the Father who gave him orders concerning all that regards the Son." He obtained access to the Father, "Who shows Himself propitious and gentle." He found himself, as it were, plunged into the most intimate mercy of the Father's heart. He recalls the day when, at La Storta, the Father placed him with the Son.[69]

This Trinitarian perspective is really the center of Ignatian mysticism. It appears in the illuminations at Manresa. We find it again in the *Exercises*. The meditation of the *Kingdom* draws men to the following of Christ in the glory of the Father. The meditation of the *Incarnation* begins with a contemplation of the Three Persons decreeing the salvation of the human race. At La Storta, Ignatius was admitted to the intimacy of the Father and the Son. The *Spiritual Journal* completes this experience. Each day Ignatius penetrates further and further, at the hour of the Eucharistic Sacrifice, into the secret of these ineffable exchanges. By means of meditation and the sacrifice of the "Eternal Word Incarnate,"[70] he draws close to the Father and sees open before him the abyss of love in the life of the Trinity.

We see to what depth grace introduced St. Ignatius to the mystery of Christ. It did not unveil for him merely one aspect of the life of Jesus—poverty, prayer, penance, zeal, humility—but it revealed to him "the breadth and length and height and depth of Christ's love which passes all understanding." It opened him to "all the fullness of God." (Eph. 3:18–19)

We have seen that Ignatius was "placed" in a very special way "with" the Crucified. In his election on the poverty of his Order, he chose especially as Leader and Model for his sons "the son of the Virgin, poor and exposed to every kind of adversity," asking his sons "to unite themselves to Him Who had lowered Himself beneath them all."[71] The cross is at the center of His spirituality and assures it a sound realism. But this humble Christ, "Whose divinity was hidden,"[72] remains always the Creator, "Who looks with an infinite love upon His creature,"[73] the Redeemer, who by His death, His resurrection, His Holy Spirit, and His Church leads back to the Father the humanity He has redeemed. Ignatius has ever present in his thought the entire achievement of the "Sovereign Goodness," which leaves the Trinity and returns to It, there to be consummated. This vision keeps him from all narrow moralism or asceticism, as well as from all individualism.

The spiritual experience of St. Ignatius is, then, after all, only a becoming aware of the Divine Love present and at work in the world through Jesus Christ and through the Church, a collaboration with His work, a docility to His Spirit. This apprehension of the mystery of the charity of God in Christ places this experience at the very center of biblical revelation. The religious entrusted in 1548 by Paul III with the examination of the *Exercises* recognized this: "The *Exercises* are without any doubt born of a knowledge of Holy Scripture and a long experience."[74] Doubtless, little inclined to speculation, a man of action before all else, for a long time uneducated, and then trained in the school of a scholasticism and a method of exegesis that was fairly nominalist, Ignatius had no intellectual tools which would permit him fully to exploit the intuitions of a St. Paul on the Body of Christ, on His life in us and on the recapitulation of all things in Him. But to the simple, grace was able to communicate notions that were the furnishings of the mind of the old student-soldier: lordship, honor, service, such a divine mandate, such a power and life. Through them there radiated freshly a singular glow of the glory of the "Eternal Lord."[75]

Christus, No. 8, October 1955

Contemplation of the Mysteries of Christ

HENRI HOLSTEIN, S.J.

"Without a care in the world he went on with his reading and his good resolutions. All the time he spent with the members of the household he devoted to the things of God, and in this way brought profit to their souls. He took great delight in the books he was reading, and the thought came to him to select some short but important passages from the Life of Christ and the Lives of the Saints. And so he began to write very carefully in a book, as he had already begun to move a little about the house. The words of Christ he wrote in red ink and those of our Lady in blue, on polished and lined paper in a good hand, for he was an excellent penman. Part of his time he spent in writing, part in prayer."[1]

It was undoubtedly at Loyola, during his convalescence, that St. Ignatius had the first idea of the contemplation of the mysteries. The prayer which interrupted his pious penmanship was inspired by the scenes of the Gospel which he recalled while copying in his fine hand the words of Jesus or those of His Mother. For the rest, Ignatius must have had under his eyes one of those illustrated lives of Christ[2] which were widely circulated at the time. We might suspect that his prayer, still more or less vague, had its beginning with the pictures which placed the Lord, the Apostles, and our Lady[3] before the eyes of the convert. The Gospel meditations of Ignatius probably began with a long prayerful look at these pictures.

Beginning with this discovery, Ignatius acquired the habit of "living" the mysteries. He "lived" the Gospel during the hours of his prayer at Manresa. In this light his vocation was strengthened little by little, and God's will in his regard became more refined. "All the time that remained free to him during the day he spent in thinking of the things of God, or on what he had meditated or read that day."[4] At Manresa the feeling of the presence of Christ never left the retreatant, who "saw His humanity with the inner eyes of his soul."[5] It seems that once cleansed from his sins, Ignatius, in a prolonged "second week," matured his vocation and little by little discovered, by means of his inner and apostolic experiences which he himself recounts, God's will in his regard, which was "to gather fruit in souls."[6]

Later, when Ignatius gave the Exercises, he shared with others the very simple method he had thus discovered. He also introduced souls to a spiritual familiarity with the Gospel, an atmosphere of election and school of union with the Word Incarnate by making present the mysteries of His life, passion, and resurrection.

The method of contemplation, as it emerges from the extremely brief and concise direction of the Exercises, sets up a number of problems, both on the ground of spiritual psychology and that of theology. We shall try to formulate them briefly and indicate along what lines solutions may be found.

First, let us read the directions given by the text of the Exercises. The method is sketched at the beginning of the contemplations on the mysteries of the Incarnation and the Nativity. [101–119]*

The preludes create a framework which is psychological and spiritual and in which is situated the contemplation properly so called. It is a matter of first recalling the history of the mystery one is to contemplate. Already known, it is recalled at the threshold of the prayer. "The first prelude will consist in calling to mind the history of the subject I have to contemplate." [102] The memory, which plays an active role in the meditation of the first week, does no more than introduce the subject here. It places the prayer of the retreatant in the Gospel context, in the temporal unfolding of God's plan. Hence the importance of this first prelude, which one might at times be tempted

*Spiritual Exercises of St. Ignatius. Westminster: Newman Press, 1951.

to consider as the simple recalling of a familiar story. The mysteries of the life and death of Jesus are the paramount times of a historical salva-tion, not the imaginary expression, the symbol or the "myth" of a truth outside time, but the concrete exploits of the Word, Who, being made flesh, entered into history and took it upon Himself. The first prelude assures to the contemplation of the Gospel its historical dimension "in the fullness of time."

The second prelude fixes the imagination by "representing the place" to it. [103] Beyond the psychological opportuneness, we must understand the meaning of this preparation in the perspective of the Incarnation. The Incarnate Word appears to us in place as in time. He is made manifest in this place and in that, and it is in a determined spatial context that He wishes to be grasped. The Incarnation took place "in the house and room of our Lady at Nazareth in the Province of Galilee" [103]; the Nativity, in the cave; and we must see "whether it is big or little; high or low; and how it is arranged." [112]

The will of the retreatant, finally, will be disposed by the eager prayer which constitutes the third prelude: "This is to ask for what I desire. Here it will be to ask for an intimate knowledge of our Lord, who has become man for me, that I may love Him more and follow Him more closely." [104] To know the Lord is not within our power; it is a grace, and it should be urgently begged, the retreatant through-out the whole prayer being in the posture of a suppliant, that the Eter-nal Father through His Spirit, may grant us the grace to know His well-beloved Son and to imitate Him.

This conformity with Christ will be obtained only by a prolonged effort at making the mystery present; that is the contemplation, properly speaking, which the Exercises teach. It takes place in an atmosphere of recollection, of concurring, to so speak, with this mani-festation of the Word Incarnate, represented by the mystery that is being contemplated: the Incarnation, which makes manifest the abase-ment of the Lord made man for our salvation; the Nativity, which is the appearance in extreme poverty of the divine good will; the Presentation, which is the first official offering in the framework of Judaic ritual of the redeeming Victim.

St. Ignatius makes sure of this presence by a threefold sensory at-titude: seeing, hearing, considering. There is less question, it seems, of three successive moments than of the breaking down into three times of a total movement of intimate union. The Directory of 1591 says clearly:

"In what concerns the points of the meditations reference must be made to the end of the book of the Exercises, where the mysteries of the life of Christ are distributed into three points according to the historical order of their unfolding. . . . What is said in the meditations of the Incarnation or the Nativity of the [successive] contemplation of the persons, their words and their actions ought to be understood in reference to the distribution indicated at the end of the book; in each point, according to the successive order of events, these three aspects ought to be considered without being obliged to see first the persons, then to hear their words, and finally to meditate on their actions. In certain meditations especially this manner of proceeding would end in confusion. What St. Ignatius wished to indicate in each point is that the attention of the retreatant should bear first of all upon the persons who are met there, then upon the words they utter, or their behavior, according to the occasion. The first point finished, he passes on to the second."[7]

It is a natural convergence of the attention which focuses on the objective and immediate reality of the mystery, as the Gospel recounts it, and not on a mechanical clipping of isolated sensory activities. This appears clearly in the contemplation of the Nativity, to which St. Ignatius invites us to be spiritually present, with a presence that is actual and active, accompanying Mary and Joseph in their movement from place to place and putting ourselves humbly at their service: "This will consist in seeing the persons, namely, Our Lady, St. Joseph and the maid, and the Child Jesus after His birth. I will make myself a poor, little unworthy slave, and *as though* present, look upon them, contemplate them, and serve them in their needs with all possible homage and reverence." [114] "The essential," says Father Casanovas justly, "is to do away with spatial and temporal distance, and to make the mystery present for us."[8]

"Then," continues the text of the Exercises, "I will reflect on myself that I may reap some fruit." [114] To this participation in the mystery which does away with distance, I should mingle some "reflection." The end of the contemplation is to conform ourselves to Christ by having ourselves take over His attitudes and adopt His points of view. It is the work of grace, surely, which demands that one surrender oneself as fully as possible to the transforming influence of these Gospel scenes. This grace, however, asks an effort on the part of the retreatant. It is not a matter of dreams or of giving oneself over to spontaneous movements of sensible devotion, or of being satisfied with flimsy, pious imaginings. Hence the need of a reflective looking into one's heart.

This reflection should be prudent. It is only a secondary activity, one which the recollection of a gaze fixed for a long time on Christ Jesus may make barely conscious. It should not transform the contemplation into a meditation and by untimely reflections interfere with the movement of grace, which bears the retreatant to a very simple prayer that has very little of the discursive about it. It would be better often to forget oneself and allow oneself to be caught up by the mystery than to become anxious and draw up a fine plan of perfection.

"He read the Scripture." Nadal says, speaking of himself, "and merely by giving his attention to the facts he nourished his love. There were no reflections. A simple, prolonged look at what was written, as if he were present. From this he drew no ordinary fruit, especially when contemplating Christ performing His miracles or dealing with men. This method," adds the close friend of St. Ignatius, "is very simple even when the mind has some difficulty in working, even when it is ill."[9]

The end of these contemplations, and the effect they ought to produce by a kind of osmosis in the soul of the retreatant, is clearly noted in the initial prayer of the third prelude, "to know, love and follow Christ." Christ shows Himself only to draw followers; but the soul must know Him to become attached to Him and walk in His footsteps. As with the Apostles, the growing familiarity with the Lord keeps pace with a forward movement, a closer adherence to His thought and to His perferences. "Lord, to whom shall we go?"

The colloquy starts this forward step in the way of poverty, of humble service: "I will beg for grace to follow and imitate our Lord more closely." [109] It is more sharply pointed towards the future (the election and its carrying out in a change of life) than the contemplation itself, which operates merely by being present to the mystery. An hour passed in contemplating the abasement of the Eternal Word, "Who has just become man for me," [109] in penetrating oneself with the sweet and realistic poverty of the crib, ends in the spontaneous desire "to follow and imitate" the Lord. Thus the ideal glimpsed in the meditation of the Kingdom, "to give proof of a greater love and distinguish themselves in the service of the eternal King and the Lord of all," is brought to a focus and made concrete: the service to which the retreatant offers himself is the sharing of the poverty, the acceptance of the humility of the Lord. When the hour comes to make a choice, the retreatant will be ready to choose that which will give him the certainty of remaining *with Him*.

The contemplations on the mysteries of the Infancy and the hidden life are prolonged by repetitions. These latter are intended to give a deeper penetration into the prayerful familiarity of the mystery, to produce a more intimate "connaturality" with it. Nevertheless, it is not a matter purely and simply of beginning the exercise over again, but of "going over the more important parts in which one has experienced understanding, consolation, or desolation." [118] The experience acquired in the first week of the movements, produced by different spirits, is here a guide to the retreatant. He ought to linger over the points where he has felt consolation (sign of a drawing, of a call) or desolation (sign of resistance, which he should overcome. If the rich young man had understood the meaning of the sorrow which took possession of him when presented with the programme of Jesus, he would not have left Him so quickly). The second week, even more than the first, is a privileged time in which interior movements succeed and jostle each other. There is nothing less placid than these contemplations. To see clearly in these eddies, to profit from them, to acquiesce in the grace, and to have nothing to do with the illusions of the enemy, such is the end of the repetitions, a new facing of the mystery to obtain its full spiritual benefit. St. Ignatius knew the value of time and the worth of repetitions.

Illusions in the second week could have the appearance of a false light. It is then that the demon "assumes the appearance of an angel of light" [332] and deceives the soul by "proposing fallacious reasonings, subtleties and continual deceptions." [329] The time of the contemplations is a time of light, but the distinguishing of the genuine light is there all the more difficult. It was surely for this reason that St. Ignatius, who in the first week asked us "to dwell on those points in which we have experienced greater consolation, or desolation, or greater spiritual appreciation" [62], here writes, "A repetition of the first and second exercises will be made, by giving the attention to some more important parts, in which one has experienced understanding [conoscimiento] consolation or desolation." [118] The word "understanding" is that which he employs in the third prelude "to ask an intimate understanding of our Lord." [104] He insists on the spiritual illumination of these days of "contemplations." The understanding is enlightened not by a process of reasoning which would come to the determination of practicing this or that virtue in imitation of Jesus, but from an inner light which is emitted by the mystery lived in prayer—precious light which we must not allow to go out and to which we must return and linger over.

The word "understanding," in the intuitive and almost mystical sense in which St. Ignatius uses it, well summarizes the fruit of the contemplations of this second week. A light penetrates the soul, which radiates, as in certain pictures of the Nativity, from the Lord entering the world.

> "The people that walked in darkness
>   have seen a great light;
>   to them that dwelt in the region of the shadow of death,
>   light is risen. . . .
>   For a Child is born to us, and a Son is given to us. (Is. 9:1–6)

Gently, by an insensible influx, this light transforms the retreatant and changes him into a resemblance to Christ. Enlightening his mind and strengthening his will, it prepares him for important decisions. The new man which he is becoming, little by little, by the time of the election, will be able to decide "according to the divine call." [172] Nothing henceforth will separate the retreatant from Him Who in making Himself known has attached him irrevocably to Himself. Who will separate us from the love of Christ?

The contemplations of the second week make us present to the mysteries of Christ, more particularly during the few days which separate the Kingdom from the meditation of the Standards, when we are brought into the presence of the mysteries of the hidden life. The retreatant clings to the movements of the Word Incarnate entering into the world by a prayer which makes him a contemporary and a participant in these mysteries.

This presence is obtained by an effort at sensory attention: seeing, hearing, considering. It is through the senses that the mystery penetrates us and that we get some understanding of it.

From the psychological point of view, this method is well advised. An idea does not strike or move or penetrate us unless it takes hold of our entire being. We are not pure spirits. Far from being ineffectual, the concurrence of the sensible faculties in indispensable. The liturgy is aware of it, since it has an interest in bodily postures and expresses adoration and supplication by movements of the body. The Gospel ceases to be a faraway history when we relive the scenes which it evokes and accept an active role in them. To place oneself at the service of Jesus and Mary in their distress is to realize "for oneself" the poverty of Bethlehem.

But above all, the Ignatian method of contemplation fully accepts the realism of the Incarnation. The Word Incarnate is the invisible God become visible, the impalpable Who makes Himself tangible: "That Which was from the beginning, Which we have heard, Which we have seen with our eyes, that Which our hands have handled of the Word of life." (1 John 1:1) Jesus is not a philosopher who proposes a doctrine, and the Gospel is not a speculative treatise. It is a history of One Who was born, Who lived, and Who died. Even when not speaking, Jesus teaches by His actions. To know Him one must take up His attitudes, walk with Him, accept as one's own His poverty and His cross. Christ does not say to those whom He calls: "This is what you will think, believe, and proclaim." He invites them to follow Him. It is by walking with Him that they will learn what His spirit is and what His message.

To walk with Jesus is to be where He is, to go there in order to find

Him. St. Ignatius leads his retreatant to Nazareth, to the crib, to the Temple, to the Jordan. He has him cover the stages of the earthly life of Jesus actively, concretely. Only this experience can reveal the Christ. In sharing His earthly condition, the retreatant takes on the feeling of Christ Jesus. He shares His preferences, he puts his sensitiveness and his heart into harmony with the Heart of his Savior.

"For in Him dwelleth all the fullness of the Godhead corporally." (Col. 2:9) To come to the Father, we must pass through the Son, and to know the Son of God, we must cling to the deeds of His holy humanity. In the newborn Infant, St. Ignatius discoveres the Word "Who has just become man." [109] Far from withdrawing us from the adorable God, the contemplation of His humanity is the indispensable means of bringing us to Him.

But because the Word Incarnate wished to perform deeds of men in a very humble human context, our contemplation must have us enter into this context and unite ourselves with the deeds which have made the Word of God one with us. "We have eaten and drunk with Him," said St. Peter, recalling without diffidence the intimacy which the Eleven knew with the risen Christ. (Acts 4:41) St. Ignatius wishes that we do what we can to make in our turn this experience of the Apostles our own. One perhaps smiles sometimes at the naïveté—inspired, some say, by the meditations of the pseudo-Bonaventure—of the contemplation of the Nativity. This supposed naïveté is the total acceptance of the law of the Incarnation; since the Word has become "God with us," we must be with Him, and we must mingle with the shepherds who have hurried to the crib to see, contemplate, and respectfully touch our Savior.

In this realism, there is, of course, some danger of puerility and excessive familiarity. But the danger will be avoided as soon as we have a care to maintain ourselves in the faith and in the recollection of prayer. The contemplations of the second week call for a great spirit of faith which seizes, so to speak, all the faculties of the retreatant and which with the help of the gifts of the Holy Spirit concentrates his whole being for communion with the mysteries of the Gospel. The grace which they suppose is surely a gift of God, but it is prepared by a prolonged and calm effort of docility to the Holy Spirit. This grace translates itself into a spirit of infancy which is far removed from puerility. "I confess to Thee, O Father, Lord of heaven and earth, because Thou hast hid these things from the wise and prudent, and hast revealed them to little ones. Yea, Father for so hath it seemed good in Thy sight." (Matt. 11:25–26) All self-complacence, all worried self-examination should be turned aside, as well as all dissipation of mind. At this price, one experiences at moments of sweet "consolation," fleeting or protracted, how good is the Lord to reveal Himself to the prolonged and unwearied gaze upon His sacred humanity. . . .

And the very simple reflection which underlies this look spontaneously takes the form of a dialogue. The retreatant speaks to the Savior "as one friend with another," as did Abraham, Moses, or the Apostles, those great friends of God. Listening to the Savior telling again the parable of the Good Shepherd, Nadal interrupts Him familiarly:

"I am Thy sheep, Lord, through Thy bounty. Thou art my good Shepherd. If Thou leadest me, nothing will be wanting to me, Thou wilt lead me to good pastures. . . . But, really, Thou art also the gate of the fold, holy Jesus? Who then is the gate-keeper? The gate-keeper is he who gives or refuses access from without to the sheep. Look at Me. You see that I am the door of My Church in My cross and in My death. I open My wounds to My true and pious sheep, I close them to sheep that are not Mine. Doing this, am I not the true gatekeeper?

"But what are these pastures, these brooks to which You lead Your sheep? It is I, I who am the pastures and the brooks; I am their sweet and delicious food. And note well, in this food, there is also drink. Received as food, I not only satisfy hunger, but I quench the thirst of the soul."[10]

Presence of faith which makes the soul a contemporary of the mystery! It does not suppress the activity of the mind, which reflects and draws fruit from what its eyes see and its ears hear. In this way, we think, the contemplation is distinguished from the application of the senses, in which the higher faculties become acquainted with a silence that is quasi mystical. But this presence supposes a recollected concentration, a fruitful and beneficial simplification of prayer.

Such a manner of praying supposes at the same time a great spiritual activity and a genuine passivity. It supposes activity because it sets into operation all the "powers"—intellect, will affection, sensory attention—and especially because it supposes a habit of recollection which permits this "concentration" on the mystery, without which the contemplation is not possible. But it supposes passivity also, for it must allow itself to be taken and modeled by the mystery, and it must allow itself to be invaded by the Lord, Who grants us an "intimate understanding" of His Person.

Indeed, frequent "desolation" at this time of the retreat makes clear the impossibility of our approaching this simplified manner of prayer without some freely bestowed help. Left to his "natural powers," the retreatant can only struggle in vain and patiently await the return of consolation. He then readily discovers that a greater exactness in the observance of the additions and the "rubrics" of the retreat would have helped him to find the Savior with greater ease. A humiliating and salutary experience which, as it makes him more humble and careful, prepares him for new lights and disposes him better to experience a relish in prayer.

"The second will be that as soon as I awake, I should place before my mind the subject of the contemplation with the desire to know better the Eternal Word Incarnate in order to serve and follow Him more closely." [130, par. 2] The fundamental disposition at this moment of the retreat is, in a word, desire. The desire of Daniel hastened the sending of Gabriel; the desire of our Lady prepared the Incarnation. Spiritual desire is at one and the same time an intense wish for the gift of God, a recognition of its complete gratuity, and a generous disposition to receive it. It begets at the same time effort and hope. To know the Incarnate Word, a great desire is necessary. God does not refuse Himself to souls of desire. The Father grants them intimacy with His Son, for which one must be disposed but which does not finally depend on our mere wishing it: "No man can come to Me, except the Father, Who hath sent Me, draw him." (John 6:44)

"In the contemplation of the mysteries of Christ," writes Father Casanovas, "we should not consider the scenes of the Gospel as removed from us in space and time, but try to make them present and actual."[11] Is there question here of a purely imaginative undertaking, a kind of pious historical reconstruction of a past that is gone? Or, as some ancient commentators would have it, of a vision of faith perfectly genuine and theologically justifiable?[12] It is worth while to give a moment's thought to this problem and to clarify, by a few considerations, that which is well founded in the method of prayer proposed by St. Ignatius.

The contemplations have a tendency to make real, as we have said, a spiritual presence with the Person of the Word Incarnate. They do not stop at the anecdotal aspect of events, but in them they attain to the Lord Jesus in the fullness of His human-divine Being. "Ut dum visibiliter Deum cognoscimus, *per hunc* in invisibilium amorem rapiamur." "We contemplate the visible things," writes Father Casanovas justly, "in the manner in which we regard corporal things; but the contemplation does not end with the visible, and it would be a serious mistake to think that it did. The inner senses are a path in the same manner as the outer senses are a path by which we come to an understanding. Sensible contemplation, which warms and illumines the soul, raises it to a knowledge of spiritual and immaterial realities. We ask, at the beginning of each contemplation, for an 'interior knowledge' of Jesus Christ. One of the purposes of this prayer is to reach the heart and the soul of the Savior."[13]

But the Savior Jesus is present in us by grace, which actually makes us members of His Body. The Risen Christ lives in us. He is not a faraway Person Whose features, or Whose deeds and actions, we recall by an effort of the memory. He dwells in us and we in Him. His mysteries are, then, our mysteries, His "thoughts" our thoughts, our life itself is His. *"Vivit in me Christus."*

It is this actual presence of Christ in His faithful that the contemplations of the second week "make real" to the retreatant. St. Ignatius does not assert this after the manner of the theologians. But he makes us aware of it by associating us with the mysteries of the Word Incarnate. In truth, Christ is born in souls at baptism, He rises in them at Easter, grows in them each time that they accept His grace and consent to the movements of the Spirit. The spiritual life of the Christian is not a life parallel to that of the Head of the Body, of which he is a member, or a life "in imitation of Christ." It is the very life of Christ, continuing in each one of the redeemed. Hence the actuality of the mysteries for the Christian and the necessity of being united with them, not as with faraway happenings, but as with immediate realities of his spiritual life.

The liturgy teaches us this, repeating each year at Christmas the *Hodie Christus natus est nobis,* and it makes us aware of the happy event by counting the days, like schoolboys just before their vacation: *Quinta die veniet ad nos Dominus noster. Ecce completa sunt omnia quae dicta sunt per angelum de Virgine Maria. Crastina die delebitur iniquitas terrae. Hodie scietis quia veniet Dominus, et mane videbitis gloriam ejus. Testatur hoc praesens dies, currens per anni circulum, quod solus e sinu Patris mundi salus adveneris. . . .*

Hodie. The coming of salvation is never for us a fact of the past; it remains for each one of us a *today.* In the very measure in which I adhere through faith to the mysteries of Christ, in this measure they are for me something actual. They are accomplished for me in the admittance I give them to my life, they become actual for me in the welcome I offer them. *"Today* is salvation come to this house, because he also is a son of Abraham." (Luke 19:9) Called, like every man to salvation, Zacheus is a son of Abraham by the eternal election which chose him "before the creation of the world." And yet he did not become so, really, until the day when he received Jesus into his house. The salvation which was destined for him from all eternity entered his dwelling only with Jesus and at that moment alone became something actual. So it is with each of us. The historical events of our salvation in Christ become *for us* a truly spiritual reality only at the hour that we accept them by a personal adherence. Does not the event of Christmas, a simple folklore feast for so many Christians, take on its full spiritual significance only at the moment when a long prayerful contemplation reveals it as an exacting and beatifying presence of the Lord? *Beati pauperes spiritu.* "It was at such a moment of the retreat," willingly admit those who have made the Exercises, "that I began to understand the Gospel."

The Gospel history does not become truly our history until we consent to be present to it, to consider it no longer as a narration of past events but as a presence of Christ in our own existence. It is the actuality of this meeting of the salvific plan with our life which the Ignatian contemplation tends to make us realize. For this, the Spiritual Exercises bring into play our spiritual faculties and our inner senses, "reformed by grace and the gifts of the Spirit."[14] It is a matter of becoming aware—actually, historically, precisely dated, so to speak—of a slumbering reality, the life of Christ in us. This life of Christ, made immediate and compelling in prayer, will bear henceforth, if we are faithful to grace, all its fruit. It will clarify the understanding, direct the will towards forthcoming decisions, transform our heart and our sensitive nature, "conform" us to Christ by making us docile to His Spirit. Decisive day, blessed "today." "Today salvation has come to this house."

The contemplations of the second week are, as we have seen, a school of faith. They are not merely pious fancies, deserving of only an indulgent compassion, but a vigorous awakening of the soul, a demand to take seriously one's situation as a Christian. In prayer, an immediate presence of Christ, in Whom we live, is made clearly manifest. It is not merely a question of going back, a return to the past. It is Christ in His mystery Who comes to us and calls for us. "The Master is here and calleth for thee." (John 11:28)

Purified by the first week, prepared by the Kingdom for the most generous offering, determined to admit nothing that would turn him aside from Christ, the soul of the "well endowed" retreatant (who alone should ordinarily be admitted to the second week[15] will not as a rule withdraw from this presence. The poverty and humiliation of Christ enter into his life at this juncture and bear their fruits. The sign of the "meek and humble" Lord is ineradicably imprinted. The retreatant is ready for the prayer of the third degree of humility.

At the same time, these contemplations teach him to pray. More than the others, this method will be of service after the Exercises and will permit him to find Christ in the Gospel each day. It is significant that the first spiritual men of the Society, Nadal,[16] St. Francis Borgia,[17] to name only the greatest, have written meditations on the Gospels which follow the suggestions of St. Ignatius and, at the same time, the order appointed by the liturgy. It is an indication of the need of finding each morning this actual presence of Christ in the mysteries of His life, of His passion and resurrection, of communing with these mysteries which are ours, of allowing oneself to be ever more and more transformed by them.

"Show Thyself to us, Lord, and give us, for our salvation, to know Thee, to see Thee, to adore Thy presence through Thy examples and Thy precepts."[18]

Christus No. 1, January, 1954

Knowing Christ

Paul Agaesse, S.J.

To the question which Jesus asked His Apostles, "and you, who do you say that I am?" each one of us should give an answer. Our faith already places on our lips the words of Peter: "Thou art the Son of the living God." And yet, in spite of this perfect faith, we have to make ceaseless progress in the knowledge of the Man-God. Reflecting on His mystery as it is revealed in the Gospel, we shall, little by little, see more clearly on what conditions we can "try to grasp Christ, as He has grasped us." in order to come to know Him as far as possible here below.

As we place ourselves in Christ's presence, we detect a twofold movement of attraction and repulsion. Jesus had hardly begun to speak and to work His miracles when men gathered about Him; jostling each other to get near Him, they crowded Him on the lake shore to the point of forcing Him to take refuge in a boat. They besieged the threshold of a house He had entered so that the paralytic had no other means of reaching His presence than having himself let down from the roof. When He stopped in a village, the inhabitants brought Him their sick to be cured. The blind, the deaf, the lepers, the possessed fringed the roads where he passed. When night fell, He was hardly able to escape for prayer, and in the early morning they began to look for Him and, finding Him, brought Him back. To hear Him, crowds followed Him, listened for hours, forgetting their fatigue and their hunger. It was not only the benefit of the miracles that moved them, but this Word, like no other in Israel, had no need to refer to other masters in Israel, even Moses, to make Itself accepted. The miracles, the goodness, the authority of Jesus had made them feel that the Messias had come at last, that the Kingdom of God had begun, the prophecy of Isaias fulfilled: "The blind see, the lame walk, the lepers are cleansed, the deaf hear, the dead rise, and the poor have the Gospel preached to them." (Matt. 11:5) A day comes, however, when the enthusiasm of the first hour gave way to doubts and murmurs. On the day following the multiplication of the loaves, the Eucharist discourse shocks the hearers of the preceding day. He Whom they wished to make King of Israel promised His flesh as food and His blood as drink. Instead of the expected triumph, He presents them with the prospect of sacrifice. The same people who said, "Never has man spoken as this man," now say, "This word is hard, and who shall bear it?"

Henceforth this alternation of confidence and mistrust runs like a rhythm throughout the Gospel. In the last days of the Lord's earthly life, the *Hosannah* of the ascent to Jerusalem is close upon the *Crucifige* of the feast of the pasch. Christ seems to discourage the hopes that He arouses. He calls Himself the Messias, He proclaims the Kingdom, He cures the sick and raises the dead. But when the Pharisees ask Him for a sign, instead of answering their official demand with a miracle, instead of clearing the way to give Himself a free passage to the first place in Israel and restore the Kingdom of David, He seems to lose interest in His success and answers the confidence of the disciples whom He has drawn along with Him in this adventure by prophesying that He must die upon a cross. Hope is turned into disappointment.

Inversely, the enemies of Christ, they who claim never to have been misled (John 7:47–49) and who place Jesus in opposition to the Law in order to denounce Him as an imposter, are, nevertheless, troubled by the radiance of His presence. They make use of threats and diplomacy in turn. But Christ is as far beyond the reach of fear as He is of flattery. They draw near, they propose insidious questions, hoping that the answer, whatever it may be, will be to their advantage. "What is the greatest commandment? Who is my neighbor? Is it lawful to pay tribute to Caesar? Must the woman taken in adultery be condemned?" Christ has a blunt solution. He becomes master of the situation and places the discussion where His opponents are beyond their depth. "A simple word, an affirmation without proof, puts them to rout more than any wonder," writes François Mauriac. It is no use for them to take refuge in their hostility. They cannot get away from this superior disputant, because He answers not the words that fall from their lips, but the secrets of their hearts. They think they have before them an interlocutor from whose gaze they can hide behind the façade of phrases and legal niceties, and they discover that Jesus has already penetrated to the depth of their consciences, placed them in the presence of their sin, and obliged them to take their place on a level where the soul is caught in the presence of God. When Jesus, finally breaking His silence, says to them as they stand about the adulterous woman, "Let him who is without sin cast the first stone," they slip away with bowed heads, embarrassed by that clear gaze. They try to put Christ into contradiction with the Law, and yet none of them will take up the challenge: "Who of you will convince me of sin?" When, in the give and take of the conversation, Christ asserts His union with the Father and His mysterious origin, which places Him above David and before Abraham, they are disconcerted and do not know what to think. "We do not know whence He comes," they admitted. So, in the group of scribes and Pharisees, some, feeling their prejudices vanish, believed in Jesus (John 12:42), admiring His answers (Luke 20:26), said, "Master, thou hast spoken well" (Luke 20:40), and did not venture to ask Him any more questions. Without craft, without magic, without miracles, Christ, by His mere presence, disconcerts even those who came to seize Him. "Never has man spoken as this man," they answered the chief priests by way of excuse. (John 7:46)

As St. Augustine says, commenting on the cure of the paralytic at the probatic pool, Christ "moved the water by His mere presence," this human water which is awaiting the visitation of the Lord. The coming and going about Christ, the flux and reflux, betrays the same uneasiness—this confidence followed by confusion, this hostility which has so poor a defense against a secret misgiving. The same uneasiness is reflected by the questions of the crowd, of the Pharisees, of the Samaritan woman, of the Apostles, of Pilate. "Where did he get this wisdom and these miracles?" (Matt. 13:54); "How long dost Thou keep us in suspense? If thou art the Christ, tell us openly." (John 10:24)

"Art thou greater than our father, Jacob?" (John 4:12) "What manner of man is this, that even the sea and wind obey Him?" (Matt. 8:27) "Where art Thou from?" (John 19:9) And the answers intercross and contradict each other. "He is a prophet" (Luke 7:16; John 9:17); "a Samaritan and hast a devil" (John 8:48); "He is a good man. But others were saying, No, rather He seduces the crowd" (John 7:12); "He has gone mad" (Mark 3:22); "This man is not from God, for He does not keep the Sabbath"; "How can a man who is a sinner work these signs?" (John 9:16) Something stranger still, the Precursor himself puts this question, he who, nevertheless, had the mission of preparing the way for the Messias: "Are you He Who is to come, or are we to wait for another?" Father Benoit comments: "Without the slightest doubt concerning Jesus, John the Baptist is surprised to see Him realize a type of Messias so different from Him Whom he was awaiting."

The uneasiness of the Pharisees, the doubts of the crowd, the surprise of the Apostles, and the question of John the Baptist betray under different attitudes which will evolve differently one and the same truth: The Messias is greater than he whom they were expecting. He fulfills that expectation, but He fulfills it by transforming it. *One knows Christ only by accepting His mystery.*

When we take a closer view of it, it is to this that the fifteen centuries of history that prepared for His coming were leading. The Jewish people knew only imperfectly the hope which they carried within them as a grace and to which they bore witness among the nations. True, the alliance, the promise, the prophetic texts had as their purpose the maintaining and the development of the expectation of the Messias, but they aimed less at giving details of the features under which He would appear than in transforming the hearts of the Jews to prepare them to receive Him. As in the Exodus, Israel, all along in its history, moved towards a goal it did not know, a movement which was a tearing away, a constant displacing. The stages and the resting places had to be left behind, and the Israelites had to give up known routes to enter on untraveled ways. The peculiar quality of hope is not to satisfy man's curiosity nor to give him an anticipated vision of the future, but to surrender him to the mystery of God. For what the prophets have a duty to maintain when Israel is tempted to sink in the mire of success or to lose courage in the hour of trial is faith in God's fidelity to His word. The promise will be kept. But when? And how? The gift of God awaited, but impossible to foresee, can only be understood by an adherence to the mystery. God's love is too strong to be shut up within the limits of our concepts or confined to the extent of our desires. He it is "Who is able to accomplish all things in a measure far beyond what we ask or conceive, in keeping with the power that is at work in us." (Eph. 3:30) The generosity of the receiver should correspond to the generosity of the gift. But just because it is a response, man's generosity can express itself only by the faith in which it enters into God's plan, giving up its own narrow views to yield itself unconditionally to the divine initiative.

Now the temptation of the Jews, easily explicable since it is a human temptation, is to upset this relation of man to God, that is, to appropriate the promise to themselves by determining its content, emptying it of mystery, arresting the revelation when it is ever progressing and, doing this, to change the sign by giving it the opacity of an event or the materiality of a letter. They interpret the future in accordance with their human views, mingled with earthly ambitions and national selfishness. They represent Christ under the features of a temporal king and the Kingdom under the figure of an area, the frontiers of which are being rolled back. The Law itself, detached from its initial meaning, which is to reveal the sin of man and the holiness of God, is no more than a mirror in which they contemplate their own justice.

But by the test of this meeting with Christ, man is drawn away from this mistaken attitude, dislodged from the refuge where he has sheltered his illusion, and forced to a choice because he is placed in the presence of the true and living God. Knowing Christ is accepting the mystery of God, for it is by discovering this mystery in Christ that man will know Who He is. Doubtless, this revelation is progressive. Excellent studies have shown by what pedagogy, by what assertions at first veiled, then made clearer and clearer, Christ brought His hearers to an awareness of His divinity. But there must be no illusion—the mystery comes first. We do not explain it after the event by a reference to human behavior. It is, on the contrary, the human behavior of Christ which is explained by the mystery of His Person and His divinity. It is the mystery which at one and the same time draws and shocks those who come near. It is He Who sets us a question: He is either an appeal, to which we answer by faith, or a scandal, which we reject by calling Him a blasphemer, a madman, or one possessed by the devil. We can make no abstraction; for, just as Christ cannot pretend to act *merely* as man, because the acts and the movements of His humanity are placed by the divine Person, so the Jews cannot see and hear without being placed in the presence of God. That is why in the very beginning, even before offering any explanation of His mission or of Himself, Christ demands and awakens in His hearers that unconditional faith which in the Old Testament was due to God and to Him alone. He must be believed on His word. He must be followed without turning back. What He asks, what He admires, is that surrender of the soul which recognizes, though obscurely, its God in Him.

Jesus Christ is Himself His own proof, by reason of His mystery, which is also light. This is what St. Augustine means when he comments on the Gospel verse "And the light shines in the darkness and the darkness grasped it not." We do not clarify the light, but it bears witness to itself by dispelling the darkness. If the Prophets, if John the Baptist, lead to Christ, it is not because they clarify Him, it is because they reflect Him. They are like the mountains touched by the rays of the rising sun. Because our eyes were diseased and we were in the night, the glow of the reflection prepared us to support the brilliance of the day. "But when Christ shall have appeared to you," continues St. Augustine, "then the great light being present, we shall have no need of torches. . . . You have felt the dew, you have been at the fountains. One ray, slipping sidewise through a chink, fell into the darkness of your heart, and now you see the light." It is the mystery of God present in Christ which clarifies and perfects this "conversion," this reversal of the heart prepared in the Old Testament. He is the holiness of God because He makes no compromise in His demands, and in His presence man becomes aware of his sin. He is the Wisdom of God because in disappointing our own conjectures, He has made us draw near the Truth. He is the strength of God because in contradicting our dreams of power, He withdrew us from the slavery of evil. He is Blessedness because in resisting our earthly tastes, He has made us enter into a joy that no man can take from us. He is the Love of

God because by crucifying our selfishness in us, He has taught us the gratuity of the gift. He shocks us and fills us at the same time because to be filled, we must first be transformed. Surely we have here the theme of the Beatitudes. "He speaks with authority," said the crowd. An authority which bruises and which, nevertheless, responds to our most deep-seated aspirations; an authority which rules and which, nevertheless, is not foreign, for it reveals to man his real capacity for Truth, for Happiness, for Love. God alone knows what is in man, and it is because He reveals Himself to him that man, delivered, recognizes God. Thus the light causes the drachma that was hidden away in the dust to shine.

The development of the Apostles shows clearly how it is by faith and adherence to the mystery that they enter into the understanding of the signs. At the beginning, without power yet to say that Christ is God, they obeyed Him as God Himself. At His word, they left all to follow Him. In the presence of His holiness, they became conscious of their sin: "Depart from me, O Lord, for I am a sinful man." They listen; they do not always understand, but they do not doubt because it is Jesus Who speaks. "To whom shall we go, Lord? Thou hast the words of eternal life." Little by little they become capable of formulating the act of faith, quite imperfect though it was, which from the beginning had governed their attitude. The day when the Lord, Who had seen this faith grow and mature, takes up as His own the question which had been asked concerning Him, "And you, Who do you say that I am?" Peter, in the name of all answers, "Thou art the Christ, the Son of the living God."

And yet there remains one last stage for the Apostles to cover. The historic fact becomes an absolute as soon as they recognize in it the action of God. If the mystery of God offers the key to the actions of the humanity of the Lord, correlatively and simultaneously, it is these steps which make us enter into the mystery of God. We have no right to exclude any of them. God is supreme liberty. It is He Who takes the initiative in man's salvation; it is He Who reveals to us the secret of His life. This secret and this initiative are fully revealed to us only in Jesus Christ, God made Man. Now if it is one kind of idolatry to enclose God in sensible objects, it is another to refuse the Incarnation under the pretext that it does not correspond to the concept we have of God. There is a permanent temptation in the history of the Church, that of wishing to save the purity of the Divinity by refusing to implicate It with feebleness and fragility in man. It seems that God cannot launch into an adventure from which He will emerge with loss of prestige. But it is not for man to judge what is worthy or unworthy of God. God is indeed the Eternal, the Absolute, the All-powerful, All-sufficient to Himself. We shall never sufficiently affirm His transcendence and His mystery. But it is because of this mystery itself that we ought to accept Him as He reveals Himself. "I cannot . . . say," writes Romano Guardini, "that God cannot do this or that, for that would be to contradict the notion of pure Divinity. But I ought to say: according to Revelation, God did this and thus shows me how it is. A fundamental reversal of thought, becoming a part of that *conversion* demanded by Christ and on which the Christian existence reposes."

Now if the Apostles were not tempted to deny the humanity of Christ, at least they were shocked at the scandal of the cross. When Christ began to foretell His Passion, Peter undertook to correct Him, saying: "Nay, that will never happen to you!" He recognized God in man, but he had not yet entered into the mystery of the weakness and humiliation by which God would accomplish His plan of salvation. What He will reveal to him will be the *fact* itself, the compulsion of the event which he will not be able to deny because it shall be accomplished. It is by this means that he will succeed in entering into the thought of God concerning Christ, in knowing Christ himself. "When you have lifted up the Son of Man," said Jesus, "you will know that I am He." (John 8:28) To know that He is fully God, we must accept Him as completely man, having made trial of all our infirmities, short of sin, because it is by not changing one iota in the Gospel, by not refusing a single deed of that history that we enter fully into the mystery of God.

It is for this reason that the confession of Peter is a beginning rather than an ending. Because the facts of history reveal to us the mystery of God, their meaning is inexhaustible. And because we understand them only when we identify ourselves with the intention of Him Who has placed them, it is necessary that the Spirit of Truth, Who searches the profundity of God, should reveal their meaning to us. Meditation begun at Pentecost and never finished, by which the Church learns to know her Lord. She cannot stop in her searching because she cannot measure out her love.

We understand better, therefore, since we participate in the life of the Church and should not be dead members in a living body, how the question "Who do you say that I am?" is directed to us as it was to the Apostles.

We begin with the answer: Christ is the Son of God made Man. But the answer becomes a question, for are we aware of what the divinity of Christ implies? In the presence of a human master, we have the right, and doubtless the duty, to maintain a critical attitude, to verify what he says, sympathetically, of course, but also with that intellectual honesty which gives or withholds its assent. The most sincere friendship demands that it be so, for he who teaches is not the Truth, but only Its witness, exposed to the same errors and the same gropings as we. But it cannot be so when it is a question of Christ. Knowing Him as God is adhering to Him without reserve, for He is Truth itself, the sole Master. We cannot distinguish in His teachings between that which pleases us and that which disturbs us, that which we understand and that which we do not understand, that which seems possible to us and that which appears impossible. We cannot, therefore, make two parts of His message; we cannot distinguish two moments in our assent, pledge ourselves temporarily, make trial for a time of the worth of His teaching, being free to reject it if it fails to satisfy us. When we begin to serve Christ, we must know that we are not able to foresee all the consequences of our engagement or all the demands of Truth. Our first adherence to Christ, like that of the Apostles, is reconciled with imperfect ideas about God, and God is not a static ideal but the transforming invasion of a presence into a life.

All knowledge of God today, as hitherto, is a departure, a going forth, a leaving of one's country. To know Him, we must forget our usual ways of seeing. He is the Absolute Truth, which becomes accessible to our eyes only when He purifies them, assimilable to our understanding only when He transforms it. We "enter into the Truth" as the Bible says; that is, it comes to us only when we surrender to it. It is not primarily of the Eucharist that St. Augustine speaks, but of the knowledge of faith, when he ascribes these words to God: "Eat Me; but it is not you who will transform Me into you. It is I who will transform you into Me." We seize the light only when we allow what is darkness in us to be dispelled. Thus we experience this twofold movement of repulsion and attraction which, in the Gospel, characterizes the meeting of men with Christ.

Repulsion is always present because there is an incompatibility between the holiness of God and the sin of man. There is need of our being torn away from our selfishness by the strength of purifying love. Whosoever has not felt this conflict between the demands of Christ and his sinful inclinations has not yet entered into the true knowledge. He makes a likeness of the Messias according to his dreams. Illusion is possible, for the play of attention clips those texts in the Gospel that verify the image which one makes of Christ and leaves the others unnoticed. Or, better still, one reads them with an accustomed eye, as the Pharisees read the Bible. We accept the crib, we accept the sermon on the mount, we accept even the cross, because habit has rubbed down the edges of the relief like souvenirs that have lost their contact with life. The reason is that we have not understood, we have not entered into the mystery. St. Ignatius, in his "Annotations" to the *Exercises,* is uneasy when the meditation of the Gospel does not awaken in the retreatant some movement of soul. That is why he insistently makes him see the poverty of the crib and, in the *Kingdom,* the invitation to struggle against his own sensuality and the spirit of the flesh and of the world. But since the spiritual attention which places one at the heart of the mysteries is a grace and since no one knows the Son unless the Father draw him, he makes us ask, before each contemplation of the Gospel, "an interior knowledge of the Lord . . . so as the better to imitate Him and follow Him."

But there is also a second aspect: the attraction, the joy, and the peace which this meeting with Christ occasions whenever one does not avoid His light. The word of God is life; it is an energy that tends of itself to grow and take possession of the soul. In proportion, as the soul is transformed, it aspires to a more luminous knowledge, a stronger love.

The Fathers of the Church, alluding to the word of our Lord to the Samaritan woman, ask how he who has a spring of water leaping to life everlasting could still be thirsty. They answer that to be hungry and thirsty for God, we must have begun to know Him and that, in-

versely, all progress in this knowledge develops a new hunger and a
fresh thirst, a satiating thirst that is ever reborn! The word of Pascal,
"You would not seek Me, if you had not found Me," has here its
counterverification, for he has not truly found who ceases to search.
We are never through learning Jesus Christ.

Christus, No. 3, July, 1954

True Love for Our Lady

Henri Holstein, S. J.

"Lord, wilt Thou at this time restore the kingdom to Israel?" The Apostles, gathered for the last time about Jesus, Who was on the point of ascending to His Father, asked the question bluntly and revealed their secret thoughts. They sincerely loved their Master, and it was with all their fervor that they had asked through the lips of Peter: "Lord, to whom shall we go?" And yet they could not forget their obstinate dream of temporal success; they had not succeeded in forgetting themselves. Their love was to be purified in the flame of the Spirit on Pentecost.

Our spiritual attitudes constantly call for the same purification. Selfish aims mingle, almost without our knowledge, with the purest aspirations of our love of God. The naïve Messianism of the Apostles remains only too lively in us. We look for tangible results and spectacular successes from our faith and piety. We must constantly rectify our feelings, even when they come from a sincere and generous love. "There are no pure feelings," says Father de Moncheuil very wisely, "there are only feelings that are purified."[1]

There is a special need for this with regard to the love we bear our Lady because in this area there is more room for illusion—the illusion of a good heart which seeks itself in the affection it bears its mother. In all love there is the gift of self and the desire for the good of him whom one loves. But in virtue of this reciprocity, which is the result of a love normally shared, there is also the deep satisfaction and joy of being loved. And one can, without being too aware if it, yield to this selfish pressure and seek oneself while thinking that one has only the interests of the other at heart. Devotion to Mary touches our sensitive nature too deeply for us not to have to guard against an awkward selfishness, against which I venture to say, we have no protection. Mary is a creature and does not display the glory of the divine transcendence. She is a woman, she is a mother, the mother of mercy. "There is nothing hard, nothing fearful in her," said St. Bernard. Wearied, tempted, discouraged, we go to her because we have been told since childhood that she repulses no one. And it is quite normal that she be there to receive the afflicted, to offer, as a priest very devoted to Mary wrote, "her bosom and her peace to my soul, disquieted by so many worries and disorders."

But may not this spontaneous love, basically correct, soon become a piece of self-seeking for us? We think that we are practicing devotion to Mary. Are we not rather interested in our own comfort and our own relief? The child who is afraid of life nestles down in the arms of its mother. It seeks protection, it wants to be defended and preserved from rough contacts and cruel blows. Is not that, transferred to the spiritual plane, the attitude of many of the clients of our Lady? For them, the Mother of God is the nursing mother who consoles and near whom it is good to remain.... Hence the need of a critical examination for the purpose of purifying our love of our Lady and of eliminating the latent selfishness in it and its too natural components. We readily speak of excesses and warpings in devotions to our Lady, and we are not wrong to be on our guard from the beginning against this pious deformity thoughtlessly proclaimed: *De Maria numquam satis.* But these exaggerations would have no hold on us except for the connivance they find in a sensitiveness that is more interested in a sentimental affection than in that strong love which unites us, through Mary, with the painful history of our redemption. We so easily transform our Lady, who remains standing, uniting herself to the sacrifice which saves us, into a honied consoler. Is it not, therefore, usual for us to make a travesty of the doctrine to satisfy the pleading of our poor hearts? ...

We must therefore undertake a necessary but difficult criticism. For there is a delicate intimacy involved which criticism must respect. We have no right to pose as censors of our brethern or to cast discredit on the simplicity of those who, like true children, place themselves under the protection of the Mother, whom Jesus gave them. Even less do we wish, without authorization, to throw any suspicion on forms of piety which the Church does not ban. It is not our business to penetrate the secret of hearts or to re-edit, after a Jansenist censor of the seventeenth century, a "warning of the Virgin to her indiscreet clients." It is simply a matter of making our own examination of conscience in order to purify our prayer to our Lady and to place more firmly in the faith our attitudes towards her who believed and who merited by her belief to be called Blessed.

For a hundred years the apparitions of Mary have held a conspicuous place in Catholic piety. This is a fact that by itself presents no problem. We find ourselves confronted with "private revelations," but made, if we may say so, on a social pattern. The seers are surrounded by a crowd which, without itself perceiving anything, is united to their prayer and receives the message, which, on the part of the Lady, they transmit to it. After a serious investigation, the Church recognizes the "supernatural character" of the facts and authorizes a devotion, pilgrimages of penance, frequently the coming of the sick, some of whom, notably at Lourdes and at Fatima, are miraculously cured—cures which are themselves recognized as unexplainable by human means, even after a long medical inquiry sanctioned by the Church. What is essential in Mary's message is the reminder of the need to observe God's law, prayer, and penance; the characteristic of these pilgrimages, which constitute the answer of the crowds to the appeal of our Lady, is an effort of faith, prayer, and conversion. "The most beautiful miracles," they commonly say at Lourdes, "take place in the confessionals." . . . The atmosphere of Lourdes, the most popular, perhaps, of these pilgrimages, is substantially that of the Gospel.

There is nothing surprising in the devotion of the faithful being particularly attached to the appearances of our Lady. Their quality of present interest, their nearness in time and space, the desire they awaken of seeing the place where Mary appeared and praying where she asked that "they come in pilgrimage" sufficiently explain the outburst of fervor provoked—and maintained—about the shrines which commemorate the great apparitions. This fervor is sound, and it testifies that the call of Mary has been heard.

But the weakness of our heart, which maintains itself only with difficulty on the summits of faith and penitent prayer, has sought for compensations. We have been tempted to dodge the austere lesson and the genuine message, to shirk the demands which the seers have transmitted to us.

First, there is a restless and ill-restrained curiosity concerning new apparitions, news of which is spreading. For a number of years—troubled times favor the growth of a doubtful Messianism—there has been frequent talk of some uncertain testimonies of our Lady, of mysterious words which she has uttered, of unpublished wonders. Today, some seem to attach to these rumors an excessive importance. They are on the watch for these manifestations, often illusory, equivocally "supernatural," in the presence of which the Church remains prudently silent, if not openly distrustful. Instead of awaiting her judgment, there is hurry; vague rumors are heard, and they are peddled about as though they were Gospel truth. . . . It is painful to discover the attraction which these unconfirmed tales exercise over the pious faithful and sometimes over interior souls. Even if they have to be pronounced authentic and recognized as such, they merit at least our respect, but for the moment they should not disturb us. For it is not accurate to say, with a certain well-known writer, that an apparition like that of Fatima "has a very special *theological importance.*" Scripture and Tradition are enough for the Church. The Son of God has told us all, and Revelation ended with the death of the last of the Apostles.

This curiosity goes further than the desire of being edified by the accounts of fresh apparitions. It also wants to know details about future events, pronouncements on the near future which disturb us, approvals or censures on world affairs. As though Our Lady of Lourdes had given her warnings on the government of the Second Empire, or Our Lady of Pontmain had communicated prophecies on the issue of the war which dangerously threatened the little town of Mayenne! The seers are questioned, some try to force them to speak, they are urged to share their "secrets," and sometimes they become a party to this little game. Or some even try to set up a connection between this or that apparition of our Lady and this or that political regime, after the manner of the good-intentioned but ill-advised lecturer who made the beginnings of Salazar's regime depend upon the events at Fatima:

"For every student of sociology and political economy," he bravely declared, "the 'Portuguese counter-revolution,' beginning with the event at Fatima, and *issuing directly from these facts,* is absolutely amazing. . . . In opposition to the economic system imposed by the Communists, the system *issuing from Fatima,* was often heroic and the work of individual patriotism. This explains without doubt why it is pronounced an *economic success.*"[2]

Is it honoring the humble virgin of Nazareth to make her the inspiration of an "economic system," to give her the patronage of its success, and to unite her apparition to a political regime? We are here in that temporal Messianism in which Christ refused to play a part: "Man, who has appointed me a judge or arbitrator over you?" And to show how far one can go, the orator is not afraid to imagine that our Lady, by an extraordinary exploit, could in like manner revolutionize eastern Europe: "If a similar miracle were worked in Russia, it could very well follow the same pattern."

The apparitions of Mary have not for their purpose the settling of the economic or political problems of Europe. Nor do they bring us new truths, unknown to the deposit of faith contained in Scripture and taught by the *magisterium* of the Church. When Mary, at Lourdes, declared herself the "Immaculate Conception," it was four years after the dogma had been solemnly defined by Pius IX. It was, rather, to enliven our faith and to make our prayer more genuine. Miracles for a weakening faith, stimulants to conversion and fidelity— these invite us to take seriously the lesson always present in the Gospel. And, to force the attention of a distracted world, our Lady maternally multiplies her prodigies and constrains us, so to speak, to lend an attentive ear to the words of our Lord.

Mary is here, as she was at Bethlehem, as she was at Cana, at the Cenacle on Pentecost eve, instructress in the faith. She who believed teaches how to believe. The Gospel shows us her attentive to "keep these things in her heart," the mysteries of the hidden life. In silence, Mary each day better understood the manifestation of the Word

Incarnate, and her faith has luminously peneterated, to inexpressible depths, "what she has seen with her eyes, and touched with her hands of the Word of life." She knew Him as her Son, she loved Him as her God, she was united with Him in her virginal heart. Her silence is the admiration of a mother, the contemplation of a creature penetrated with the splendor of her Creator, the mystical ardor of a virgin. No word can express what she discovers in her peaceful ecstasy. Mary then remains silent, but her silence is the fullness of intelligence of the mystery of Christ.

It is this silent Virgin who has come upon our earth, who showed herself to Bernadette, to the seers of Pontmain, to Lucy and her cousins at Fatima, to Sister Catherine Labouré. She has spoken little— a few words only, which have locked these privileged souls in silence rather than encouraged them to speak. Mary showed herself, smiled, manifested her sorrow, uttered a few sentences. . . . And that was enough for the seers for the rest of their lives. And that ought to be enough for us. For faith does not melt away, but thrives silently on the rare words it meditates. The most authentic lesson of these apparitions, of which there is perhaps too much talk today, is the prayerful understanding, in the faith, of the mystery of Christ the Savior and of our union with this mystery. It is enough for us to receive this message from our Mother, to get to the bottom of it, and to try to conform our lives to it.

Commenting on the request of the mother of John and James, who sought the first places in Kingdom for her sons, St. Ambrose remarks that "this widow, aged and deprived of the consolation of her grown sons," thought only of the profit there was for them in having followed Christ. . . . A touching bit of motherly selfishness, for which the good bishop invokes extenuating circumstances. . . . Does not a certain selfish individualism sometimes mark our devotion to our Lady? Devotion with an eye to gain, more often isolating and tending to separate one from the great current in the Church, not only because it grows on complicated practices which are multiplied and hard to bear—the refuges of souls that like to retire apart from the crowd in the comfortable security of little closed circles—but especially because it seems to offer convenient means of making sure of these heavenly rewards: *mercedem sequentium Christum*. . . . Hence these promises, these assurances, these recipes which are passed around in a low voice.

Caricature is easy, and it would be unfair to prolong it. Is, however, the sordid candor of the Messianism to the devout improbable? Does devotion to Mary alway imply a sufficient disinterestedness?[3] The Lord, as St. Ambrose said, smiled at the mother's prayer, concerned as she was over the future of her sons. His mother should not be more severe on the men and women who before her image multiply infallible prayers to obtain eternal salvation. And it is quite possible that our pharasaical smiles will not find as much indulgence. . . .

We must, however, denounce this deviation of devotion to Mary, which might cause her to turn away or make her less sympathetic and which, especially, betrays the truth.

First of all, devotion to Mary is not a matter of practices but of attitudes found in the Gospel: "Do whatever He tells you." To please our Lady is to meditate ceaselessly on the Sermon on the Mount, the parables of the Kingdom, and the Discourse at the Supper and to steep one's life in them. Devotion to Mary is not an unfailing recipe for salvation. It is an opening to grace, a spur to greater generosity, the secret of a theological prayer. Devotion to Mary is not the setting up in the Church of a chapel where a few lovers of solitude and a few eccentric people with leisure on their hands may gather. But Mary is in the Church and of the Church, at one time the most eminent member of the community of the redeemed and the mother of these redeemed whom her Son had entrusted to her from the height of the cross. And here we touch upon the most intimate aspect of the mystery of Mary—the mystery with which our devotion must be penetrated if it is to be genuine and avoid shrivelling up into spiritual selfishness. The mystery of Mary is this, that Our Lady remains a creature who is redeemed and yet elevated by God's gift above her condition. Mother of her Creator, she is also, in virtue of her vocation as mother, the mother of this Church of which she never ceases to be a member.

Thus founded in theology, devotion to Mary, far from opposing the broad dogmatic perspectives which are dear to us—Christ the Mediator and "head of all men," the Mystical Body, the devotion to the Kingdom of God—brings us back to them and sets us firmly upon them. And, from the point of view of religious psychology, devotion to Mary appears like a source of apostolic strength and daring. It has been accused of representing a kind of infantile regression, of leading the adult back to the behavior of the child who cries for tenderness and protection. This objection has no force against a devotion that is well understood, which turns us, on the contrary, towards the future and strengthens us for the present task, which will be finished only in the heavenly Jerusalem. Mary and the Church are inseparable. This strength, of which Mary gives us the example, is itself the strength of the Church, which follows her path unweariedly through contradiction, persecution, and sometimes apparent failure. But this strength is not a hardening. At the foot of the cross, Mary knew the immobility of ecstasy, not the twitching of stoic regidity. Strong, she is gentle; constant, she is engaging; an enemy of sin which has never besmirched her, she is all pity for the sinner. Her welcome and her consolation give greater courage. At her school we learn manly patience, courage in suffering and failure, a contagious peace which He Himself radiates Who knew temptation and solitude . . . Mary's secrets of prayer, when prayer endeavors to be selfless and to prefer God's will to our own whims.

It is perhaps at Lourdes that we must learn this simple prayer to our Lady, especially in the cars of the sick as they are jolted under the summer sun, those who agree to go to Massabielle, not so much to be cured (the majority of them return in the same condition in which they left home), but, as one of them said, "to have the strength to suffer and to give some meaning to sickness." They pray, indeed, but rarely with the selfish intention of obtaining *their own* cure. They do not go to "win over" a magic power to their side, but to offer themselves to the invasion of the grace obtained by Our Lady. This unaffected heroism is contagious. The benefactors are frequently the sick and the well the benefited. . . . It is an atmosphere of faith, of penance, of confidence and self-surrender. . . . And the summit, if we may venture, so to speak, in each day is the devotion to the Eucharist, Mass, the procession of the Blessed Sacrament, in which the Immaculate Virgin seems to efface herself before her Son. For, far from monopolizing the attention of her children, Mary, by a tactful gesture, willingly yields place to Him. Handmaiden to the Lord, she is handmaiden to her Son.

Our examination of conscience would remain incomplete if it were not prolonged to the point where fervor itself runs the risk of drawing to itself the confidence it professes in the Mother of Jesus. It thinks that it honors Mary and wishes to exalt her suppliant omnipotence. In fact, it tends to place it at the service of a retiring timidity which does not venture to appear before Christ, which shies away from the Christian mystery. It is question of a presentation familiar enough, but a little incorrect, and has been named "Marian mediation." On the exact measure of Mary's participation in the work of redemption and of her causality in the communication of grace, the Church, as we know, has not yet officially taken any stand. She permits her theologians to discuss, and to come to an agreement, not without difficulty, on a vocabulary which is still rather fluid. Without going into their discussions, let us be satisfied with recalling the incident of a too sentimental representation of the role of our Lady—Mary, necessary "intermediary" between Christ and us—in devotion and the spiritual life.

Father Congar has emphasized the mistake in the "theme that Christ is God in such a way, so lofty that he appears far away, and that between Him and us we have need of Mary's mediation."[4] The theme finds frequent support in St. Bernard; the fine sermon on the twelve stars is here quoted:

"Of course, Christ Jesus is the mediator, completely faithful and all powerful between God and men, but His Divine Majesty fills them with a reverential fear. In Him the humanity seems to be absorbed by the Divinity, not that there has been a substanial change, but because all His actions are divine. We sing not only of the mercies of Christ, but also of his judgments, for, if He learned through suffering, the compassion which makes Him merciful, He does not remain any the less our judge. How can the sinner not fear to perish when he approaches God, just as the candle melts in the presence of fire? And so . . . we have need of a mediator to go to Christ our mediator, and we cannot find a better than Mary. Why should human weakness be afraid to draw near to Mary?"[5]

Although he maintains perfectly the unique mediation of the Word Incarnate, we may be allowed to think that in pronouncing these words, the great client of Mary has allowed himself to minimize slightly the importance of Christ's humanity in order to exalt the place of our Lady in the spiritual life. Far from being "absorbed by the Divinity," the Humanity of Jesus remains in the union which causes it to subsist in the Person of the Word "without confusion or change," as the Council of Chalcedon puts it.

Marian literature accentuates too readily two characteristics borrowed from this touching sermon: "On the one hand the connecting of the role of Mary, particularly in her title as mediatrix, with the consideration of a Christ, Who, if we may say so, is too divine; on the other hand, the idea that Christ is a severe judge, while Mary is only merciful."[6]

A few texts will suffice to give some idea of these excesses. It is said in a manual of devotion:

"Is not the hour of divine justice ceaselessly sounding for too great a number of sinners, who do not cease to irritate Him by their offences? How much need we have, therefore, of causing it to pause by appeasing this God of all holiness! Who shall do that, who shall be able to offer Him satisfactions and merits, a love and an innocence capable of staying His arm and of inclining His merciful heart towards us, if not the most loving Heart of His immaculate Mother? 'My heart is all powerful over that of my Son. He can refuse me nothing,' she said at Pellevoisin. This mother, all good, wishes to use her immense authority in behalf of her unfortunate children! We honor her, we give her joy, we show our love for her in the manner most acceptable to her heart, when we have recourse to her powerful intercession, and help her to bring souls to the Heart of Jesus."

A writer recalls the pilgrimage of La Salette:

"Moving toward the summit, the Christian thought he saw his *Advocate* in tears, holding up in her sorrow his *Judge* with pierced hands. . . . The Immaculate Conception, the Virgin priestly by a unique privilege, has come to ask "victim" souls of her *reconciling* Compassion."

In a penetrating study, we are sorry to find the following formulas:

"Between Christ and us there exists an *infinite* distance, and we are drawn to seek a being if in some manner such can be found, who would be able to *lessen* it from the side of creatures: there must be a privileged creature, all holy, and it is here that the thought of Mary presents itself."

We transcribe, finally, this paragraph, which is plainly in error:

"We are tempted to believe that the hearts of Jesus and Mary, sharing the two natures in eternity, subsisting of spirit and matter, are in most intimate association in the work to carry out together the decisions of God's justice and mercy—the Heart of Jesus leaning towards Justice, the heart of Mary leaning towards mercy. That is why acts of reparation of all humanity for 'the offences against my Immaculate Heart,' acts of reparation which Our Lady expressly asked for at Fatima, are of the highest importance for the final destiny of men and the universe. What strikes us and inspires us with fear is the impersonal manner, we might say, in which Our Lady speaks in this regard. It is God's mercy which has formulated this request, so that the Divine Justice in the Heart of Jesus may be aware of His Satisfaction. At the end, 'my Immaculate Heart must triumph.' "

It remains to be said, with an ill-inspired publicist, that "Mary is taking over more and more in our day the government of the Church."

We are putting the finger on a sentimental exaggeration which thinks it honors Mary by giving her a place ever higher, without being careful to see that it is at the expense of Christ. These exaggerations cannot be admitted just because they are candid and devout.

For "there is but one mediator between God and man, Christ Jesus, God Himself Who is given as a ransom for all." (1 Tim. 2:5–6) And this Mediator, Who possesses our human nature, does not ask to be relieved by anyone. There is no need of an intermediary between

Christ as Man and us. Jesus reaches us immediately; there is no void to fill, no interval to clear between "Him Who has taken upon Himself the condition of a slave and become like to men" and those whom he calls His brethren.

In particular, we are not to imagine in our Redeemer an ascendancy of rigorous Justice which must be tempered by the constant influence of a suppliant mercy. In Jesus, Justice and Mercy, divine attributes, are perfectly united in the mystery of a conciliation which we have not succeeded in representing to ourselves, especially if, yielding to a sentimental anthropomorphism, we bestow upon God at one and the same time our vindictive severity and our emotional compassion. He Who forgave the adulteress also said, "Woe to you scribes and Pharisees, hypocrites"; Who called to Him all those who were heavily burdened and declared unworthy of Him those who were unwilling to follow Him by bearing their cross. . . . Mystery which makes insipid the sentimentality of those indiscreet clients who seek to find in Mary a shield against her Son . . .

Must we then set aside all notion of the "mediation of Mary" or reduce it to a pious metaphor? Certainly not. For Jesus wished to associate with His salvific work her who was His mother, who not only gave to the Son of God a genuine humanity, but in the strongest intimacy of mind and heart was throughout the length of His life on earth and at the foot of the cross His "faithful companion" and the unfailing co-operatrix of our salvation:

"The consequence of this community of thought and of suffering between Mary and Jesus," wrote St. Pius X, in his encyclical *Ad Diem Illum,* "is that Mary merits very legitimately to become the reparatrix of fallen humanity, and, therefore, the dispensatrix of all the treasures which Jesus has acquired for us by His death and by His blood.

"At least, one cannot say that the dispensation of these treasures is not a right, proper and particular with Jesus Christ, for they are the exclusive fruit of His death, and He Himself is the unique Mediator between God and men.

"And yet, by reason of this sharing of grief and anguish between Mother and Son, it has been given to the Blessed Virgin to be, after her only Son, the all-powerful advocate and mediatrix of the whole world.

"The source is then Jesus Christ, of Whose fullness we have all received. But Mary, according to the expression of St. Bernard is the aqueduct. We do not go so far as to attribute to the Mother of God, as is clear, a power productive of grace, a power which is God's alone. Nevertheless, because Mary excels all in sanctity and in union with Jesus Christ and because she has been associated by Jesus Christ in the work of redemption, she has merited *de congruo,* as the theologians say, what Jesus has merited for us *de condigno,* and she is the supreme minister of the dispensation of graces."[7]

This sound theology, by giving Jesus Christ His place of unique Mediator, throws a light on the part given to Mary in our sanctification and gives stability to the conviction that every grace is given us through her maternal hands. It justifies the fervor and the confidence of the prayer to our Lady and allows us to understand why certain forms of spirituality are so exclusively and totally Marian, even to the mystical experience of a "Marian presence" that is continuous and transforming. There is nothing disturbing in that, no more than in the spontaneous affirmation by the Christian people of the "Marian mediation," since, according to the expression of Scheeben, "by her collaboration in the sacrifice of Christ, Mary has become the depositary of redeeming merit for all of humanity and for all time."

And the great theologian expresses very happily, it seems to us, the precise meaning of "Marian mediation."

"It is not at all that we do not receive grace without ourselves having implored the intercession of Mary; that none of our prayers is heard without the help of this intercession. A positive and deliberate exclusion of her in the intention of him who prays should certainly cause fear that the prayer will not be heard. This teaching does not claim either that the intercession of Mary is universally necessary to determine Christ to use His intercession for us, as though He were not disposed of Himself to do so. The meaning of the doctrine is rather that, according to the order fixed by God and by Christ, the merit and the intercession of Christ should not be used in favor of anyone unless the intercession of Mary is added. No grace, therefore, is granted except that which is also obtained as it were by Mary's prayer."[8]

"The truth will make you free." Our devotion to Mary must be true in order to be freed of the dross which weighs it down and incurs the risk of hiding its genuineness. Exaggerated exaltation is no honor to Mary.

The worship paid to the Mother of God will be true if it produces in us an increase of the theological virtues; if it makes firmer our faith, which is ceaselessly threatened by an effective restlessness that is interested in "consolations"; if it causes us to live in hope, without running ahead of the plans of Providence or foreseeing the happenings which are not dependent on us; if it increases in us theological charity, the love of God inseparably united with the love of the neighbor . . . and if, far from locking us up in some remote chapel, it helps us better to understand in prayer the salvific plan of the Father, in which Mary occupies so beautiful a place—this salvific plan which terminates with the Church, Christ's Mystical Body, and which is brought about by the slow maturing of the Kingdom of God, to which we should contribute the collaboration of our prayer and good works. . . .

But, for all that, this devotion to Mary will not lose its way in an exclusiveness or in an intellectualism which is somewhat disdainful of the naïve piety of "good Christians." It will remain simple, as becomes the homage given to the "humble Virgin" of Nazareth. Truth and simplicity call to each other and are not exclusive. Many say that they are repelled by certain aspects of Marian devotions; they have not the courage to mingle in the crowd and to recite without affectedness the rosary of their woe . . . and of their distractions. It is monotonous, indeed, full of routine, and "conformist," and the mind easily strays while the lips murmur the *Aves* mechanically and the fingers let the beads of the rosary slip through. . . . But for him who prays with faith, there is something there which keeps us in communion with the nameless throng of the generations, with all those who have implored the help of Mary, who have placed confidence in her, who are frequently wearied and disheartened. But, properly understood and truly lived, devotion to Mary shares in this simplicity, which is a treasure of Catholicism. It would be dangerous to cut oneself off from it, to believe oneself "too evil" or too modern to be satisfied with the piety of good people. . . .

True love of Mary causes Christians to grow in the divine life and to develop in those virtues which unite them with Christ. It is the sign of its genuineness. It is also the wonderful answer which our Lady gives to our confidence. The Mother leads to her Son, and forms Him in the souls of those who give themselves up to her. . . .

Christus, No. 3, July 1954

Born of the Virgin Mary

Robert Rouquette, S.J.

Born of the Virgin Mary. The Word of God, placing Himself in the current of time, chose to be born of a virgin.

Here we meet with the creature who comes closest to God. The Church soon saluted her with the inconceivable title of Mother of God. Not bearing the weight of original sin, she brings to realization the very idea of human perfection as God wished it before the beginning of the ages. This perfect creature is and remains a virgin. In the act of supreme liberty which expressed her fiat and by which she gave humanity to God, she remains a virgin.

We are so accustomed to this affirmation of the ancient Creed that we no longer measure the reversal of values which it introduced into the history of humanity, in the privileged history of Israel first of all. There was no greater misfortune for a woman in Israel than to remain unmarried. We have only to recall the daughter of Jepthe whom a barbarous vow of her father condemned to death! She went to the mountain with those following her to "bewail her virginity," to weep over her shame in dying a virgin. Certainly it was not virginity itself which was a misfortune in Israel, but its consequence, the absence of posterity.

The absolute novelty was that with the virgin Mother of God, virginity ceased to bear the curse of those who were sterile. This is announced by the long series of childless women, ancestors of Christ, who, by a miraculous grace, became mothers; from Sarah, who laughed with doubt when the angel of Yahweh announced to the aged Abraham that she would conceive; from the praying Anna, mother of Samuel, whose triumphant canticle the Virgin took up in her Magnificat, to Elizabeth, the wife of Zachary.

Thus the virginity of our Lady takes on meaning only in the Divine Maternity. It is not an end in itself. It is destined to bring forth Christ.

We shall not attempt to guess why it was becoming for the Word Incarnate to be born of a Virgin. Such speculation, while not forbidden, is indeed without profit. It narrows the mysterious intentions of God down to our human measures. Instead of asking ourselves why God has acted in such and such a manner, it would be better to accept these divine interventions in time as provindential manifestations of the transcendental rule of values. The acts of God reveal to us that which the eyes of Eternal Wisdom is beautiful and good.

The transcendent fact which forces itself on us here and which reveals the inner thought of God is that the Divine Word, when He entered into history, chose to be born of a virgin who was to remain a virgin. This divine choice by itself reveals to us that for Divine Wisdom, virginity has a lofty merit and that it is in close relation with the mystery of the Incarnation, with the manifestation of the saving love of God.

This revelation of the merit of virginal chastity in the eyes of the Eternal Wisdom of God, its essential relation to the mystery of Christ, is deepened and clarified when we reflect on the fact that the Word Incarnate lived a virgin.

And this seems to us to be so natural that we experience a kind of instinctive repugnance at the thought that it might have been otherwise.

Did not the Word wish to run the whole gamut of human experience? Do we not see Him in the Gospel bearing all the burdens of man? He willed to be born of a woman and submit to the laws of growth which the Creator had laid down: "For thou hast possessed my reins: Thou hast protected me from my mother's womb. . . . My bone is not hidden from Thee, which Thou hast made in secret, and my substance in the lower parts of the earth. Thy eyes did see my imperfect being." (Ps. 138:13–16)

Hers was an infant Who grew like the children of men and Whose

human understanding opened little by little to the earthly knowledge
of this universe which He launched into being in the beginning,
when the Word was. He knew hunger, thirst. He asked a little
water from the Samaritan woman. He wept, he shuddered with fear
before the tomb of Lazarus. He shared even in the troubling mystery
of sleep which makes us discontinuous beings. He slept, His head
upon a pillow, in the stern of Peter's boat.

To human eyes it would seem that virginity is not a logical part
of this will of total incarnation which the Word Incarnate thus manifests. Is not the human creature, as it comes from the hand of God
in Genesis, man-and-woman? As long as Adam remains by himself,
he is a being unfinished. Yahweh must create a companion for him,
like to him. Even before the Fall the pair received the command to be
of one flesh. At least there is no a priori repugnace that to be man,
the Word of God, Who has known friendship, would have con-
descended to a chaste and spiritual love for a woman in a virgin marriage, such as the mutual love of Mary and Joseph.

But all that is the human way of looking at things. Quite different
is the Eternal Wisdom of God which the Christ of the Gospels reveals
to us in His being and His behavior.

Christ, even more than Mary, is the ideal creature, and He is virgin
in both body and heart. The Gospel is transparent chastity. The Gospel is virgin. The pair, in which man and woman complete themselves mutually, are not, in the eyes of Eternal Wisdom, the final
perfection of the creature. In Christ, creation mounts to a state in
which man goes beyond the limitations and the incompletions of sex.
In fact, the Lord teaches explicitly that in everlasting life, the sole
and real end of humanity, sexual relations will come to an end. (Matt.
22:30) And yet the ideal of virginity, as realized in Christ, is not
presented as an inaccessible state to men in this temporal existence.
(Matt. 9:12)

That is why, beginning with Christ the Virgin, born of a virgin, the
extraordinary phenomenon of virginity, or voluntary chastity, spread
so irresistibly. Paul observed chastity and said that it was better. Very
soon there appeared in the Church consecrated widows and virgins
who constituted a true state, an Order in the community. Then, in

imitation of Paul and of John, who, according to an old tradition, remained a virgin, monks especially consecrated to the contemplation of divine truths observed chastity. The ideal of chastity won the clergy. It was imposed on bishops and priests in the West and on bishops in the East.

At certain periods in the eleventh and the sixteenth centuries, it might have seemed prudent of the Church to give up her requirement of chastity for her priests and her monks. But she never yielded to this human prudence, and at the worst moments in her history she concentrated all her strength on the reform of chastity with an almost miraculous success. The ideal chastity of Christ, born of the Virgin, is carried on in the chastity of consecrated virgins, monks, and priests.

Such is the extraordinary fact. We might stop with that. It is enough to adore in silence the virginity of Christ, Son of Mary, as a divinizing ideal revealed to us, as a supreme value lived by the Lord.

But it is also allowed us, without seeking to pry into God's reasons, to analyze what religious value the ideal of virginity and Christian chastity[1] affords humanity. They are human and frail views indeed, but they can help us better to adore Christ the Virgin, born of the Virgin.

We can consider chastity from two points of view: as it renounces a carnal act and as it renounces a spiritual love which the carnal act signifies and maintains.

With respect to the voluntary renouncement of the carnal act, the chastity of some men and some women among the mass of their brethren is the permanent sign which efficaciously recalls the higher merit of the spiritual. It does so in several ways, but first because voluntary chastity is the renouncement of the satisfaction of the most powerful human instinct among those which we have in common with animals. The symbolic value of chastity thus considered is very profound. By it, humanity freely approves the creative act by which God raises men above the animals.

It is a general rule of God's activity, revealed in the Bible, that the Creator freely associates the free activity of man with all the divine works in history. It would be easy to prove this. Thus the biblical Adam received delegation from God to name the animals, that is, to have them come out of the undistinguished mass, to finish off, in some sense, their creation. This general law is applied even to the creation of man. The creature capable of reflection is called upon freely to approve the act by which God, a pure spirit, draws it out of nothing and creates it in His own image.

But this image of the spiritual God is placed in an animal body. The process of creation makes little difference, whether the human body be the result of a long evolutionary progress, drawing out the creative act throughout the length of time, or whether the animal body of man was called into being without a previous history. In any hypothesis, the human creature who has a body that is animal in its structure and in its physical functions is, however, absolutely different from the animal. The Creator did not find for the first Adam a companion like himself among the animals.

Chastity renounces the satisfaction of the sexual instinct, which is common to us with the animals and which we can master without danger to our physical life. It thus enters into the creative movement of God, Who raises us above the animal; it shares in it by loving it and approving it innerly. For this reason it is the freest act that a man can place, the most human and the most humanizing, because the most spiritual, the most creative act permitted to the creature.

This act of supreme liberty is not asked of all. It is a token act, a mediation placed by a few in the name of all, in the solidarity of the mystical body of the human fraternity. Thus chastity participates in the sacerdotal meditation of Christ. One might even say that it restores all things in Christ because it is the meeting place of the material creature and the spirit divinized by the grace of Christ.

There is no question of proposing voluntary chastity as a universal ideal, less still of seeing in sexuality and marriage simple manifestations of concupiscence and the results of sin. In the Bible narrative, it is before the Fall that man is created, *vir et virago,* male and female, and that he receives the command to increase and multiply, in being, husband and wife, one sole flesh.

But in the human race a small number of men and women are called by divine vocation, and free choice on their part,[2] to be, as it were, representatives of humanity. In the name of all their human brothers and sisters, they approve by their voluntary chastity the act by

which they are created images of God, animated with the divine
breath, in an order of being other than animal.

Chastity is also the sign of our eternal destiny. It is essentially a
Pauline idea that, thanks to the risen Christ, we possess already in this
present existence the pledge, the anticipation of life everlasting. The
Church forms beforehand the heavenly city upon earth. The
Assumption of the Blessed Virgin is the first act of the resurrection
of the flesh promised to glorified humanity. Consecrated chastity is one
aspect of this penetration of eternity into time. Men and women
vowed to voluntary chastity by a divine vocation are the witnesses of
our everlasting existence, of our only true life, where, as we have
seen, marriage will disappear. Quite explicitly, Christ also affirms,
but not without some bluntness, that they who choose to preserve
their chastity are "eunuchs *for the kingdom of heaven*." "For the
kingdom of heaven," that is, this complex reality, the eternal city and
the possession of God, the goal now of the Church and of grace.
Chastity is a witness, a sign that our eternity has already begun. Let
him who can, understand, adds our Lord. To understand the deep
religious meaning and the impressive beauty of chastity is a grace.

Up to now, we have simply regarded what we might call physical
chastity—the voluntary renouncement of the satisfaction of the sexual
instinct. Physical chastity is not really a religious virtue unless it is
the manifestation of a more spiritual disposition, *chastity of the
heart*—the voluntary renouncement of the personal and reciprocal
love between a man and a woman.

And yet chastity of heart and marriage are not two divergent ways
of life. They are two means, quite necessary in the Christian community, of practicing the law of love proposed by Christ.

This law is the same for all the disciples of the Gospel, in marriage
or in voluntary chastity of heart: to love God and His Christ above all
and in preference to all, and to love men with the same love that God
loves them:

"And if any man come to me, and hate not his father and mother
and wife and children and brethren and sisters, yea and his own life
also, he cannot be my disciple." (Luke 14:26)

"For you, my brethren, have been called unto liberty. Only make not liberty on occasion to the flesh: but by charity of the spirit serve one another. For all the law is fulfilled in one word: 'Thou shalt love thy neighbor as thyself.' " (Gal. 5:13-14)

Christ teaches explicitly that there is no limit to this universal charity.

As a rule, charity, to attain this breadth, passes beyond the narrowness of the exclusive and mutual love of the pair. This narrowness is not a last end. Love in marriage, to be genuine charity, the image of the Trinitarian life and the life of Christ and the Church, should make the spouses readier to pass from individual and family self-interest, to be more attentive to others, better members of the community, and more capable of bearing witness to the life of the Lord in them.

This expansion of charity to which the Christian couple ought to tend does not consist only in a kind of philanthropy. It aims at God, God the Infinite Being, through Christ, the Head and the Life of the whole Mystical Body. The mutual love of the spouses ought to be for them a means of loving God and in God of loving their neighbors more generously.

The restricting of love in a couple has, therefore, for its end the making more universal the forces of charity so condensed and of opening them to the infinite measure of God's love, like a stream of water, under pressure, spreading into a vast spray.

Chastity of heart tends to the same love in God, to the same universal love, but without passing through the restriction of the total giving of self to a creature. St. Paul clearly reveals this meaning and this finality of chastity of heart:

"But I would have you to be without solicitude. He that is without a wife is solicitous for the things that belong to the Lord: how he may please God. But he that is with a wife is solicitous for the things of the world: how he may please his wife. And he is divided. And the unmarried woman and the virgin thinketh on the things of the Lord: that she may be holy both in body and in spirit. But she that is married thinketh on the things of the world: how she may please her husband. And this I speak for your profit, not to cast a snare upon you, but for that which is decent and which may give you power to attend upon the Lord, without impediment." (1 Cor. 7:32–35)

St. Paul does not mean to say that one cannot belong entirely to the Lord in and through marriage, but simply that chastity chooses God and Christ as the direct, immediate, and exclusive object of love.

Of course, the love of others is implied. But chastity, instead of rising from the beloved creature to God, descends from the love of God to the love of the creature. It is not attached to a particular human being in order to concentrate its power of loving on him in order to see in him a privileged image of God. It is an unattached love, open on all sides. In fact, this love will apply itself to a limited number of human beings without being attached in any exclusive or definite way to any one of them.

Chastity, therefore, resembles the vocation of the Virgin Mary, such as we recalled it at the beginning of these pages. The virginity of Mary is not sterile but essentially fruitful. It is not a falling back on self but a total gift of self to bring forth Christ. And since Christ is not only an individual, but the first-born of a multitude of brethren, the universal Head of the race of the divinized, the virginity of Mary is indeed a universal fruitfulness of love.

Our chastity of heart, total consecration to the glory of God, imitating Mary's virginity, has a special value as a sign and witness if the love of man and woman in marriage is to keep its authentic meaning. The conjugal love of the couple should, in fact, be ordered to the love of God, should be a providential stage in the advance towards the possession of God, without which it would be only idolatry. It is good that in the common fraternity of Christians there is a love of God which does not pass through any human intermediary. Thus we are reminded that no love has meaning or fullness unless it is ordered to the love of God.

It is again necessary if we recall that the restriction of love in the couple is the means of universalizing charity. It shows, in addition, that Christian love ought to be the negation of selfishness, ought to be diffusive of itself.

From this point of view, it has, finally, an eschatological value. It constitutes the pledge of heaven. It causes the eternal reality to penetrate into time.

Thanks to the veiled teachings of Christ and the Apostles on the life of heaven, we know that in the Eternal City, men and women, in their mysterious, glorified bodies, will see the limitation and the exclusiveness of earthly life fall away. By their common participation in the life and joy of the Holy Trinity, there will be a kind of transparence between them, a reciprocal intimacy, a perfect agreement of wishes and thoughts, a total and universal charity. After the image of the Holy Trinity, the heavenly city will be a community of persons. It will admit of centers of affection, which doubtless will prolong the loves of earth, but will not be opposed to the perfect universality of the charity towards which voluntary chastity of heart tends here below.

I think that within this perspective, there is no room to set up an opposition between virginity and the conjugal life. Marriage is the ordinary vocation of the greater number of Christians. Voluntary chastity is in the Christian city like a living reminder of the finality of all love; both vocations are necessary. And yet we understand the profound meaning in the Church's traditional assertion, which recognizes a higher vocation in virginity simply because Christ, born of the Virgin and the ideal of man, chose to live as a virgin and because the sexual realities of today are called upon to disappear in the divinized life.

Men and women who by special grace are called to this special vocation of virginity, or of consecrated chastity, bear this vocation not as a burden, but as a joy. It is beautiful and great in itself, it is the sign of a divine predilection, it impresses a special resemblance to Christ, it introduces us already and beyond time to the reality of our eternal life.

PART III

The Problem of Prayer and Action

Christus, No. 8, October 1955

Some Thoughts on "Prayer and Action"

FRANÇOIS CHARMOT, S.J.

Number 6 of *Christus* has posed the difficult and important problem of union between prayer and activity. It is not a matter of reminding informed readers that contemplatives are active in their own way. They are convinced of it and look upon the apostolate through prayer, sacrifice, and the radiation of holiness as an essential duty. There would be on this subject some beautiful truths to make known for the consolation of religious souls and for the laity, to whom God has given the grace of contemplation. It would mean dispelling the errors of unbelievers, and of Chritians, who do not sufficiently believe in the immense and profound fruitfulness of union with the God of love in solitude and silence. But that was not the purpose the review had in mind.

Union with God Through Action: Proposed Method

The authors of the articles take a different point of view. To apostles by profession, to militants of all orders, and to every Christian worker, they wished to show *how* union with God, man's supernatural end, is possible outside the cloister and by means of the duties of one's state in life—whatever that may be—a teaching on which all are in agreement and which St. Francis de Sales has notably made the most of. The problem, which is centuries old, is to discover how activity, profane by nature or religious because of its end and its means, can sanctify souls and unite them with God. For experience has often proved that activity in the world meant a dissipation of the spirit, that it attached the heart to earth, that it developed self-esteem, and that the surest means of living with God was to contemplate Him "in the desert." Against all kinds of preconceived notions, *Christus* has taken up the combat with competence and confidence. Number 6 shed much light on the subject. Has it, however, completely solved the problem of *holiness through action?* Perhaps a few complementary thoughts, without any claim to call them definitive, will help to present a fuller teaching for the "activist."

What *method* do most of the authors in this issue propose for uniting oneself with God and sanctifying oneself in action? They look for it, and think they have found it, in a close dependence of activity on prayer. It is a purely objective method of approach, progressing from one object to another, from an earlier to a later stage, *from prayer to action.* Is that not announcing at once our conclusion, a road without an exit? Would it not be good to renounce such a method if it is true that the solution of the difficulties is of a *subjective* character? It is in the state of soul of the apostle—or simply of the Christian— who prays and gives himself to action that we must look for a solution of the difficulties that are forever cropping up. The same spiritual perfection permits, at one and the same time, prayer and action which sanctify and unite with God. The development of our thought will clarify, we hope, these slightly puzzling prefatory statements.

Is the Problem of Action Solved By Prayer?

Many think so today, as they did yesterday. Against the contemporary exaggerations of some "activists," we meet today with spiritual writers who, taking up certainly the echo of a long tradition, profess only a moderate confidence in sanctification by action.

Thus a former Superior of a major seminary, Canon Cuttaz, recommends, in the *Dictionnaire de spiritualité,*[1] that the apostolate be used only with discretion. We are "not to undertake a work when we foresee that it is going to cause the omission of the indispensible minimum of devotion." In the same vein, Père Pinard de la Boullaye[2] advocates recollection or diffused prayer as the preservation from total cooling of the fervor acquired in prayer.

These authors have no trouble in showing that this teaching is traditional. We read similar counsels in the *Imitation,* in Bossuet, in Dom Chautard,[3] in Père Lallemand and his disciples, as in all the works written by contemplatives. The instances of a Lallemand, a Surin, a Rigoleuc are remarkable enough. These spiritual writers are apostles, and Père Lallemand had the task, in the third year of probation, of forming religious destined to an almost superhumanly active life. It may be that we do not know his thought completely. The statements which have been preserved for us lead us to suppose a great mistrust of action. "One should undertake but very little external activity before one has acquired a virtue perfectly." "If we are advanced in prayer, we will give much of our time to action; if we are only moderately advanced in the interior life, we will give ourselves only moderately to the exercises of the exterior life; and, if we have only a very little of the interior life, we will not give ourselves at all to the exterior, unless obedience orders the contrary."[4] This is, we can see, a radical subordination of action with relation to prayer.

But we must take a closer look at the problem and ask, on the one hand, what is in quantity and in quality the prayer necessary to permit a man in the active life to unite himself with God, and, on the other hand, what is the kind of activity under discussion.

a) What sort of "dose" of prayer is meant?

On the quantitive level first, the following questions may be asked. If daily Mass and communion, the sacrament of penance received every two weeks, the rosary, morning and evening prayers, with a short examination of conscience, are recognized as sufficient, why ask that a mediation be added? If, on the contrary, these spiritual exercises are not enough, are we going to ask an hour, a half-hour, a quarter-hour of mental prayer? And if a half-hour is not long enough to keep the soul from the dissipation and the more or less deliberate faults to which action inclines it, would it not be good to impose an hour of prayer? Then, if this whole hour, unfortunately, did not obtain better results, there would be nothing left to do but give the advice to persevere with confidence and avoid discouragement. . . .

But it is more important to determine the quality of the prayer, which ought to sustain the active life and preserve it from temptations. What level should we attain? It is not enough to say: "Make the meditation." An hour of meditation in which we do not succeed in overcoming boredom, sleep, torpor, inertia, and dryness is evidently not enough. The demon of distraction, of dissipation, of imagination, of intemperate zeal, of restlessness, of anxiety, of hope of success and fear of failure roams ceaselessly around the apostle seeking to devour his hour of meditation. And we must not forget, either, the demon of resentment, of bitterness slowly and fiercely relished, of spites entertained, in a word, an hour of struggle on both knees, renewed almost every morning, which is doubtless very meritorious but which does not seem to establish the soul in a lasting union with God during the day as much as does a quarter of an hour of thanksgiving after holy Mass, in which the love of Christ would have inflamed it with charity. A resigned prayer in which we await the striking of the hour and freedom from a duty fulfilled does not at all seem more effective.

The authors who claim to solve by prayer the spiritual problem of action evidently suppose that the apostle has overcome the temptations which assail his prayer. They admit, as a matter of course, that for the greater number of men of action, the morning meditation has established them in a union with God which will last the day through. Now it is a fact of experience that many in the active life ask themselves, after many disappointments, how they should pray. For them it is a primary and difficult question. It proves that the problem is not solved as simply as one would like to claim.

Will it be solved by *infused prayer?* A number of spiritual writers of all schools, and among them important Jesuit authors, claim that it will.[5] Father de Guibert, summing up their opinion, writes: "A certain number among them (the spiritual writers of the Society) are clearly of the opinion that there is no high sanctity without *infused contemplation,* that, consequently, to aspire to sanctity is by that very fact to aspire to this very contemplation, which is presented as the aim of the interior life, the end towards which it ought to tend, which it will normally attain if the soul is truly faithful to the attentive anticipations of grace."[6] Should those in the active life be taught this doctrine, which is more likely to discourage than stimulate them? Are they to await the hour, desirable, certainly, but unforeseeable, when

God will grant them this great grace of infused prayer, when they will begin to give themselves to apostolic work? "How long, O Lord?"

The difficulties inherent to prayer are aggravated by those that come from activity itself.

b) What kind of action is spoken of?

Even if, by an impossibilty, a teaching as traditional as that of so many spiritual writers who insist on the necessity of infused prayer for the apostolic man were an illusion, it still remains that action requires a sufficiently great perfection in ordinary prayer. It is not any kind of meditation, even faithfully kept up for an hour, that will solve the problem of the holiness of the apostle.

To this quality of prayer will respond a very high perfection in action. The statements we find throughout the articles of Number 6 of *Christus,* notably in the article by M. Lochet, suggest that activity is entirely penetrated by prayer. "Prayer should not stop at the threshold of action. It should penetrate it and vivify it. Intimacy with God is at the center of all."[7]

But how are we to reach it, if not by a long practice of prayer? The very high perfection of apostolic action requires and supposes an intimate familiarity with God, constant attention to His Spirit—in a word, that interior attitude, quoted in this same issue of *Christus,* which Père de Grandmaison calls "virtual prayer."[8]

Briefly, we expect from the true apostle in the world *an action that is mystically very elevated.* The whole problem is to tend to that, to make every effort, with the help of grace, to reach it. Of this growing perfection of an action "in the presence of God," such as the apostle, according to a formula of Père Surin's, "relishes and tastes in all things only Jesus Christ, thinking that in all things he sees his Divine Master, having no affection or feeling of joy but from Him and through Him,"[9] we can distinguish three stages, three ascending steps in the spiritual growth of the "contemplative in action." Perhaps it is along this line that it would be good to seek the solution of the problem.

First Step: Seeing the Will of God in All Things

The first stage is that of "servants," of whom Ruysbroeck speaks.

The soul, attentive to God's will in all things, works like an apprentice under the eyes of his master, like a servant who obeys the head of the family, like a child who does not wish to displease his father. Whatever it does, it does according to the command it has received. And in this commandment, it sees God. "He who says that he knows Him and does not keep His commandment is a liar, and the truth is not in him. But he who keeps His word, in him the love of God is truly perfected." (1 John 2:4) To see God's will, is not that to see Him in faith? To unite oneself with God's will, is not that to unite oneself to God also in faith?[10] When the will of God becomes the sole end of a life of action, can it not lead us straight to heaven and transform us into co-operators with God's designs?

Does this first step in union with God require infused prayer, virtual prayer, or merely the separate hour of daily meditation? It seems that in order to persevere in this union of will with God, it would be more important to participate in the spirit of sacrifice at holy Mass and to receive the Body and Blood of Jesus Christ than to make a separate prayer. Prayer, evidently, is power. But the reception of the sacraments seems still more necessary, and it is probably sufficient. The problem of action at this lower level of fidelity is solved by obedience and by as complete an adherence as possible to our Lord's holy will.

Second Step: Seeing the Love of God in All Things

At a higher level, the soul not only sees the will of God in all things, but it bows to the aspirations of the Holy Spirit which on all occasions suggest the means of "bringing about the Kingdom of God." One seeks not merely to avoid sin, but positively to please God, to respond to His love, to co-operate with Him in procuring His glory and the completion of redemption.

These souls live on a level of *love* or *friendship*. They are contemplatives, not merely by the attention they give to external commands, but by their possession, in addition, of an "interior life." It is through an attention, ever deeper and purer, to the demands of *charity* that they are illumined concerning the presence and activity of God in them. *Contemplatives in action,* they contemplate God as fervently as she who is married "thinks of all things . . . how she may please her husband." (1 Cor. 7:33) Such a soul is not only a servant of God, but also His Spouse. And so it puts order and beauty not only in its moral life, but also in its spiritual life. The hidden virtues of humility, purity of intention, detachment, self-forgetfulness, and delicacy in charity have greater value in its eyes than the virtues which regulate its external activity.

To reach this degree of contemplation of God in action, there is need of a more lively faith than that in the simple seeking of God's explicit will. We also think it necessary that the soul then add to the fervent reception of the sacraments and the generous offering of self in the holy sacrifice of the Mass two methods of preparation and training: mental prayer and spiritual direction.

Why does mental prayer then become necessary? Not only, as was once said, because we cannot be united to God in action unless we are faithful to the rule of mental prayer, but also because prayer is part of the profound demands of friendship with God or of love. Prayer is no longer considered as a means towards a self-centered end, which action would be, but as an end to which friendship tends. It is not here a matter of infused prayer or average prayer, but a life of intimacy with God, without distinction of limits, hours, or activities. This point of view permits us to say that prayer and action are, in a parallel sense or at the same time, the luscious fruits of a single source of life, which is *friendship* or the *spirit of love*. Here the solution is subjective and interior. It springs from grace and the heart, in the interest of prayer as well as action. Besides, is it not evident that without mental prayer it is almost impossible to lead an interior life that is at all serious and to make progress in it? The hidden virtues of this profound life develop only if, in the light of God's countenance, one keeps a loving eye on everything in the soul that could please or displease His heart. And this labor of trimming and planting ought to be taken up daily if we wish to offer God those flowers and the fruits which are not too unworthy of His love.

Spiritual direction also prepares us to take part in a healthy spiritual pedagogy. The spiritual life does not develop successfully without encouragement in trial, without obedience in obscurity, without discernment of spirits in perplexity, without certitude in ambiguity, without theological truth in new ventures, in a word, without the guarantee which the Holy Church alone can give. The love that comes from the Holy Spirit is daring but prudent. How far should daring and prudence go, each in its own direction? Who will know it in the concrete without obedience to a director, in whom a docile faith recognizes the authentic representative of the Church?

Third Step: Seeing God Through the Holy Spirit

The spiritual ideals proposed by the articles in Number 6 of *Christus*—"seeing God in all things," "contemplation in action," " 'virtual' prayer," "constant," "filial"—represent a perfection so elevated that we must recognize that the pedagogy pointed out in the proceding pages is not sufficient to establish it. It is no exaggeration to assert that there is an abyss between the second step, which we have just analyzed, and the third, which remains to be explained.

Spiritual authors of all schools are one in teaching that there is no achieving sanctity except through habitual docility to the Holy Spirit, Who leads us "by means of His Gifts."[11] It is the perfection itself of those who are led by the Gifts of the Holy Spirit which called forth the articles in *Christus*. "Seeing God in all things" and "continual contemplation in action" correspond exactly to the splendid light which the Gifts of Knowledge, Understanding, Counsel, and Wisdom shed on the attributes of God in the conservation and government of all creatures, visible and invisible. What the Vatican Council teaches us about an infinitely wise Providence, powerful, loving, merciful, infallible in Its views and plans, is precisely the object which the Gifts reveal to the human mind, according to the measure of grace which only the Holy Spirit determines. It is the same as St. Ignatius' meditation *For Obtaining Love* at the end of the *Exercises*. He invites us to contemplate God present, working, and uniting us to Him in all created things. God is like the sun, and creatures come from Him, in all their details and their movements, like the rays from the sun. What the Holy Spirit has the soul contemplate, He, at the same time, makes it love, through the *Gifts,* in a higher manner than ordinary charity, which the simple light of faith gives us without the Gifts. We are persuaded that apostles in the world are called to the same perfection as contemplatives and can attain it by the Gifts of the Holy Spirit. There are those whom He permits to attain *in action* this very elevated contemplation proposed by *Christus* and judged necessary for holiness by all theologians of the mystical life.[12]

The purpose of these pages is not to describe the perfection of the Gifts and this contemplative ideal of an active life, already explained in *Christus,* but to suggest a method leading towards it.

It is only a matter of pointing out, specifically, what systematic spirituality permits us to attain the Ignatian ideal recalled by Number 6 of the review. We may note that on this point there is no divergence of view among the authors. To a fervent interior life already described, we must add *devotion to the Holy Spirit* and the active and passive purifications. We might be satisfied with speaking of passive purifications since active purification in itself is a part of the interior life described earlier.

Passive purifications are accomplished in us by the intelligent fire of the Holy Spirit. They are in close connection with the action of the Gifts, which in a certain manner disposes the soul for a more perfect resemblance to the holiness of God and which, in proportion as the soul becomes purer, is exercised in it with a greater and more habitual intensity.

On the level of spiritual pedagogy it is important to convince oneself that every soul which thinks itself loved by God can reach the perfection of prayer, or the perfection of action, only after it has passed through the passive purifications.[13] This is the sure road, and it is here that the solution of the problem is found, the answer to the question which we asked ourselves when reading Number 6 of *Christus.*

Père de Montcheuil has clearly shown the importance in the spiritual life of the passive purifications:

"Being at the root of our activity, the ailment is not curable by our own activity. It is therefore useless to wish to correct oneself. We must ask to be purified. That does not mean, evidently, that we deny the validity and the necessity of asceticism. Personal effort is required. But this effort can be effective only in the measure that it comes from a will that is already purified. Otherwise, we could correct one fault only by a contrary fault. St. John of the Cross has set this essential truth into clear relief, that all true purification is passive, and in the measure that the purification must reach the deepest zones of the soul, there is need of a fresh passivity. The night of the soul must follow the night of the senses. Such a teaching is not, as is sometimes imagined, a subtle truth, applicable only to certain extraordinary states of the mystical life. It expresses, and that with depth, the elementary law of all Christian living."[14]

St. John of the Cross is not satisfied with asserting the necessity of the passive purifications to achieve union with God, but he has shown how souls that have not yet passed through these purifications deceive themselves. Beginners, that is, virtuous Christians who have not yet been purified, imagine that they have reached a certain perfection when they are still "covered with the stains of leprosy."[15] They need to be cured by the action of the Gifts of the Holy Spirit. Not to tell them this, under pretext of keeping them to the common way, is to entertain dangerous ambiguities and to expose them to serious disappointments, to a kind of panic, when these graces which are passive purifications come from God. "These generous, but ignorant, souls think of turning back when these trials are only the narrow gate which leads to the true life."[16] And this teaching is valid for all, for those in the active life as well as for contemplatives.

The advanced, who have triumphed over temptations of sense, imagine that their purification is ended. They are more mistaken than beginners and are in danger of becoming headstrong in their ideas. St. John of the Cross says the same. "They entangle themselves so early in these illusions of the devil, and become so hardened with time, that their return to simple virtue and to the true spirit of devotion is very doubtful." And again, the holy doctor is considering only defects related to the interior life. What illusions, and what possible defects, from which only passive purification can preserve, are there not in an apostolic life, in dealing with souls, in relations with superiors, in government, in teaching or in giving direction!

The prayer of contemplatives must undergo terrible trials, without which it will remain quite imperfect. But contemplatives are on the alert and know that these trials only serve to unite them with God. Those in the active life are perhaps more tempted than contemplatives to do their own will instead of preparing themselves little by little for perfect docility to the Holy Spirit. It often happens that they wish to defeat or overcome anyone who places an obstacle to their will to dominate instead of allowing themselves to be purified by the Spirit. The Spirit would give them an ever increasing intensity of faith, hope, and charity. To resist the action of the Gifts is a serious indocility to the Spirit of God, Who would like to sanctify them. Even in prayer it happens that those in the active life are slow in giving themselves to the action of the Holy Spirit. They find too easy and too interesting a diversion in the thousand cares of activity, past or future, when the Spirit intends to make them progress and draw near a higher form of prayer through the trials of dryness and aridity. Passivity is re-pugnant to them. They have prejudices against it which faintly mask a resistance to the divine action. And since their activity is sterile in proportion to their resistance to the Gifts, they give up prayer and condemn themselves to a life of mediocrity.

Conclusion

The conclusion which flows from the laws of Providence for the sanctification of souls is the same that we offered in a veiled form at the beginning of these reflections.

We succeed in "seeing God in all things" or in becoming "con-templatives in action" or in reaching the sanctity which God asks of apostolic men not by prayer alone nor by action alone. We do not pass from one to the other on the level of perfection. But the *same road,* the *same method,* the *same pedagogy,* all lead to contemplative and apostolic holiness. We must absolutely pass through the stages we have pointed out and, finally, submit to the passive purifications and accept for ourselves the action of the Gifts of the Holy Spirit.

Must we begin with prayer or with action? A question of minor importance. We must pray and act *at the same* time and in both spiritual activities surrender ourselves generously to the action of the Holy Spirit. Purified little by little in action and in prayer, by an active asceticism and by interior trials, we shall succeed in being always ever more and more moved and directed by God's light and strength. Our action and our prayer will then become like those of the saints. We will, as a rule, live according to the mode of the Gifts. Our con-templation in action will not be the passing effect of a conviction founded on principles of faith, but an almost constant illumination of the mind through the power of the Gifts of the Holy Spirit. And every night we shall be able to thank God for His blessings, repeating Psalm XXXV:

O how Thou hast multiplied thy mercy, O God!
But the children of men shall put their trust under the covert of Thy wings.
They shall be inebriated with the plenty of Thy house,
And Thou shalt make them drink of the torrent of Thy pleasure.
For with Thee is the fountain of life,
And in Thy light we shall see light.

Christus, No. 6, April 1955

The Cycle of Activity and Prayer According to Father Jerome Nadal

RAYMOND HOSTIE, S.J.

Father Jerome Nadal undeniably played an important role in the establishment of the Society. He had met Inigo de Loyola in 1533 at the University of Paris, but it was not until twelve years later, at Rome, that he began to follow him. To do this, he had to get the better of a number of apprehensions and overcome a morbid dejection of spirits. But once he made up his mind, he responded with an unflinching attachment to the fatherly tenderness and interest of Ignatius. His lively and penetrating mind assimilated the founder's ideas with an almost disconcerting ease. His far from ordinary intellectual gifts, his profound knowledge of Latin, Greek, Hebrew, Scripture, and theology, made him capable of expressing the thought of his "Father" with a clear incisiveness. He quickly became a "man according to the heart of Ignatius, the *alter ego* of the General of the newly born Order and his authorized spokesman."[1]

Although he never gave indications of creative ability, Nadal has left an immense amount of work: instructions and notes on or about prayer, apologetic writings, a treatise on spirituality. Through it we can follow a thought that develops with a lucid and intelligent fidelity the thought of Ignatius.

All his spirituality is strictly Christocentric, and even there he wished to be faithful to Ignatius. Ignatius was filled by the Lord with abundant graces, with a providential work in view. Nadal thought that the *companions* could hope for the same graces, for they had to follow the same ideal along the same way. Thus it is not surprising that he felt moved to make such efforts to wrench from the silence of Ignatius a few confidences on his interior life. It is because of his insistence that we have today *St. Ignatius' Own Story,* that we know better the importance of the vision at La Storta, that we have some idea of he Trinitarian mysticism with which Ignatius was favored.

Nadal never forgot, however, the humility of Ignatius, who always sought to efface himself behind the efficacy of the *Exercises* so that the call of Christ might be heard. For it is Christ alone Who is the source and mediator of all grace. It is in Him and by Him that we have been created, redeemed, and invited to the service of God's greater glory. Nadal summarizes this fundamental truth of Ignatian spirituality in the formula "Jesus Christ, our Creator, Redeemer and Lord."

In the Christocentric perspective inherited from Ignatius, Nadal tried to clarify the reciprocal relations between activity and prayer. We shall make an effort to follow him by commenting on three of his formulas, rich in their brevity—*spiritu, corde, practice:* apostolic and practical prayer, cycle of prayer and activity. We shall conclude by grouping all our explanations around the central formula *In Christo Domino Nostro.*

Spiritu, Corde, Practice

These three key words summarize the principle which ought to preside over "all our activity in Christ." That is why Nadal, in his instructions, commented on them at length. Rather than give an explanation which would be unavoidably abstract, we shall try to bring their meaning into focus by referring to two beautiful texts of the *Annotationes et Meditationes in Evangelia.*[2]

Nadal was convinced that the Society is not merely a human realization, but an implementing of the choicest graces. It was not Ignatius who conceived the Society and its apostolic activity in order to promote the greater glory of God. It was God Himself Who through Christ communicated His light and His strength to associate Ignatius with the redemptive work according to "his" vocation. Every apostolic activity which claims to be inspired with his spirituality must draw from the same source. This divine origin was meant to guarantee all spiritual and supernatural activity in the Society. It must not be thought that Nadal is here turning to Illuminism or openly commending private inspirations and revelations. It is in the acquiescence of faith to Scripture, interpreted by the Church and competent superiors, that we become aware of the word that the Lord addresses to us in spirit, *spiritu*.

The spirit is at once God's call and His grace permitting us to answer it. It does not depend on man. No effort on his part can confer it on him; God disposes of it freely and dispenses it to whom He wills and when He wills. That is why this call constitutes a grace which we have to beg humbly by recognizing our fundamental unworthiness: "Offer us, good Jesus, the strength of Thy spirit." (p. 90)[3] "Impress on me, Lord, the sentiments of the spirit." (p. 200) God is faithful. From the moment that He has awakened a vocation to His service, He will not refuse the graces and light needed to follow His call to the end. In this sense it is possible to speak of "our spirit," to designate the vocation which God bestowed on St. Ignatius under a special form. Nadal points out at once that God, in His astonishing liberality, has communicated an entirely special grace to the founders of Orders. The spirit of the Society is only the form proper to the divine vocation which, through Ignatius, is directed to all those who take him as a model and seek God in the same spirit. To have us note well that this spirit is given us through grace, Nadal says that it takes possession of man and "surrounds him"(*occupare*).[4] Such a mastery could be manifested even when man opposes it. Was not this true of Caiphas, who prophesied *per spiritum?* "For God's grace still dwelt in His Temple; but although it spoke through the mouth of Caiphus, it did not touch his heart." (p. 213) This movement, which does not penetrate to the heart, can only remain sterile.[5]

In fact, it is not enough that the spirit of God be manifest to us; we must also welcome Him. Here appears the role of what Nadal understands by the word *corde*. In this context the heart means the whole man, transformed by supernatural grace. It includes the will, as well as the understanding, and considers these two powers, not in their purely natural exercise, but in their supernatural elevation. The understanding, left to its own strength, could not believe without the support of the will, which helps it to trust itself to faith. The purely natural will, in turn, cannot be drawn by God, the direct object of faith. God must therefore draw this will as Jesus did when He spoke to the Samaritan woman, by the inner spirit more than by the outward word: *loquebatur illi Jesus et exterius ore, simul spiritu interius in corde.*[6]

On the other hand, we must not be satisfied with hearing this call of God in a cold analysis. The great danger then would be that faith would limit itself to recognizing and registering the divine movement. It is here that the delicate interaction should take place between the grace which inspires man and man who is inspired by the grace. In this way it is not surprising that the *heart* is for Nadal the place of meeting between the divine operation and the human co-operation. On the one hand, "the Lord knocks at the door of our hearts," "He speaks to the heart," "He pours His light into our hearts," "He penetrates our hearts with His word." On the other hand, we ought "to open the eyes of our heart," "adore with all our heart," "understand in our heart," "answer Christ from the depth of our heart." The double role of the heart, which receives grace and responds to it, is abundantly described by Nadal. Let us point out a final example. Nadal begs Christ: "Jesus, all-powerful, enlighten and strengthen our hearts by the bright, strong and sweet spirit of faith in Thee." (p. 90) He exhorts us insistently: "Let us receive in our hearts the heavenly virtue of the divine word." (p. 70) Always and everywhere we must carefully watch, "not to withdraw from the guidance of Thy spirit, Lord Jesus. . . . Teach me to see Thee always in my heart, to follow Thee everywhere." (p. 140)[7]

This last prayer shows clearly that the operation of the spirit of God, with which our heart co-operates, should brighten in us by activity. Nadal indicates it by the key word *practice*. In the meditations, he rather rarely repeats it explicitly, but the idea underlying this word is, nonetheless, always present. Just as the Magi experienced the effectiveness of the spirit "who urged them to undertake their journey," so do we ask "that in finding Jesus as they did, we adore Him with all our heart, thanks to the light of the Lord *(e corde meo et luce tua, Domine),* and that we draw from this contemplation the fruits of the spirit." (p. 37) Nadal often recommends that we express in our actions what has been impressed on our hearts. (pp. 244, 537, *et passim*)

. One might be tempted to conceive the practical execution praised by Nadal as something inferior to the order of the spirit and the heart. The spirit, or the divine movement, would be degraded by entering into matter, the heart, little by little, would lose its purity in outward activity. Such an interpretation does not square at all with the thought of Nadal. Just as the spirit remains sterile and without fruit if the divine movement is not accepted by the heart, so does the heart remain caught in the nets of a speculative faith, impoverished and idle, if its charity does not express itself in fulfillment.[8] Far from being a secondary effect of the movements of the spirit and of the heart, the practical execution is, in the eyes of Nadal, the end always aimed at in the preceding exhortations. It constitutes their *raison d'être*. The execution is at once the fruit and the realization itself of the divine movement which is communicated to the heart. By it, the heart fully manifests the goal to which the spirit has carried it. For God, in His mysterious plan, wished to obtain the collaboration of man in order that the grace which comes from Him and returns to Him may bear its fruits through the creature and creation.[9]

The formula *spiritu, corde, practice* briefly offers us, therefore, a complete theology of the grace that God imprinted by the illuminations of His spirit in the mind and heart of Ignatius to the end that he communicate its *practice* to all those whom the Lord would call to join him.

By way of conclusion, we shall transcribe a part of the meditation for the feast of the Epiphany. (p. 42) It shows how Nadal was penetrated with the principles which he described, in his instructions, in a manner which is unavoidably a little abstract but on which he lived, even to making them the substance of his spiritual life.

"Moved by the spirit, the gentiles recognized in the infant the God Who had just been born. But do you, after these miracles, do you not recognize Him? Deplore, therefore, the hardness of your heart. Turn to the Magi and the angels who have led them. Implore their help. Do not let them go until they have led you to Christ in the manger, until they have obtained for you the interior light which will make you recognize the new-born Jesus.

"Follow the Magi. For they are guiding you, they are going before you. Contemplate the interior star in your heart. In it you possess the help of the Angel and the strength of the Infant. Look upon this light and follow it. Do not, however, neglect to accept from the Princes of the Church the Scripture and the traditional teaching, that is to say, the truth of the faith. Notice moreover that the Magi are very well insructed by the Jews, the lost people. God knew their perversion. Still He sent to them for instruction those Whom He Himself had already instructed. Make an effort to recognize in your heart both the interior illumination as well as the truth of the Scriptures and the interpretation which the Roman Church gives them.

"Thus, under the impulse of the Spirit, you will find Christ in the crib, Him Who is so great in humility, so powerful in weakness, so divine in His humanity. By the devotion of your whole being you will proclaim Him true God and true Man. Although mortal and dying for mortals, He lives forever.

"Offer Him your faith, your hope, your charity, and in these three virtues all the others. Offer your vows: your poverty in the gold, in the myrrh your chastity, in the incense your obedience. Or else your spirit of poverty, of mortification, of chastity, according to your state of life and your fervent zeal for prayer. Kneel before the Virgin Mother of God. Present her your devotion and your service forever, and ask her to present to you the Infant Jesus, as she presented Him to the Magi, to to adore Him in a total devotion. Amen."

Practical or Apostolic Prayer

Up to this we have been trying to bring forward the spiritual import of activity as Nadal understood it in the wake of Ignatius. It is time now to examine more closely the peculiar character of Ignatian prayer. Nadal had made it a principle that the graces granted the founder are destined for all his sons. Now it was his prayer and his spiritual illuminations which awakened in St. Ignatius an unquenchable thirst for the service of God through the help of the neighbor. The prayer of the Society should therefore be directed in such a way as to awaken the same thirst in its members.[10]

Before giving ourselves to the study of this special orientation of Ignatian prayer, we must clearly distinguish it from the different concrete "forms" with which it may be clothed. More than five instructions of Nadal are exclusively devoted to prayer. Others without number speak of it at less or greater length. But he did not, however, clearly set this orientation and these concrete "forms" against each other. The distinction between these two elements is none the less important. In fact, the concrete "forms" of Ignatian prayer may vary infinitely. Nadal recommends vocal prayer as well as mental prayer, meditation as well as contemplation, spiritual relish as well as the complete destitution of the spirit. Even when he treats of ecstasy and rapture, he speaks of these extraordinary gifts without any false modesty, or systematic distrust, and without excessive admiration. Recalling, with a mischievous smile, that the ancients spoke of them much more briefly than the moderns, he describes with some penetration these mystical graces, taking it for granted that his hearers have had some experience of them.[11] In the eyes of Nadal, no form of prayer, whether common or extraordinary, is specifically Ignatian. Each one will decide, according to the drawing of the Spirit and the movements of the Lord, what form of prayer helps him most to serve God. In the perspective of Ignatius, as in that of Nadal, only the direction is fixed once for all. This is something which clearly results from Nadal's way of defining prayer.

When he comes, in fact, to define prayer, Nadal offers three definitions. The first, traditional above all, is well known. All prayer is "an elevation of the soul to God." Nadal hastens to add that this elevation is not purely speculative. It proceeds as much from the will as from the understanding. It is this which is specified in a second definition, the scholastic: "Prayer is an actuation of the powers (of the soul) which grasps things according to their true import." Nadal goes on, finally, to a third definition, which is undeniably the most important in his eyes, for it is made the subject of a long commentary. "Prayer," he tells us, "consists in living spiritually according to a special grace."[12] Here there reappears the grace *supernaturalissima,* gratuitous in the highest degree, which God grants to the Society.

What, then, is this characteristic grace? Nadal answers without hesitation: It is that this prayer, completely steeped with the love of God, is orientated *ad majorem Dei gloriam*. This prayer, in fact, proceeds from God, Who is the very plenitude of charity, because it is awakened by the spirit, *spiritu,* by an invitation on His part. Since as the Son is placed into our human history by His Incarnation and since He has elevated our human condition to the divine level by His Passion and Death, it is in Him that our prayer is rooted. But we become aware of Christ's call, Who in the Kingdom and in the Two Standards invites us take part in His redemptive work, only in the measure in which we perceive the presence of grace, which is always ready to be realized in and through us. Every light in the spiritual domain, Nadal does not cease to repeat, is at the same time an effective force *(vis efficax)*, ready to translate itself into works. Prayer, then, must incline us *practice* (in our daily actions) to express the plenitude of the divine charity as completely as possible. By its very nature it urges us to seek God's greater glory, that is, the most complete service possible. This prayer will then illumine our intelligence and inflame our will. It is as necessary in hearing the call of Christ as in obeying it faithfully.[13]

The fundamental and distinctive character of Ignatian prayer is its *"practical"* orientation. It arouses at once to apostolic action. This supernatural grace which urges to the apostolate and accompanies activity is called by Nadal *affectus*. Normally the *affectus* produces the relish for the work to be undertaken. The relish is the inner conviction that the work is good. It goes without saying, therefore, that Nadal considers spiritual relish—that is, the desire of the will moved by the spirit of God and the attraction of objects proposed by this same spirit—as a powerful stimulant and precious help in apostolic activity. It must be received joyfully and exploited wisely.

Here Nadal shows his spiritual wariness. If the relishes are excellent means for promoting the fervor of the apostle, they may, however, degenerate so much that they become obstacles as soon as he becomes attached to them. From that moment he loses sight of God's reason for giving them. These relishes, in fact, are not grace itself; they are at most its manifestation or an indication which may be deceptive. Thus Nadal does not hestitate to declare, in referring to the third degree of humility of St. Ignatius, "that it is more perfect to be deprived of them, provided that one does not slacken for that reason in the fervor of his pursuit of perfection."

However, even where spiritual delights are lacking, prayer should lead to *devotion,* which is always in demand. Devotion is "a readiness of the will determined to give itself promptly and deliberately to

God." Such an unconditioned devotion is the true result of prayer. Thus it is really much more a gracious gift of God than a victory won in a hard struggle by human effort. It is this supernatural character of gift and grace that is the foundation of its true worth and the cause of the spiritual relishes "which commonly accompany it, having a spiritual efficacy." It is true that the relishes may be asked and desired as stimulants for our zeal, but only the devotion ought to be sought for itself. God will dispense, in addition, His "heavenly sweetness," and He will do so "all the more abundantly as we are less anxious to obtain it."[14]

This devotion, which is permanence of prayer in the apostolate, bestows all its supernatural meaning on activity. The apsotolic works of the Society, by the particular grace of "its" vocation, are directly born of prayer. Prayer, in turn, expands and finds its perfect realization in these works.

Here we are brought back by our analysis of practical and apostolic prayer to the very perspectives of Ignatian activity. It is not surprising, therefore, that Nadal should speak of a "cycle of prayer and activity."

The Cycle of Prayer and Activity

The views of Nadal which we have just explained permit us to assert without hesitation that Ignatian prayer is wholly orientated towards activity. Again we must not be mistaken concerning the scope of this assertion. It does not mean to devaluate prayer by reducing it to the role of a pure means which might or might not be indispensible. The activity we treat here is quite different from a distracting occupation or an amusement for recreation. Activity is the end of prayer in that it is its realization in the full sense. He who loses sight of this essential truth is undermining at its base the whole edifice of the Ignatian spirituality of activity. For such a man, as a matter of fact, activity could only be weakening, and he would have to have regular recourse to prayer to retemper himself in it. For Nadal, on the other hand, activity should normally strengthen us. It is the enrichment itself, secured by activity that brings us back to prayer with an increased purity.

We are not to think, however, that Nadal was naïve to the point of ignoring the dangers of activity. Activity often remains stained with impurity. But Nadal saw, as an experienced and keen-eyed observer, that the spirit could grow weak in labors. Because of them, we no longer perceive with the same keenness of ear "the call of the spirit," which should give direction and animation to our activity. Success itself in activity, understood on the supernatural plane, asks that in this case we again temper ourselves in prayer with the purpose of discerning God's call more clearly. This process constitutes a circular movement, moving from prayer to activity and from activity to prayer.[15] The idea of such movement is too classical to stir objections. But the most important item for Nadal is not there. There is another truth which, on his own admission, he had to learn from Ignatius himself. The following is a description of his modest experience.

"I remember in the early days of my coming to the Society, Father Ignatius suggested that I give myself to preaching and to the service of the neighbor. I excused myself on the score of my ineptitude coming from my sins and my wretchedness. But the Father answered me: 'It is precisely in this way that you will make progress, by seeking the salvation of the neighbor.' "[16] In fact, activity, if it is undertaken according to God's will, concretely expressed by the order of the Superior, causes us to enter with all our being into the divine plan. That is why this *devotion,* or the engagement of a man who devotes himself to apostolic activity, not through dissipation of mind, but by acquiescing in the will of God, will have a twofold result. On the one hand, God will certainly grant certain graces more abundantly when the man returns to prayer. On the other hand, his devotion will render him more available, receptive, and open to divine grace. He will know how to receive with a more limpid purity the divine movements which will be communicated to him. Activity, by uniting us with the work of grace, predisposes us to a more intimate and a purer prayer.[17]

This is the positive justification of the cycle of prayer and activity and of their mutual enrichment. Nadal is delighted to see therein a grace proper to the workers of the Society, as the following anecdote, which he recounted on various occasions, bears witness. "A man very learned and well known in Spain asked me, 'What is it, then? I am just as learned as you. I have the same books, and yet I can never succeed in preaching like you.' The reason is that grace can vary. In our activities we have the grace of the Society. You have another." And Father Nadal concludes, according to Father Rosefio, who had this story from him, "If it were possible for us to simplify our soul by this grace, we should be no longer troubled interiorly in our activity, fretting about from here to there, but we should work calmly with the grace that is imprinted in our heart. We do not come to this result as long as we have not acquired the habit of working under the effect of this grace and this light which God communicates to us (*infundit*)."[18]

This text in its conclusion reveals yet once again that the "cycle" does not imply two realities, one of which is set aside for the good of the other, but rather a single divine grace with which we must be always more penetrated in order to radiate it more and more purely. The cycle must be closed again and again until the two component parts, prayer and activity, compenetrate each other into a perfect harmony, a supreme triumph of grace in man, whose activity is entirely submitted to the divine activity.

In Christo Domino Nostro

Even more than a competent theorist, Nadal was a man of prayer. Surely we can hardly conclude our explanation more effectively than by following in his own spiritual notes his constant co-operation with the spirit that appeals to the heart. We shall there find the cyclic movement of prayer and activity.

In the *Journal,* there is a remark of two lines that ought to strike every attentive reader: "The spirit of the Society is a light which surrounds us and directs us." (p. 690)[19] The brevity of this formula, stripped of every commentary, calls for some clarification. We instinctively have some idea of its importance. The expression "brilliance which surrounds us" *(claritas occupans)* returns à propos of the mystery of Christmas: "In the mystery of the Incarnation a light descends from heaven to earth and surrounds it, and a strength is communicated to men." This notation is at once followed by a comment: "The Nativity of Christ is the grace which leaves (heaven) to become active. Hence, the prayer of the Society is that from which proceeds the movement to activity." (p. 692)[20] It is clear, therefore, that the *claritas occupans* of which Nadal is speaking with a view to define the spirit of the Society is a heavenly grace which surrounds the heart of man to orientate him towards the apostolate and to direct him in his activity, an activity which, in its turn, is inspired and borne by grace. This permits us to get a better grasp of the effect of this "light," but it does not yet reveal its nature to us. It seems, however, that it is intimately bound to the Incarnation and the Nativity; in other words, to Christ as Man-God. Is not this precisely what is essential?

Soon, in fact, the circumstances of the death of St. Ignatius—nobody was present when the founder breathed his last—awakened the reflections of Nadal. In his eyes, this solitary death revealed "an outstanding humility, as of a man who counted himself as nothing, and was counted as nothing by others. By that Christ makes us understand Who is the head we have had and Whom we shall always have. It is Christ Himself in our General . . . so that in the death of Father Ignatius all our affections mount from him to Christ Who is our General forever." (pp. 697 and 698–99) Ignatius leads us, not only by the *Exercises,* but by his very death, to the Christ Whom we must follow by conforming ourselves to Him.

In one of his spiritual notes, Nadal gives us this recommendation: "Enter into the Person of Christ as if you felt Christ within you, and as if in this condition and with this feeling, you could pass judgments, or dispel temptations, in Him." (p. 683) A little later, he takes up the same idea: "We should find Christ in such a way that in everything we feel what Christ would do or decide at that moment, if He were there." (p. 684) We ought, therefore, to act in everything as though Christ were present. But a number of reticences break through here in that "as though" so often repeated. Soon Nadal penetrates more deeply into the mystery of imitation and union with Christ. Then the tone changes, and with an assurance which at first sight might appear to be rash, Nadal tells himself: "Be vigilant to accept and practice union with Christ and His powers, which is the gift of the spirit of the Lord. For this you ought to know in spirit that you understand through His intelligence, that you desire through His will, that you recall through His memory, that altogether you are, you wish, you act, not in yourself, but in Christ. Here below this is supreme perfection, divine power, wonderful sweetness." (p. 697) A little after this exhortation to intimate union we come upon the secret he shares of the graces he has received: "A certain man was seeking by all means to come to the aid of Germany, and offered his Mass with this intention. He noticed at the beginning of the Mass and almost throughout the whole Mass that Christ preceded him in his prayer, in particular during the Pater and the communion[21] Christ showed Himself to the Father in His weakness, His humiliations and His sufferings. He had the clearest thought of a glory of God without alloy in Germany, of that glory which ought to be desired without any condition. This sentiment was perceived in the clearness, full of sweetness, of that light which in Christ was to drive out all heresy." (p. 699)

The grace which Nadal here describes is one of the most lofty. And so it demanded a fundamental humility before the divine activity, as one of the last notations in his *Journal* assures us. The remark stands out in full relief when we recall what he had previously said: "Make an effort to work under the effect of a real and humble feeling of God's work in you. That is what Father Ignatius meant when he said, *In Domino Nostro*. Add to it the thought of the merits of Christ. Add also *cum Christo*. And if you do not perceive the activity of the Spirit, believe at least that He is acting." (p. 721)

These few texts will reveal how, little by little, the thought of Christ's presence worked to the depth of Nadal's soul. It is a radiant light which surrounds a man even to the very depths of his being and directs all his activity by bestowing on it a supernatural value and efficacy. We understand, then, the promise made to those who follow St. Ignatius and allow themselves to be led by him to Christ: "If you dwell habitually in Christ, it can very well happen that while you are busy with something else, your heart will be united with God, not only in some habitual or virtual way, but even by a prayer properly so called." (p. 722)

Is not this the perfection of the "cycle of prayer and activity," such as we see it realized in the marvellous *Spiritual Journal* of Ignatius? All the activity of the founder is shown, impregnated with the highest mystical graces of the most authentic and most explicit prayer: *spiritu, corde, practice*. In his turn, Nadal, confident from his own personal experience, assured us that God will grant us such graces, even when we do not perceive them directly. These graces are, in fact, in line with the vocation by which God calls Ignatius and with him all his disciples, who are humbly disposed to welcome the divine operation.

Christus, No. 6, April 1955

Apostolic Prayer

Louis Lochet

The difficulties of prayer for him who is engaged in an active life are so well known that there is no need to insist on the fact. Every re-treat-master who talks to priests or to persons devoted to religious activities does not hesitate a momont to reprove them for their lack of fidelity to prayer, their lack of generosity in the matter of prayer. He is certain to touch unerringly upon the reproaches which they level against themselves. But if he is sincere, he who speaks thus should at once turn his words upon himself and recognize the fact that his theory often condemns his own practice.

Without a doubt, there is in this obstuseness of our soul to the divine light, in this dullness of our relations with God, one of the heaviest consequences of the state of sin in which humanity finds itself.

And yet we can ask ourselves whether the helplessness at prayer of so many men engaged in the apostolic life does not sometimes come from the fact that they have not been careful enough to get a clear idea of that form of prayer which is suited to them. Could it be that in certain cases they will never succeed because they are seeking the impossible? Could it be that they will remain frustrated in their own impotence because they have been led into a blind alley? In this great stream, which passes through the Church in search of a com-pletely apostolic spirituality, could there not be many clarifications ad-duced as to what ought to be the prayer of an apostle?

To approach this subject in depth, it is not enough to concentrate our attention on what is habitually called "prayer," considered as a particular exercise of the spiritual life. It is only by taking a complete view of a life that this special point can be cleared up anew. For the fountainhead from which all flows might be called "the spirit of prayer." Not an act, but a condition; not a given exercise, but a certain climate of the soul, the very source of its intimacy with God.

The Spirit of Prayer

The best way not to understand prayer is to justify it by the advantage one draws from it. One is easily tempted to do so. To men engaged in the apostolate, whose principal concern is to work for the salvation of others, it will be easy to say: "Be careful, your apostolic activity is going to lose its vigor, its rectitude, even its efficacy, if you do not nourish it at the fountains of prayer. Consecrating a little more time each day to prayer is still the surest means of succeeding in your undertakings." We might likewise say to them: "See how your activity dissipates and exhausts you. See all the imperfections and faults that slip into it. Your spiritual life is in danger if you do not support it at the fountain of prayer. For you it remains the only means of preservation and progress."

We cannot note at one and the same time all that is strictly accurate in the remarks and what risks they run of falsifying the chief orientation of our apostolic prayer.

A businessman weighed down with occupations could well say to himself: "The preservation of my health depends upon the relaxation I find within my home. A good conjugal understanding is absolutely necessary for a real relaxing of body and mind. I have absolute need of my health to be able to continue in business. I must, therefore, assign all the time that is needed for this conjugal intimacy. It is not time lost, even for the progress of my business."

The reasoning is faultless, the conclusion unanswerable. It remains that if he approaches the intimacy of his home with the intention of devoting to it the minimum of time necessary for resuming his business with success, there is every chance that he will meet with complete failure. He will never be devoted to his family, never completely with his wife and his children, never relaxed. And his business will be none the better for it.

It is the same with the apostle who devotes to prayer the time strictly needed to refreshen him to resume his activity.

He who stingily measures out the time for his prayer and is yet obliged in addition to find excuses and reasons for it in the work he has undertaken has no understanding of it. First of all, prayer is not an obligation, an exercise, a preparation for activity. Prayer is the first need of the soul and its joy. What must be done first of all, to enter into prayer, is to liberate at the very sources of life this first gushing forth, which the world holds captive and which is made for love and intimacy with God. We should never count the time given to prayer . . . but rather time which is passed away from it. We count our working hours, but the man who loves his family does not count his hours at home.

If we do not make prayer burst forth from this central point, where man is made for God and where all his being expands in the intimacy of this meeting, everything wears out and goes wrong. Life is then like a wheel, the axle of which is never fixed at the center. We have been made for this love. It is for this meeting that we live and for this intimacy that we exist. There is nothing to seek beyond.

It is our happiness, our joy, our life. And he who knows it does not seek to leave it, but to remain in it.

There is no question of denying the value of prayer as an exercise, but exercise supposes life and is at the service of life. It is on leaving the life of prayer that we find the meaning, and sometimes the relish, of the exercise of prayer.

Take the case of a child who loves music. His parents have been quick to recognize his gifts. They make him learn it, and every day for two hours, he grows wan over the scale. How long the time seems!

But when the teacher has at last gone, he slips to the piano. He is alone, and he plays with so much joy that he does not count the time, and he does not hear the hour strike.

No one will claim that the exercises are useless. They undoubtedly help the artist to a better expression of his personal performance. But they are worth while only when they are sustained and nourished by an atmosphere in which taste for music flourishes. Thus the prayer of the Christian is first inspiration, liberty, expression of first love. It does not count its minutes, it does not measure its steps. It goes, it comes, it breathes, it sings with the freedom of a child who plays in the presence of its father in the garden of the world.

There is no need of canalizing the waters from the spring if they have not first been allowed to break forth in freedom.

He who enters into prayer through the center of his soul, he who has access to God daily and at every moment, as a child to its father, he it is who knows why he is made and that the deepest joy is there.

They are like friend meeting friend. They speak of everything without constraint, as a man who returns to his home and does not ask himself how long this is going to last.

It is thus that we must solve the famous problem: "How find time for prayer?" First, by praying all the time. The paradox is the very teaching of the Gospel. It does not impose on us any limit to prayer. It invites us to pray without ceasing. "Always" is the sole measure that is proper to Christian prayer: "Pray always, and do not faint."[1] And St. Paul: "Pray without ceasing, and give thanks in all things."[2] In secret or in public, in affliction or in joy, the Christian soul lives and breathes in prayer.[3]

Does this seem impossible? A new Nicodemus, we are apt to put precisely the questions which show that we have not yet understood anything and that we take according to the letter what ought to be taken according to the spirit!

"What is to be done? Must we be saying prayers all the time?" The Gospel simply adds another piece of advice which completes the first: "Avoid sounding phrases, complicated phrases, swollen words, the 'multiloquium'; do not multiply words, after the manner of the pagans who think that by saying a great deal they will make themselves heard."[4]

True prayer, that which the Spirit suggests to our hearts, is always simple, always the same and always new, like the spring which breaks fourth and flows over the grass. It is that which the Father hears, even when it finds no words for expression.

It consists, first, in that movement of the heart which is for it more eloquent than speech, in that silence which is acquiescence, consent, and praise, in that inarticulate cry which is the call of His child. "For we know not what we should pray for as we ought, but the Spirit Himself pleads for us with unutterable groanings."[5]

Here again, what false attitudes we must correct from the very beginning of prayer! We have been taught to make it in a reflective, abstract, intellectual manner or, on the contrary, in one that is sentimental and affected. We must have a plan in three points, as though for a good dissertation. One of the first theorists of the methods of prayer in the Middle Ages, William of Auvergne, compared it to the speech of an orator. He imposed all the rules of rhetoric on it.

All the books of meditation drive home the idea of a prayer that is written, didactic, composed.

Who of us will succeed at that in the morning, or in the evening after a day of labor?

But perhaps we are seeking only affections, the comfort of a fervent prayer. Even that escapes us. The sentiment experienced and the affective outburst are as absent as the intellectual invention and the literary composition. Poor prayer! What is there left?

Why not surrender to this evidence? Our habitual prayer is a family life with God. Prayer is the language of children. Family life is not made up of either daily discoveries or habitually great outpourings of feelings. It is, rather, the same words every day, the same actions, which express the same peaceful fidelity in affection: aglow with joy, with sorrow, or marked with effort or relaxation, according to the happenings of the day. It rises superior to absence and survives separations.

All through this we well know that total devotedness is practiced and becomes deeply rooted . . . and the course of events will show clearly one day that they loved each other to the point of being able to give up their lives for those they love. And that suffices.

The love of God likewise does not ask for many surface inventions and outpourings. It feeds on daily tasks. It becomes rooted in the soul by humble acts of devotion. It expresses itself, in very simple words, on the level of daily life and more still by silence itself, where there is an exchange of everything between those who know each other well. It is practiced in the aridity of the night as well as in the joy and light of day.

Thus the Gospel brings to the plane of prayer a liberation similar to that which has been noted on the moral plane, not by suppressing the obligation, but by going beyond it.

Prayer is rooted at the center of the heart. It has a tendency to fulfill itself with that spontaneity, that ease, that joy, that overstepping of all constraint and of all measure which is the characteristic of anything that is done for love.

In this perspective we should add, as we should always do when we speak of Christian liberty, that this liberty is not the suppression of the demands of the law but a going beyond it, a perfect assimilation of all that the law asks in love. Thus the value and the importance of the exercise of prayer are not to be minimized for him who wishes to live in the spirit of prayer. If the spirit of prayer is genuine, it has a tendency to do and to go beyond all that is of rule for prayer.

But we must notice further that the law has a pedagogic value. In the history of the people of God, it was a necessary stage towards fullness of liberty in charity. The fulfillment of the law remains in each one of our lives a basic element which we cannot overlook. To refuse obedience under pretex of behaving as free men would be, in reality, behaving as free men who "use their freedom as a cloak for malice." (1 Pet. 2:16) This is why the exercise of prayer remains for all the necessary way which leads to the spirit of prayer and fulfills it in our lives. But what dwells at its goal is the communion, in the center of the soul, with the life of God.

Prayer is the theological life in exercise. It is the life of the soul in the state of grace, the life of the soul in God, and more still, the life of the Three Divine Persons in it. It is for this reason that it was made. Prayer is not first a part of the unfolding of time. It is present to the whole of this unfolding, it makes a unity of it, it gives it its meaning, it raises it above itself and allows it to fulfill itself in God in the peace of eternity.

The Rhythm of Prayer

In its source, prayer is divine life. Its roots are beyond time. It coincides with the life of grace. It has a natural tendency to become habitual or continual.

But life does not present itself among us as a continuous line, uniformly stretched and immobilized, as it were, in its effort. It unfolds in time. It is made up of tensions and relaxings, of expenditure of energy and recovery. Life has its rhythm.

The life of the body is exertion and rest, building up and breaking down, expansion and contraction, waking and sleeping. Attention, which is the essence of intelligence, is concentration and diffusion, relaxing and contracting. It is the unity of life exerting itself through these alternations.

So it is in the spiritual life. As long as we are in the state of way-farers, there is never any fullness of repose, only quest, rotation, bal-ance. It, too, has its rhythm.

It is important to note, first, that this rhythm is not rupture or discontinuity but a condition of unity.

Thus family life is, in turn, rest in the family and labor for the family. It remains that if there is a family spirit, the heart tends spon-taneously to be itself again, the atmosphere of the home. When it is within reach, it relishes its joy; when at a distance, it feels its drawing.

Nothing is more characteristic of the spiritual life of a soul than the level of the concerns, the centers of interest it finds, spontaneously, as it were, as soon as the importunity of its cares loosens its bonds with the outside and leaves it to itself.

The miser finds himself close to his treasure, the lover close to his beloved; the mother flies to her home, and the prayerful soul finds itself in the presence of God. That is, as it were, its natural place. It falls back into God.

These moments in which it thus finds the contact with the nourish-ing principles of every spiritual life are innumerable and do not fall under the measure of any law. But life itself ought to contrive these privileged moments when the release from external importunities allows the soul to find itself in finding its God.

These hours, which are exclusively devoted to Him, are not arti-ficially determined. They are marked first by the rhythm of life.

The fundamental rhythm which governs our life is that of the alternation of day and night. Superficially, it is the first rhythm of the physical life. Essentially, it is also the rhythm of the spiritual life.

The day is work, external work; the night is intimacy and rest. The day is activity; the night, prayer. It is essential to recall here this funda-mental affinity between night and prayer. It is a basic truth of our spiritual life. Night is made for prayer.

The Old Testament had a secret intuition of it: "In the night I have remembered Thy Name, O Lord." "My soul desires Thee in the night and my spirit seeks Thee." "I rise at midnight to give praise to Thee, to give thanks because of Thy goodness." "Lift up your hands to the holy places, and bless the Lord every night."[6]

Well beyond all these premonitions is the example of Christ. For it was for us that He kept vigil. All the day He labored, and at night He prayed for us, giving us an example. At the decisive hour when He finally chose the Twelve and began His public teaching, Jesus retired to the mountain for the night.

"He went out to the mountain to pray, and continued all night in prayer to God. And when day broke He summoned His disciples, and from these He chose Twelve."[7]

At the last hour of His agony, we know that is was His habit: "And He came out and went according to His custom to the Mount of Olives. . . . He said to them, 'Pray that you enter not into temptation.' "[8]

It was in the middle of the night that He rose. It is in the middle of our night that He will return, and we are invited to watch, in order to be ready to meet Him, the Bridegroom. "At midnight a cry arose, 'Behold the Bridegroom is coming.' "[9]

The nuptial theme which runs through the whole of Christian spirituality meets and enriches the theme of night.

The first purpose of the Divine Office, the rhythm of which we preserve in the Breviary, is to consecrate all hours to praise and to prayer. But the essential part, the primitive kernel, is the watching, the night office, a vigil, a watching while waiting for the coming of the Bridegroom.

The monks alone have the privilege in the Church of keeping the nightly Office; the intention holds good for all.

Night is the hour of rest and of return to the sources of life. It is the privileged moment when obscurity dims the contours of the world that is passing, brings the worker home, and gathers the soul at its center, where it finds its God.

It is the moment when the procession of time loses its harshness and its limitations and opens up to meetings where all counting of hours is abandoned.

It is the hidden moment when man is no longer a worker, an artisan, a buyer and seller, the moment in which he becomes a father. For the apostle, it is the moment when he finds, without din, intimacy with the Savior and in which he ties the bonds of love between the soul and God, source of invisible fruitfulness. It is the holy hour of prayer.

There is no balance in the spiritual life of the man of action without this relaxing, this surrender, this remaking, this spiritual intimacy of the night. Someone may observe that the night is made for resting. That is the voice of common sense. There is question not only of the mystic repose of the soul in God by prayer, but also of the humble repose of the body in sleep. Common sense is right. The night was made for sleeping. The man of action has need of his sleep.

Well, then, our spirit is torn between two evident facts: The night is made for prayer, and the night is made for sleep. The Church knows it well. With a wisdom truly maternal, she sacrifices neither of these essential facts.

But it is only a superficial and mathematical spirit which can think that these two facts are opposed and contradictory. Every man, every husband, every father knows well that the evening and the night are altogether a rest, a relaxation, intimacy, sleep. He does not count in instants, but he knows that life resolves the problem in a sense in which the body finds its due at the same time as the spirit. Thus for the apostle, the whole night is altogether a moment of repose, of intimacy, of surrender. It has its development and its liturgy. It supposes an evening and a morning.

The evening is this return, this recollection, this meeting, this remission, this gift of self and of one's work. The hour of Compline delicately marks for us its essential themes. This is the glance over the work of the day, the regrets, the pardon. The world of which we have taken charge today we place tonight in the hands of God again. Here man sinks into this peaceful night, the image of death, this definitive and blessed meeting with his Savior. Behold the infant who falls asleep in the arms of the Father, Who holds up for him the whole universe. "Into Your hands, O Lord, I commend my spirit."

It is not good that our prayer be transformed into sleep. But it is not forbidden that our sleep be transformed into prayer. This total and definite surrender of the man at last relaxed, if, first of all, it is deliberate, offered up, and spiritually lived, becomes the night office of him who has labored all the day and who has need of refreshing his strength to labor again tomorrow at the perfection of the world for the glory of the Father.

But here is another day arising, a temporal image of that day beyond all days, when Christ will come, the Sun of a new world, and shine in the darkness of our night: "Awake, sleeper, and arise from among the dead, and Christ will enlighten thee."[10]

The morning, we know, is the time for prayer, and this first hour of the day is the Lord's hour. It is what everybody calls "prayer," the exercise of prayer.

There is nothing wrong about it, but it must be replaced in this general arrangement, in the essential rhythm of the spiritual life. Not only in the life of an apostle is it "the time consecrated to God," for all time should be given to Him. No more is it the "moment of intimacy with God," for all moments are made for this intimacy. It is not "the time of prayer" for we should always pray and never slacken. It is the awakening of the soul to the spiritual life, the conscious resuming of its life in Christ and of its duties in the Church. It is the call to grace which is passing into it to spread out to the world and the assent to the order of the day which is directed to it this morning.

A necessary, indispensible exercise, for everything begins from there, from this light, from this strength. The liturgical activity itself only takes on its complete validity when it is enlightened by this watchful faith, which discerns its sacred meaning and consents inwardly to what it expresses outwardly. This is why the exercise of prayer normally precedes everything else.

It is the time when the spirit awakens in God and time is given to God; the first fruits of the day which are consecrated to Him. That is true. And it is that which marks the supernatural orientation of the whole day.

The time offered to God denotes from the start, and in the actions we are awaiting, the success of the day, not from the strength of man or the ingeniousness of his mind, but from the help of God. This offering is the sign that we are disposable. We are not the engineer who calculates or the artisan who plans the day's work, but the apostle who places himself in the Church at the disposal of God for the fulfilling of a mission. The morning prayer is the conscious resuming of the intimacy with God and the total offering of our strength to receive from Him the grace which is going to sustain us and the mission which is going to direct us, for the whole work of the day is now beginning.

Prayer remains for each of us on each day, which is a moment in the history of the redemption, something similar to the first act by which Christ, coming into this world, asserted His complete readiness in the hands of the Father for the whole of His passage on the earth: "Behold, My God, I come to do Thy will."[11]

With Him and in Him we enter anew into the world each day, there to accomplish the will of the Father and to inaugurate His Kingdom.

Apostolic Prayer

From this outlook it is easy to see that not only does prayer prepare the apostolate, but it is itself apostolic. This needs resaying: it is not ordered to insure the value or the fruitfulness of apostolic activity. It is ordered essentially to the praise, the adoration of God, and to the total surrender of the total being into His hands.

It is because of this very fact that it is at the source of the apostolate. God disposes of one who gives himself entirely to Him as an envoy to men. Those who are disposable in His hands He uses for the work of the world's salvation. It is very remarkable that the great prophetic vocations of the Old Testament all begin with a vision of God and all end by a mission to men. It is always the same.

It is even that which constitutes the apostolate. That is why there is no true apostolate which does not have is roots in contemplation. It is by the adoration of God, by the discovery of His transcendence, that man hands himself over to Him wholly. And it is only in this surrender of his being and of his strength into His hands that he can be sent and that he becomes an apostle.

We should be careful, however, not to conceive the apostolic life as being divided between two currents running in opposite directions— the current of prayer, which turns it to God, and the current of activity, which turns it towards men. As though to enter into intimacy with God, we had to forget others; to go to men, we had to leave God.

It is nothing like that. From the very moment that a mission is given, when a man is sent to others, his mission itself binds him to God and to the world. He is an apostle before God and before men.

He presents himself before God as burdened with his mission. He enters into his prayer, he penetrates to intimacy with God, but not by an impossible abstraction which separates him artificially from all his burdens, from all his functions, and from the whole inhabited world.

He enters God's presence with all those who have been entrusted to him and whom he bears in his heart. He is an envoy who brings a report of his mission. He is a man "with a job" who goes to prayer with the bonds of his family, his neighborhood, his profession. It is a father, it is a priest, it is an apostle who prays.

In him and through him, it is his family, his parish, it is all humanity that adores, prays, implores pardon, and hopes for salvation. It is thus that God loves him. It is thus that God wishes him.

It is quite the same when he turns towards others; he does not turn away from God. He bears Him with him. He is charged to carry Him to the midst of men and to make Him manifest to their eyes. For that He must preserve His presence and live His life. That is why, in a true sense, prayer does not stop at the threshold of activity but penetrates it and gives it life. Intimacy wih God is at the center of everything. Just as incense does not burn, or ascend, or give its perfume unless it is cast upon the coals, so all our outward actions, our prayers, our gestures, have meaning and mount to God only when they are in the heat and the light of this inner fireplace.

The life of the apostle is not divided into two movements in opposite directions: activity and contemplation. By prayer it is made one in the theological life. It is the light of faith which incessantly reveals to it God's plan in what takes place, His presence, His activity, His goodness in lituragical mysteries, and in other men the countenance of Christ. It is the Father who sends him, and it is for the Son he works, and for the mystical body which is the Church. That is why his activity does not withdraw him from God. He moves in Him Whom He loves.

Even more, it draws him close to Him. For apostolic activity itself is an exercise of the theological life. For him who has received the apostolic vocation, prayer and activity are the two wings with which he should fly towards his end. Prayer marks from the beginning the supernatural orientation of apostolic activity. It prevents apostolic activity from wallowing in a natural activism, which would be nothing other than a display of man's strength which is incapable of realizing God's plan. But activity denotes the realism of charity; it keeps the supernatural life from going astray into false mysticism, of being lost in sentimental emptiness or in vapid outpourings. For some, it will guarantee the authenticity of a prayer which is not the falling back of a soul little gifted for activity but the real gift of self to God in order that He may make use of us.

We thus find our true place in God's plan. For we must emphasize it: Prayer and apostolic activity are not only the individual or personal meeting of a soul with God. Our destiny is collective. God sees us, knows us, and loves us in the Church and for her. Each one of our actions thereby receives all its scope and meaning. Each time that we go to God, each time that we serve Him, it is the bridegroom coming to meet the bride; it is the Church in us who answers by her assent to the previous love of the Savior and who obtains everything from Him by giving herself entirely to Him.

In Christ Jesus

This mysterious exchange in which everything is summarized and consummated, in which God gives all and Himself to humanity which consents and delivers itself entirely to Him, takes place in Christ Jesus.

When we say, "God loves us in the Church," we should also say, "The Father loves us in Christ." When we say, "Humanity assents in the Church to the love of God," we should also say, "Humanity assents in Christ to the love of the Father." All is perfected in this mystery. All our activity and all our prayer are comprised in the mystery of Christ. Every prayer ends with Christ Jesus: *Per Dominum Nostrum Jesum Christum.* That is why our apostolic prayer can never be separated from the center which is its life. It is in Christ that we pray, that we act, that we exist.

Our prayer binds us to Christ. It is this which gives it, without pretense its cordial, simple, familiar character. In Him we speak to

God as to a friend. To Him we confide our human reactions, and we are certain of being understood. That is why our prayer begins at the level of daily happenings and the most humble of daily devotions. It espouses the very contours of life.

But in Christ, also, through His Incarnation, it mounts to the Father and enters into the mystery of God. It enters into the prayer and the gift of the Son: the only prayer, the only adoration, the only offering worthy of the Father.

Through grace, it is granted us to lay hold of it, to make it our own; more still, to be taken into it and to have access to the Father in the Spirit.

Our mission is the mission of the Son. As the Father sent Him into the world which He loves and which He wishes to save, he sends us to finish the redemptive work of the Incarnation.

Our activity is the activity of Christ, Who, through the Church, carries His teaching and His sacramental acts, His life, and His light to the ends of the world.

Our life is the mystery of Christ, which is completed in us by our insertion into the Church, our participation in His Passion and in His glorification.

Apostolic prayer consists of consenting to that with all one's being, to renewing and deepening our insertion in Christ Jesus. Through all the year it operates, bringing into contact all the events of our life, the smallest as well as the greatest, with the mysteries of Christ. Contemplating these mysteries, we discover the meaning of our life, and uniting ourselves with them, we enter into the deep reality of what we do and what we are. Truly, we live in Him.

To conclude, we must at length realize in God's light that our insertion into this world, that our love of men, that our activity in their behalf, that our suffering of their misery and their sin—all this is only our participation in the mystery of Christ. He gives everything to the Father, even to the death of the cross, and receives everything from Him in glory. Our whole life is to give all to the Father and to receive all from Him. It is the gift and the surrender of the Son in the offering of his death and the joy of His resurrection.

The center of our life and of our apostolic prayer is the mystery of Easter. Our life is Christ.

PART IV

The Discernment of Spirits

Christus, No. 5, January 1956

Discernment of Spirits and Spiritual Direction

FRANÇOIS CHARMOT, S.J.

Our moral life develops like a network, the human threads of which intercross, without our knowledge, with the dark and unperceived threads of heavenly and diabolical spirits. This is a truth vouched for by Holy Scripture and by the teaching of the Church. Experience shows that we make a mistake in attributing to it only an ordinary importance. It would be very interesting, therefore, and very profitable to study from this point of view the subtle wiles of the demon in the course of temptation: how, for example, he brings into agreement his external snares with the perverse tendencies which he has discovered or aroused in a nature which is itself inclined to evil, thus paving the way for falls.

But we should like to restrict our subject to a more definite point, the study of the advances made by the evil spirit in the sincere seeking of an unquestionable spiritual good. For, in spite of ourselves, the spirits of light and those of deceit mingle in the most innocent measures adopted by the soul. Those who have the happiness of acting with a good conscience are not for that reason sheltered from illusions. A fatal error may be hiding under the appearance of a generous impulse. One of the tasks of a spiritual director is precisely to point out errors of this kind. He should have a habit of "discerning," a difficult science which is not acquired at once and without effort. We should like to offer here a few principles from the fruit of experience, limited, of course, acquired by a director of souls.

There are, it seems, two ways of passing a sound judgment on the behavior of a soul; we may come to a conviction by examining either the state of mind which inspires one in action or the tactics of the "good and the bad angel" who work upon one's faculties. Experience proves that souls, without wishing to, without knowing themselves, without resolving their problems, without dissipating their darkness, show with sufficient clearness the character of their conditions and the tactics of the good spirit or of the demon.

We shall pause only on the light cast by the *states of soul*. In such delicate analyses, numbered paragraphs seem to be out of place. However, they answer a need of the mind, and we have a special need of seeing clearly.

1. *All* good states of soul, lofty as they may be, even the most mystical, in that they are human, sensible, and objects of psychological, scientific, or medical analysis, may be produced by the bad spirit, as well as by the good. The most enlightened person, the most consoled, the most transfigured in his intelligence, in his sensible nature, or in his heart cannot be immediately certain that he is not deceived by a diabolical invention. His director does not know either. Presumptuous, thoughtless, naïve indeed would be the priest who should make a snap judgment and who, dazzled by the brightness of this elevation of soul, should think at once that he had met with a privileged soul or that the direct action of God was being made manifest. We do not say that he would be mistaken, but we merely assert that there is the probability of error in every case. The most elementary prudence asks that we warn this soul, favored with extraordinary manifestations of a higher being, to mistrust itself and not allow itself to be led astray by admiration or esteem of these supposed favors, to have at first even an unfavorable prejudice, and to prefer the most faithful practice of the evangelical virtues[1] to everything that would induce it to leave the common way.

We must say as much about ordinary inspirations when they are unaccompanied by visions or audible words or violent movements, the result of which is that sometimes, souls take spiritual or apostolic initiatives which would raise them above others or place them in opposition to the hierarchy of the Church. We should not begin by flattering these souls. That would be contrary to the wisdom of God and of man.

In temptations where the soul feels itself drawn to sin, there is no discernment to be made, for the demon declares himself by the impulse of evil. But this is not the place to speak of that.

2. Light is to be found in the succession of states of soul. In time, a first state of soul is followed by a second, a third, a series which is sometimes long, sometimes confused, of thoughts and interior feelings which form a continuous line, the direction of which it is not difficult to see. Thus the same point, if it stands by itself, might enter into a curved line which turns to the right or left or into a broken line. The same note, if it is sounded by itself, could enter into very different melodies and multiple chords. It is the same with ideas and movements of the soul. What is of special importance is the evolution of the thought, the desire, the wish. We should not be in a hurry to judge. We can wait weeks, even months, to give us time enough to perceive progress in a determined direction. One might intervene to accelerate this development. But it would be imprudent to leave the soul to its own resources and the spirit which animates it and is still questionable.

The succession of states of soul produces the light because it is done in reverse direction, depending on whether the spirit is good or evil. The ends which each proposes being opposed, the curves of the interior movements are opposed as well. The attention of the director (or of the soul, if it wishes to see clearly in the matter) ought to bear principally on the inclination of the affections.

Before indicating which is the good and which the evil inclination, by means of which we judge the direction of the spirit, it seems worth while to be on guard against a simplification that could be misleading. There is no electronic brain to answer all our questions.

3. In the course of its path, like a small stream which follows the slope and strikes against obstacles, an evolution of states of soul can be turned from its original direction. From the right it can turn to the left and vice versa. The good direction will then become bad, the bad good. It is certain that an initiative which is praiseworthy on all points and certainly inspired by the Holy Spirit can end in spiritual disaster. It is rightly said that we should discern the spirits by the end to which

an undertaking is leading us. But a director who is too *simpliste* runs the risk of forgetting that between the happy inspiration and the regrettable end, the demon has intervened to turn the soul from her excellent plan. "The feelings which were leading us naturally to God, which were putting us on the way to God, which were causing us to end with God," writes Péguy, "provide him [the evil spirit] with the means for drawing us away from Him. It is by means of the passions, the waves of passion which were casting us upon God, that he draws us back. And the waves of grace, poor child, the waves of God's grace, it is in these waves, it is even in these waves that he drowns us in sin. That's how he works, my child, and that is pride."[2] This subtle game of the wicked spirit is so frequent in the spiritual life that we should always foresee the demon's counterattack against the inspirations of grace. Frequently enough, it is a sign that the first inspiration was good and should produce great fruit.

4. Let us now put the great question. What are the stages in the evolution of states of soul that is guided by the good spirit, and what are those of an evolution led by the evil spirit?

The soul that is under the dominant influence of the Holy Spirit receives the first manifestations of this Spirit with "confusion"; then it feels itself to be "indifferent," that is to say, ready for anything that God may wish. It then experiences a profound peace, whatever happens. And, finally, it obeys with an unselfish heart, in spite of obstacles, a strong impulse of charity. This is always the action of the Holy Spirit on souls. It must be so if the director is finally to be persuaded that "the finger of God is here."

The procedure of the demon goes in the opposite direction. But before exposing it, we should further characterize the states of soul of which we have just spoken.

Every inspiration and, all the more so, every vision or extraordinary voice, every project, every plan, every apostolic ambition which causes the idea to be born in the soul that it is preferred, chosen, elected by God for an exceptional virtue or for great work beyond the ordinary ought to be received by this soul with a deep feeling of confusion. This confusion should be sincere, spontaneous, and almost instinctive.

By "confusion" we mean the certainty that one is unworthy of such a favor, of which one is aware for a number of reasons, and that one is naturally incapable of bearing this honor and this burden with profit. The first movement of the heart is to suppose that the choice is the result of a mistake of which one is unaware. One is, therefore, inclined to withdraw from or refuse the proposals through humility, without suspecting, however, that one makes oneself grow through this virtue of humility.

This first stage is absolutely necessary. As long as the soul has not passed through this preliminary renouncement, it is useless to pursue an inquiry concerning these heavenly communications and to encourage it to curiosity and docility.

Before every other question, the director will try to assure himself that this "confusion" is real, that it is not an involuntary pretence, an artificial modesty, or a timidity of character, but the feeling, awakened by the breath of grace, that one does not merit the attention of God. "Depart from me, O Lord, for I am a sinful man." (Luke 5:8) It will be good for him to be convinced by a test. The simplest and the surest is to show that every word of unworthiness that the soul allows to escape is taken literally, to insist on the doubt which results from this evident unworthiness, and to lead this person by the exercise of virtue in which pride, vanity, and self-complacence find no satisfaction. If the soul takes offense at the little esteem of the director or at the method he uses in its regard, there is a strong probability that it is not under the guidance of the Holy Spirit. From now on there is reason for considering all its spiritual pretensions with added prudence. No vigilance would be exaggerated.

5. The first stage passed, the humility of this privileged soul should inspire the director with some confidence. But this favorable prejudice at the beginning cannot give any certainty. The second stage is that of "indifference," for the Holy Spirit is not tied down by the words or actions of men. No one knows where He goes. Who can foresee the succession of things God wills? Neither logic nor length of time rules His activity. The danger would lie in becoming attached to the hopes which the first sketch of God's plans caused to be born in the heart and in refusing to accept the holding up of their execution or their delay by men or events. One wishes the early success of the idea which the plan has awakened in the understanding, and one thinks that that is God's will and makes it one's own. Very soon, stub-

bornness, self-will, and the obsession by the end to be attained rob the soul of all liberty, of all pliancy. Unfavorable circumstances, the deliberate or indeliberate opposition of men, failure of superiors to understand, perhaps even the silence and the slowness of God, surprise, then irritate this poor soul, which is not aware of its illusion and which will not tolerate the suspicion of delusion, much less a word about it. Irritated, it complains and criticizes even authority. In a word, it is not detached, ready for success or failure, disposed to carry from its modest adventure either a good or a bad reputation. This state of soul is an evident sign that the first inspiration came from the demon or that the demon has been able to interfere with the work of the Holy Spirit, bringing the soul, by his deceits, to abandon the way of God to follow that of the Liar.

6. The "indifferent" soul will soon feel that the Holy Spirit is flooding it with that secret joy which we call peace. If it had not already received the grace of detachment, it would never come to taste this higher joy "which passes all understanding." Nevertheless, solid peace is a victory; it supposes a combat. The soul, led by the Holy Spirit, preserves it unchanged in the midst of all kinds of difficulties: criticisms, slander or calumny, spiteful words, persecutions, sometimes even condemnations coming from a community or from persons who enjoy the reputation of good judgment. More secretly, God permits that the director, by his advice, his counsels, and even his orders, torture the conscience and the confidence of this soul, which is at the end of its endurance. Why does the Holy Spirit thus allow creatures to harrow one whom He has chosen to raise to a much higher holiness? Doubtless because these purifications are necessary. But if the theory is simple, the reality is not. It is clear, however that an experienced director will do all he can to keep the soul in peace. And if he sees that, in the darkness and the storm, it actually maintains itself in peace, it is an indubitable sign that the Holy Spirit has given this peace to it and that the soul is advancing under His guidance. What a consolation for the director! And what strength he draws from his conviction to help such a soul to fight on and to fear nothing, borne up by the grace of Christ!

One of the difficulties of this task is to distinguish true peace, which comes from God, from false peace, which comes from nature or the demon. In just the same way, it is difficult to know the source of the trouble and unrest, more especially since supernatural peace is frequently hindered by temptation, scruples, and weaknesses and since it does not reign without its struggles. We cannot enter into the analysis of a psychological phenomenon where good and evil are inextricably mingled in a perpetual variation. However, divine peace is recognized by the sign that the soul feels the approval of its Father in heaven because it faithfully seeks that "His Name be hallowed," that "His Kingdom come," and that "His will be done." On the contrary, false and counterfeit peace results from the satisfying of self in the well-being and the enjoyment of contented instinct. We can recognize the first and fortify it in the midst of the most revolting and determined temptations. But we must try to destroy the second, with the assurance that we are collaborating with the good spirit.

7. The soul that has made a happy journey to the heavenly peace may still suffer shipwreck if it trusts the helm to the demon. Its director, whose confidence has grown strong in the course of this evolution of the states of soul conformed to the spirit of God, cannot yet conclude that there is here question of an activity of the Holy Spirit which will produce certain supernatural fruits until the last stage has been cleared.

This stage is that of the gift of oneself to the neighbor. We can never be sure of a soul that has been filled with graces and then turns back upon itself and sets itself up in a kind of spiritual comfort where its life becomes barren. Recollection, the interior life, and the contemplative life may become more intense and more profound after a more abundant outpouring of the Holy Spirit and a more urgent appeal for union with God. Far from being surprised, the experienced director will find it normal to see a diminution in this soul, and sometimes a cessation, of any need of expressing itself exteriorly, of spreading itself without, of communicating its divine favors in secret conferences, of distracting itself, of interesting itself in profane activities. But the director should be on his guard that this return to the interior life and to the exclusive relish of remaining inactive in God's presence does not detach the soul from the service and the devotion which the duties of its state, as well as the needs of the neighbor and the requirements of the apostolate, demand. Should it be noticed that these new graces which it has just received make it slothful at its labor, in a hurry to do it carelessly and to be rid of it as soon as possible, dissatisfied with the cares caused by family life, or the common life, slow to obey, sullen with others, all this would be a sign that it is no longer, if it was at first, under the guidance of the good spirit. It would then be necessary to awaken in it a sense of the apostolate, a care for others, zeal for the salvation of souls. Even more, it would be good to entrust it with work which makes it tend to forget itself and to practice charity with regard to the neighbor. If it resists obedience, if it resigns itself to fulfill its task reluctantly, ill humoredly, without that zest which the Holy Spirit gives in active charity, one could be sure that this soul is living under an illusion.

To resume, the curve followed by the soul which the Holy Spirit is directing according to God's wisdom begins with confusion, otherwise called humility; then, growing in "indifference," peace, forgetfulness of self, and the giving of self to the neighbor, it ends by the supernatural expansion of a more fruitful and more profound union with God.

The curve of the demon develops in the opposite direction. It begins with vanity and pride, progresses to disquiet, stubbornness, self-will, and revolt, and ends in discouragement and inactivity—when it does not end in the striking manifestation of the spirit of evil. We must be able to expose this sequence of action and reaction in order to recognize at one time the two sides, the reverse and the obverse of the same problem.

Not wishing to have the last word in a matter so delicate, we will be satisfied with referring our readers to the *Imitation of Christ*. More than once, especially in Chapter 54 of Book III, it returns to the "movements of nature and of grace." Condensing the lesson of an ancient wisdom, it throws a flood of light on the illusions of our times. We would be failing in the most elementary prudence to make little of its counsels or to think ourselves sheltered from the errors it points out or even to pretend that these warnings are good for monks but superfluous for laymen. Every soul that wishes to remain faithful to God will have to meditate on them: "Son, observe diligently the motions of nature and grace; for they move with great contrariety and subtlety, and can hardly be distinguished but by a spiritual man and one that is inwardly illuminated. All men, indeed, desire good, and pretend to something good in what they say and do; therefore, under the appearance of good many are deceived."

Christus, No. 4, October 1954

Movements of the Spirit

Maurice Giuliani, S.J.

Preceding articles have made an attempt to analyze in their relation and their effects the two currents which divide our soul—the driving power of holiness and the driving power of sin. We have seen how the progress of our spiritual life at once requires attention to the drawing of the Holy Spirit and a clearness of view in the presence of temptations which paralyze and vitiate the most generous impulses. In this world, where the tares are always mingled with the wheat, there is no submission to the Holy Spirit which does not also imply a struggle against the busy presence of evil.

We can, however, consider the progress of the "new man" under a more positive aspect. Born of the Spirit, he should never cease to grow and be perfected in the Spirit. St. Ignatius himself, so attentive to the "discernment of good and bad spirits," seems more than once to give us to understand that the spiritual life ought to lead to a deeper attitude still.[1] Along with the conflict between good and evil, it is important to discover, little by little, that the good itself, that is God's grace, works in each of us in a manner all its own. We must know how to "discern" this action, recognize in what direction it is working, and yield ourselves to its prompting. There will never be a moment when the struggle between light and darkness ceases. But a quiet reception of the light is already a more definitive assurance of victory than could be expected from the most taut of struggles.

It is of this positive experience that we wish to speak in this article. Consolations and desolations constitute the "movements" of which

St. Ignatius so often speaks and are the signs of the living presence of the Holy Spirit in the soul. To feel them, to interpret them, and to follow them is the work of a spiritual fidelity on which finally depends the holiness of him who wishes to live only for God's service and the coming of His Kingdom.

Docility to the Spirit acting in our souls is a part of the most traditional teaching of the saints. But this teaching comes to us only through their own testimony. That is why, for a better understanding of the exact thought of St. Ignatius, it will be good to review his own spiritual experience and that experience in particular which, in the days at Loyola, gave a definite and final direction to his life.

It unfolds in three different stages.[2] In the soul of the convalescent cavalier there meet, first of all, worldly thoughts which offer him delight, his human desires, his ambitions, his delight in deeds of military prowess or daring gallantry, and the spiritual thoughts suggested to him by his reading in the *Life of Christ* and the history of the saints. These thoughts were accompanied with inner feelings, the novelty of which hitherto contrasted with the uneventful calmness of his soul.[3] Here was sensitiveness to an inner world on which, in a second stage, he "began to reflect." The fact of such a diversity of thoughts and feelings, the awareness he had of them, the recognition of their spiritual origin and their meaning "were the first reflections he made on the things of God." Already the cavalier has become a pilgrim, determined to imitate the penance of the saints and to leave for Jerusalem. "Holy desires," indeed, but they do not seem to be enough to insure stability and depth to his return to God. In a third stage these desires are "confirmed"[4] by an extraordinary grace. It was "a vision of our Lady and of the Holy Infant Jesus," and at the same time a consolation of exceptional intensity, which confirmed him, together with a disgust "for things of the flesh." This grace thenceforth was to allow him to overcome temptations which had been so dangerous for him. Only then could he speak of "a change which *was worked* within his soul." His conversion received the seal which left the soul strong and certain of itself because it was, in reality, certain of God's grace.

Thus the soul *tasted, discerned,* and was finally *confirmed* by grace. This spiritual rhythm, infinitely pliant and graded, will be characteristic of the experience of Ignatius as it appears in his life, in his work, in his spiritual direction. The first stage is expressed most often by the words "to feel." It is a matter of experiencing in oneself "interior knowledge, consolations and divine inspirations" [213] which do not have their origin in us, or their cause, but are the fruit of the Holy Spirit. The second stage consists in "discerning" by a reflection, which grace enlightens without taking its place, the spiritual value of these "movements" by means of which God is at work in the soul and in bringing to them a complete adherence. Finally, the "confirmation" is a supreme gift from God which is a guarantee of the decision taken and gives to the soul the certitude and the light it needs for undertakings that are of more than ordinary importance.

The secret and success of the spirituality of St. Ignatius reside perhaps in this manner of bringing souls to a full consciousness of the Holy Spirit, Who is active in them, and of leading them to a decision in favor of sanctity for which they have more need of perfect submission to a transcendent will, which is "moving" them within themselves, than they have for heroism.

The first stage, we said, consists in feeling interiorly "the movements of the Holy Spirit" as a grace alien to our own sensible nature. St. Ignatius ordinarily supposes that these movements are many. He invites us to heed them, to ask for them at the beginning of prayer, to receive them at the end as the normal fruit of the spiritual effort made. He multiplies words which show the diverse repercussions in the soul of "consolations" (fervor, relish, joy, calmness, sweetness, peace, etc.). In the *Exercises,* he insists, in a manner which has disconcerted more than one commentator, on the necessity "of feeling an interior knowledge of our sins" [63], of "feeling what is more to God's glory" [179], and even of "feeling that the love borne an object comes from the love of God." [184] It is plain that the Spanish word *sentir* can have more than once a weakened meaning. (Cf. [10], [27], etc.) But it remains that we would be unfaithful if we were to transpose, as happens, in terms of conviction, reflection, or understanding what St. Ignatius clearly means as an experience, interior to ourselves, of a divine action felt and accepted.

We do not yet come to the full spiritual life by the fact that we obey, or practice virtue, or exercise charity, but only when conscience offers itself to the "movement" which, coming from God, bears it to attitudes

which the Holy Spirit Himself inspires. Even in prayer we must
know how to speak to God "according to the light one has received."
[109]

He who submits to the pedagogy of the *Exercises* will pay very close
attention to these touches, more or less repeated, more or less certain,
more or less decisive. He will be neither surprised nor disturbed at
them. Experiencing these feelings that come from God, he will
slowly familiarize himself with interior realities. He will learn to
recognize them in himself. In his prayer, as in his activity, he will
allow to expand the perpetually different movements of fear or of love,
of humility or confidence, of ardor or of peace. Little by little, his
fidelity will turn into a submission increasing in wonder and love
for Him Who, living in him, communicates to him the infinite riches
of God Himself.

It is thus that the spiritual man is, in his spiritual effort itself, a
living being who participates in the fullness of God. His inner life has
no false stability which becomes fixed and hardened like death. It
is, on the contrary, an extremely varied history, marked by divine
events which lay upon him a rhythm, the law of which he himself
cannot regulate. To one who has begun to experience such effects of
the Spirit, a strained and mercenary generosity is no longer sufficient.
Having become at home in the divine life, he submits in a happy attention to the "movements" which transform his prayer into a real
dialogue and his activity into an alert service where toil is absorbed in
love.

Some interpreters of St. Ignatius, fearing possible mistakes or mis-
understandings, tend at times to turn souls from such a spiritual way.
We must in fact admit that it is easy to confuse the "spiritual sentiments" [62] which are pure gifts of the Spirit[5] with the sensible manifestations which are due to laws of a purely human psychology.[6] In
spite of the risk of illusions, it is nevertheless necessary to orientate
even beginners to this docility to the Spirit. Besides, supposing an
abnegation and a purification of self that is ever more demanding, it
is a guaranteed means of opening the heart to the higher and, at the
limit, to graces really mystical. It is certain, at any rate, that St.
Ignatius never asks us to refuse these movements which the Holy
Spirit causes us to feel. When they disappear, our attitude should be

one of patience and courage, "awaiting in patience the consolation of the Lord."[7] A passing trial permitted by God, the end of which may be hoped for with the fervent wish that "the Spirit of the Lord," or "devotion," return;[8] this is the devotion which St. Ignatius makes a goal for us to seek in all things, in prayer as well as in activity.

Will this help us to state precisely the nature of Ignatian mysticism? The last effect of "consolation" is that "all the toil becomes pleasure and all the weariness repose. To him who advances with this fervor, warmth and inner consolation, there is no burden so great but seems light, nor penance or other affliction so great as not to be very sweet."[9] The movement of the Holy Spirit, far from being a restraint, a stiffening or a breaking, makes the soul, on the contrary, very pliable for activity and multiplies the forces it can use to serve God, Who is at work in it.

It is, in fact, to know exactly God's will concerning it that the soul directs its attention to the "movements" it feels. "May God give us His grace so that we may know His most holy will and perfectly fulfill it." This wish, which St. Ignatius places at the end of his letters to the greater number of his correspondents, clearly shows that the "spiritual feeling" never finds its end in itself. We must "know" (*sentir*) the way God acts in us so that we may become more faithful to what He thus wishes to make known to us. The movement of the Spirit is a sign which ceaselessly specifies the activity toward which God is drawing us.

Perhaps we can discover one of the most original aspects of Ignatian thought. The *Exercises,* in particular, ask us less to do God's will than to "seek it and find it." [1] How are we to seek it? Not only by obedience to commands or rules[10] (This will of God, objectively expressed, is sufficiently clear.), but also by the discernment which is exercised through the movements we feel. These are the "aspirations of the Spirit," which we must welcome if we are to know in what direction they are drawing us.

From this point of view, prayer is the most wonderful field of experience, we might almost say of experimentation, "to know the most holy will of God." Certain light, certain "spiritual relishes" are there made known; they seem to fade away and then return to become more definite and imperative. Certain aspects of the life of

Christ exercise an ever growing charm. The soul can vary its efforts, its method, the subject of its prayer. If the Spirit is drawing it to the same inclinations or, to use the language of St. Ignatius, to the same "devotion," it ought to yield itself even to the point of overcoming all its hesitations. The will of God then takes on a clarity, all the more indisputable, since the soul shall have been at the same time interiorly prepared to accomplish it. Aridities and repugnances themselves have the value of a sign, whether they indicate that the Spirit is not drawing in this direction, where the soul remains desolate, or, on the contrary, that there is a necessary purification or a specially exacting presence of God.

In this way we can understand the high spiritual value of the exercise which St. Ignatius called the "repetition," which consists in remaking a preceding meditation, to review "the points in which one has felt greater consolation, or desolation, or a greater spiritual relish." [62] It is a matter, so to speak, of confronting the Spirit with Himself, the better to see the goal He proposes to us by His action. The "memory," a veritable mystical faculty, makes us relive the moments of the greatest graces and thereby strengthens their effect. These repetitions will doubtless have as a result a gradual simplification of prayer by making it less discursive, but more still, they will contribute to the revelation of God's activity in us and thereby of His will.

We will say even more. We have a duty of positively interrogating the Spirit; to go over again certain subjects of reflection or of prayer or, on the contrary, to modify them, to wait for grace to answer us in causing us to feel certain new or already experienced sentiments which will enlighten us concerning God's will, the object of our search. "We may," says St. Ignatius, "present one view to God our Lord today, and another day, another view; as for example, one day the precepts, and another the counsels, to observe in which our Lord gives greater signs of His Divine Will, just as one would present different dishes to a prince and observe which one it is that please him."[11] Inviting the retreatant to penance, he advises him now to do more, now less, and to await enlightenment from God, for in these varied experiments God "often makes each one feel what is suitable for him." [89]

This calls for the humble submission of the creature, which "allows its Creator to act directly with the creature." [15] Far from an arbitrary application of rules and methods, it makes use of them to allow God to cause the exercitant to feel all the more His presence and His will. In fact, by the rhythm of these spiritual experiments, "God Who knows our nature infinitely better than we do" [89] permits us to feel our strength, to judge our delights or our fears, to measure the weight of our "feelings," to discover the spiritual world proper to each. The *Exercises* thus lived expectantly and submissively are not only one instrument of spirituality among others, but a path to lead souls exactly over the route which God illumines for them. The example of Bérulle is well known. At the end of an "election" carried out from beginning to end by "movements and feelings," he concluded that God did not call him to the religious life. "Must not every soul recognize and follow principally the path by which God is accustomed to come to it?"[12] Examples could be multiplied, but suffice it to recall the many retreatants who, in the lifetime of St. Ignatius, decided to join the Benedictines, the Dominicans, the Carthusians, the Franciscans, and so on. The *Exercises,* Ignatian in spirit, remained, nevertheless, a universal instrument of perfection.

Such a spiritual discernment is effected more easily in the course of a retreat, when the best conditions for prayer and attention to grace are realized. It constitutes that which St. Ignatius calls the "second time of the election" [176], on which he makes the following comment in his *Autograph Directory:* "To know what his vocation is by experiencing consolations and desolations, so that when he goes on making the meditations of Christ our Lord, the retreatant studies when he is in consolation just how God moves him, and the same when he is in desolation."[13] But the retreat only makes more familiar and more fruitful a manner of behaving towards God which ought, therefore, to continue after the retreat to enlighten one's daily life. In the numerous instances where the soul freely exercises its choice, fidelity to grace takes the form of a dialogue with the Holy Spirit, which is ordinary attention given to the movements He inspires. Every human situation, historical and concrete, thus becomes a spiritual situation. God's will is manifested much less by imperatives of conduct determined in advance than by the form of an inner response received and welcomed, fruit which is the offspring of grace and human psychology through which it has traced its way and found its expression.

Privileged moment of this inner docility, the examination of conscience made at regular and short intervals remains the means of encouraging the activity of the Spirit and of insuring our fidelity. It is indeed a school of the will. But it is more a school of submission to the action of God leading to the learning of His immediate wishes. We "observe" where these "thoughts" come from, where they lead, what they demand. The "examen" of the obstacle introduced by sin should yield more and more to the "discernment" of the action of the Spirit. We must not forget, moreover, that the *Exercises* do not offer merely the type of examen described in the first week, but also the examen of prayers [77], of consolations, [333–36], of affections. [342] The insistence which St. Ignatius puts on the examen is explained as much by the attitude which we have just described as by his desire to see us "freed from all inordinate affection." Or rather, the most rigorous asceticism remains in his eyes always ordered to a perfect submission to the Spirit. Voluntary and generous activity and passivity to the "movements" will be like two poles, equally necessary in his mysticism of service.

In more than one instance the inner response, under the form of these movements, which are a visit of the Spirit, does not succeed in clarifying the soul, or at least it does not bring it the light which permits a perfect decision. St. Ignatius then asks us to come to the "third time" of the election, the "time of tranquillity in the course of which the soul . . . has free and peaceful use of its powers" [177], which Nadal interprets with no uncertainty "under the action of ordinary grace by the exercise of its own faculties: reflection, reasoning, counsel, prudence, and everything else submitted to our natural faculties."[14]

But this third time does not find its end in itself, and it opens for us a new attitude: "After such a choice or decision, the one who has made it must turn with great diligence to prayer in the presence of God our Lord, and offer Him his choice that the Divine Majesty may deign to accept and confirm it, if it is for His greater service and praise." [183. Cf. 188]

This *confirmation* brings us to the third stage of the spiritual experience of which we spoke at the beginning of this article. After the movement has been experienced, after the discernment has caused us to discover and accept the direction in which God is moving us, St. Ignatius orientates us towards a grace which will be the guarantee of our fidelity. As the spiritual life unfolds in ordinary submission to the Spirit, such as we have described, the soul finds itself, as it were, already confirmed by the inner response it has received. It does not call for any new certainty. But when the "tranquil time" has left it to its "natural powers," it offers itself anew to the Spirit in order to receive the movements which will give to it the efforts it must have to make the "seal" that guarantees them.[15]

This will help us to understand why the *Exercises* continue after the election has been made. Doubtless the decision is taken. But, especially if it has been taken by the effort of the "natural power" rather than by the light streaming from consolation, we must earnestly ask God to confirm it by making us feel interiorly that He accepts it and that He will be answerable for it. Père de Guibert notes this very firmly: "Election which all the rest of the retreat will only confirm. We would not understand the thought of the saint if we were surprised at seeing him, once the election was made, prolong the *Exercises* for ten or twelve days. We know from his own example what importance he attached to having God confirm the decisions made."[16]

We think from this fact that the third and fourth weeks of the *Exercises* are given an importance which often passes unnoticed. We insist, properly, on strengthening the will in the resolutions it has taken. It is for this purpose that the meditations of the suffering of the glorious Christ are made. But is the retreatant sufficiently orientated towards an attitude of passivity and of acceptance which will permit the Spirit to confirm him?[17] Meanwhile, does not the consolation which the risen Christ bestows [224] assume, under this prospect, all its spiritual depth by giving to the soul determined to serve God the full reality of the Easter joy through the interior gladness coming from the gift which God has just accepted?

This complete openness to the Spirit seems, indeed, in the thought of St. Ignatius, to mark an admittance to the mystical life. At any rate, it was so in his own life. We have already related the first "confirmation" received at Loyola in the vision of our Lady and the Infant

Jesus. It gave his conversion its cornerstone. Later, the grace at the Cardoner, after the months of groping and searching, that of La Storta, after the years at Paris, consecrated in a solemn and definitive way the form of life he had chosen. Later still, at the end of his life, "he frequenty had visions," he said, "and it often happened while he was speaking of matters of importance, and caused him to take it as a confirmation: *venire in confirmationem.*"[18] We know from his *Spiritual Journal* how long he waited before considering his choice irrevocable, until God wished to "confirm him inwardly."[19]

However that may be, concerning the mystical realities which explain this inward confirmation, we must admit that the soul who is faithful to the Ignatian method is eminently disposed for grace. It seems to us that this recourse to the Spirit justified what Nadal said of St. Ignatius. "He wished that the *Exercises* should be the first experiment of those who asked admission to the Society, for he knew that in them could be found the principles and the strength by which we should be able to reach all perfect and even sublime prayer."[20]

Will it be necessary to specify clearly that the perfect prayer mentioned here does not lead us to a loss of selfhood in a contemplation which would be an absolute union with God, independently of the salvation of the world in Christ? It does assure us of the progressive revelation of His will for us to do and serve. The soul becomes more and more sensitive to the activity of the Spirit, welcoming His inspirations and His directions, capable of seeing whither He is leading it and of finding the actions to perform in complete passivity to the movements received. The "sublime" prayer does not cease to make it freer for the unique service towards which God is turning it. If it does not feel the inward certainties of this "feeling of consolations," it will, first of all, be satisfied with doing its best to fulfill with its "natural powers" the duty already laid down by obedience. But it will remain attentive to the "confirmation" desired, that is, to the interior response given by the Spirit, Who will develop in it His "very holy gifts." In a letter to Borgia, St. Ignatius specifies what effects he looks for from the Gifts: "I do not say that we ought merely to seek them only for the satisfaction and enjoyment we find in them; but with the purpose that all our thoughts, our words and our works—which without these gifts we know to be mixed, cold and troubled—may with them be warm and clear and just, for the greater service of God."[21]

In a number of instances the confirmation of the Spirit may not be manifested in interior movements that are felt. This last text leaves that to be clearly understood. He may be satisfied, for example, with the manifestation of conscience and the approval of the superior, with the unfolding of events, with a certain ease in finding God, with a renewed strength to act cheerfully and effectively, even in the midst of difficult circumstances, and so on. God's answers are manifold.

Ignatius himself recounts[22] how at Manresa he sought, not without a strange anxiety, "spiritual persons" with whom to converse. Why this desire on the part of a soul filled with the loftiest favors and determined, moreover, to place its confidence only in God? The answer is given by Ribadeneira, who merely reports a confidence of the saint: "During the first two years of his conversion, whenever he heard speak of one who was noted for his holiness, he sought him out, less with the hope of gaining some advantage from the visit than of seeing whether his spirit was in agreement with his own. But after two years, he made no more visits with this purpose. The father told me that in those two years he had hardly met one or two persons whose spirit and manner of life agreed on all points with his own."[23] In this agreement of two "spirits," was not Ignatius seeking a new confirmation of the way in which God was placing him?

This confirmation by a human intermediary is found, moreover, in the *Exercises*. We have already spoken of the spiritual confirmation furnished after the election by the third and fourth weeks. But the presence and the role of "him who is giving the *Exercises*" assures a confirmation which offers no less a guarantee, even though it is of another order. For Ignatius, every election should be checked and ratified by him whose essential role is to help in discerning the effects of the Spirit. Far from leading to a dangerous subjectivism, the *Exercises* thus insure a double submission: to the Spirit and, in the person of the director, to the Church.

These three stages, which we have tried to set off, define, we think, a very firm spiritual attitude. We began with the experience of St. Ignatius at Loyola. We should have pursued our analysis much more profoundly and enriched it with many other documents. But the harvest would have been too abundant, the problems encountered too serious, to be dealt with in the limits of a single article. We have preferred, at the risk of appearing to simplify, to be satisfied with sketching a few main lines.

The *Exercises* are the luminous focus of such a spirituality. They constituted for St. Ignatius and his first companions the surest instrument in a spiritual diagnosis. This especially appeared in the choice of candidates who asked admission to the Society. The *Exercises* were given them to "obtain a sure knowledge of their characeer or their constancy, their temperament, their tendencies, their vocation"[24] or, again, "to learn by what Spirit they were being led."[25] The director of this "experiment" of the *Exercises,* himself submissive to the call which God made the retreatant hear by the manner in which He "moved" him, accepts the candidate only if he knows that he "is led by the same Spirit,"[26] that is, by the same divine movements which constitute one and the same vocation.

But, especially adapted to those who must pledge their lives by a definitive decision made in God's light, the *Exercises* retain their efficacy for choices which are apparently more humble. At every turn of our lives, almost at every moment of the day, a burning question is placed before us. Are we faithful to God? The attitude, which is that of St. Ignatius and which is transmitted to us by the *Exercises,* consists in progressing from a fidelity still exterior and moral to a fidelity properly spiritual, from duty done by submission to an objective rule to duty for which the Spirit prepares us and stimulates us. This progress can be accomplished only if we succeed in accepting God's will as a gift which constitutes our spiritual "present." The situation most determined by the logic of events and states of soul becomes, then, the place where the Spirit makes Himself known and where there is already sketched the immediate future towards which He is drawing us.

"Sacrament of the present moment," spirituality of the "duty of the state of life," docility of the "instrument united with God"—formulas inherited from the Ignatian tradition which translate into the concrete facts of our lives this submission to the Spirit, without which we shall never be anything but paid employes in the service of God.

Part V

Characteristic Ignatian Virtues

Christus, No. 7, July 1955

The Night and the Light of Obedience

Maurice Giuliani, S.J.

This article, which supposes the preceding analyses, is not offered as a theological or moral synthesis. It purposely omits certain aspects which an exposition of the subject as a whole ought to develop in an effort to lead us to the heart of the mystery of Ignatian obedience. The attitude which it describes could lend itself to many abuses if one should claim to derive from it a teaching in which authority becomes a spiritual tyranny because it took advantage of the submission of an inferior for its own ends. But we feel that these pages, taken on their intended level, can, in fact, throw some light on the true grandeur and fruitfulness of obedience and, at the same time, on the the duty of superiors.

Obedience, therefore, before being a virtue to be practiced, is a mystery to be lived. Through it we enter progressively on an order where the gradation of values is no longer established according to human evidence but according to a divine arrangement over which our reason could neither possess the initiative nor indicate the laws.

It has been noted how, from many different angles, St. Ignatius was led, in various tests of his legislation and in his letters, to clarify the fundamental points of his teaching. We think that this teaching can be fully understood only when we view the mystical horizons which were so habitually his. Following to their last requirements the spiritual experience of one who obeys, obeys as he is expected to, we will in this article distinguish three stages, or rather three different aspects, of one and the same act. Obedience will appear to us as a way, capable of leading us through *the night of the soul* to a *light,* in which the apostle *contemplates* the eternal will of God in order to submit to it his own sanctified activity.

Obedience, Mystery of Night

The first step which the religious takes on entering the mystery of obedience plunges him into a night where his liberty and his power to judge things according to his own views seem to perish and actually do perish. It is a night which can be desired and passionately loved by one who vows himself completely to Jesus Christ and who seeks only to imitate his Lord. But it is a night of pain, for it strikes him much more profoundly than the surrender of all his human possessions, or the denial of all enjoyment to his body. "Another will bind you and lead you whither you would not," said Jesus to Peter, signifying the martyrdom with which he was to glorify God at the end of his earthly apostolate. "Another shall bind you," He repeats to the religious who pronounces the vow of obedience, a man who will be your superior and will set limits to your liberty, within which it will be exercised. More still, he will be at the very center of your heart, the principle and rule of your desires and preferences.

This, obviously, is the ideal proposed by St. Ignatius. To carry out an order received is to obey like a slave; to wish for its success is still not very much and doubtless would be the wildest dream if the inferior did not succeed in seeing in such an order the actual making known of God's design, for him to adore its wisdom and love it, as that which for him from now on is the most lovable and desirable thing in the world. St. Ignatius constantly invites his sons to this last degree of obedience, obedience of the *judgment,* by which the truly obedient man endeavors to adhere to the order received by so conforming his *thought* to the thought of the superior that he approves it and makes it his own.

Only this obedience is "perfect." Our readers are already acquainted with the texts where St. Ignatius says so, says it unweariedly. Let us recall only one, which is conclusive on this point:

"There are two ways to obey; the first consists merely in obedience of one's will, while reserving one's judgment. The second, which is perfect, is not merely obedience of the will, but also of the understanding. This latter is called blind obedience."[1]

This text is also conclusive in that it closely unites obedience of judgment with blind obedience.[2] It is true that St. Ignatius generally speaks more of the "denial of one's judgment" but was it not natural that this denial of one's self, which bears upon the intelligence, should express itself by the image of night or blindness? "Blindness of judgment"[3] makes sure of the progress and the perfection of obedience in order to be transformed into a light, the nature of which we shall have to state precisely.[4] Far from calling to mind, as one may sometimes think, ideas of the foolish or absurd, the vocabulary of St. Ignatius is, on the contrary, related to that of the mystics.

Such formulas, however, have led ill-informed readers into mistakes. In them they have seen a surrender of intelligence, something quite close to spiritual suicide. They have condemned the irresponsibility or the servitude of him who, blind in the face of evidence, is no more than an instrument in the hands of an arbitrary authority. Even in a kinder mood perhaps they have refused to recognize any religious worth in a government which is satisfied with such resignation. These formulas, however, have a long tradition in the Church. In the Society of Jesus they have been faithfully repeated from one century to another by its saints and martyrs. They must be capable of a wealth of meaning other than the ridiculous disguises in which they have sometimes been decked out in order to deride them the better.

Blind obedience, in which one's own judgment is denied, has its roots in the depths of Christian abnegation. We must die to be born again; die to every kind of selfishness to be reborn to grace which builds up the new man; die with Christ on the cross to be reborn a sharer in His glory. In "denying" his judgment, the inferior brings his abnegation to bear on "the most precious part (tan digna) of man."[5]

The obedient man is blind first to the multitude of difficulties and objections that confront him the moment the command is given him. This dust cloud of reactions, most frequently irrational and superficial, rises from a sensitivity that is all astir. We must say the same of some spontaneous and ambiguous acquiescences which run the risk of engaging the soul in a path of sluggishness and faintheartedness. Confidence in obedience, instant and deliberate, a quality of faith, ought to allay these movements, which, moreover, have very little likelihood of involving spiritual values. This confidence should cause us to remember that every order given us calls for an answer to a question which, perhaps, we had not yet posed to ourselves in faith. By that very fact, it makes us humble and receptive.

When he enters into these vistas of faith, the obedient man is blind to every human aspect affecting him. The command of the superior can doubtless be opposed to his health, his success, and his reputation, against his preferences, his tastes, his plans, against his ordinary way of passing judgment, and so on. They are so many sacrifices to which he must consent if he is henceforth to cling to the one certainty born of his vow of obedience: He has become the instrument chosen by God to achieve His purpose. He finds it his joy to be not the judge of this purpose, but its pliant and ever available servant. For him it is enough that God has spoken. He submits with a humility which is going to be transformed into a force for activity.

But God must have spoken to him. It is at this point that blind obedience properly begins to be practiced. Just as he is blind in his own regard, to see in himself only God's instrument, so is the obedient man blind regarding the person of his superior. He will dwell neither on his good points nor on his defects; neither on his breadth of mind nor his narrowmindedness nor on the human motives (despicable, perhaps) which have dictated his command. These points of view can only obscure his faith and thus turn him aside from the real discovery of God, Who makes His will known through the mediation of the superior. Doubtless, in a large number of instances, it may happen that we can offer the superior a confidence that is founded on human reasons. More competent, more enlightened, more capable of seeing as a whole the event in which each is playing a part, the superior easily obtains our support for the order he gives. But even when that would seem to be a help, the danger that one is succeeding in obeying only a man will be great. Were he gifted with a thousand good qualities, this man has no right to the abdication of our judgment in his favor, and if one were actually deciding against him, one would dishonor himself by obeying him. To support our obedience by motives of which we are the final judges would be to barter the glory of God for idols.

By remaining in faith, blind obedience exercises ever more and more profoundly its work of purification. Blind to the person of the inferior and of the superior, it is likewise blind to the very content of the command it received, not that conscience relinquishes its essential freedom in order the better to submit. It is attentive to the moral value of the command and would stop short in the event of sin. It remains quite as much aware of the consequences, fortunate or unfortunate, which it involves. Obedience will not be blind if conscience does not see, just as blind faith is proper to the intelligence which sees the difficulties of the doctrine and not to the truck driver who ignores them. But the obedient man carries his view, in the faith, far beyond the natural connections of causes and effects. He does not justify the command at the price of having recourse, humanly speaking, without hope, to a God Who will know how to bend the decisions of men to His own ends and, in spite of all, find His glory through our weaknesses. We are, of course, certain that God can turn everything into good, but obedience does not set its blindness in the belief that a command can become good because God will have finally modified its effects! The obedient man, accepting the order given, does not justify it by a conditional development of history in which God will be served, despite all, because He shall have adapted Himself to our errors in order to change them to the benefit of His Kingdom. But getting to the bottom of the demands of faith, which is at the base of his abnegation, the inferior accepts the order as it is given by the superior. It is to the *transmission* of the order that faith is attached.[6]

When blind obedience succeeds in purifying our way of looking at things, it then places us in the presence of the mystery which is the foundation of all obedience. It knows that the Holy Spirit and His power of sanctifying the world is made known by the human intermediary of the hierarchical Church. Instead of looking for a miracle to come to transform the object of the command he received, the inferior, at the very moment that he receives this command from him who is commissioned to give it, receives, at the same time, the grace which is attached to this *arrangement* wished by God from the beginning of the history of salvation. Recognizing this necessary mediation, he makes the sacrifice of all his personal plans, even if they were born of charity, to conform himself to the divine plan which in its realization remains hidden and mysterious to him. Together with the command given, he accepts the Holy Spirit, Who rules the Church and sanctifies the individual through the human intermediary of His choice. Blind obedience is then the perfect obedience of faith and of submission to God alone. It does not bow before the superior to the extent that he is man, but to the extent that he is (perhaps unknown to himself) the one through whom God gives His Spirit.

It is to the structure of the Church, the necessary and only dispenser of the Spirit, to which blind obedience leads us in revealing to us, through the agency of the superior, the function he performs and against which no apostolic fulfillment can hope for a guarantee or, when all is said, success.

Taking up St. Ignatius' teaching, Blessed Peter Faber, in a page which deserves a word-for-word commentary, explains this teaching on blind obedience. In it, one senses his experience as apostle, at once tormented by boundless desires and mastered by an obedience that was often crucifying:

"Obedience ought to be blind; that is, true obedience should not place its confidence in the charity, in the reason, or in an appreciation of the fruit there is in the action commanded.

"If it happens, however, by the grace of our Lord and as an effect of blind obedience, that we are given a knowledge and an appreciation of the fruit there is in what we are commanded, we must still, in the event we are given a contrary command, make every effort, not to lose the spirit which inclines us to such an obedience. He who obeys must never therefore stop to repose anywhere, in spite of the very clear and very holy spirit he may find there. What I mean to say is, that we should never repose in such a way that we lose promptitude in every point of obedience.

"If it happens that the will of him who obeys, informed by charity, wishes very zealously to do something for an abundant fruit which he clearly sees, and that obedience commands something else in which he clearly sees no fruit, it will be good then for him to reflect that he has not taken a vow to obtain that fruit of charity, but the fruit of obedience, and to consider that a man does not take a vow to save souls according to his own judgment, nor even according to the desire which our Lord has given him, but to that which is commanded him by his superiors.

"We must note also that our Lord, wishing to open every good to us, often disposes our own will and judgment to feel that a thing is good, and that in spite of that, He wishes us to do the contrary, following the will of him who commands the carrying out of the work."[7]

Neither zeal, nor reason, nor assurance of success can be the final standard of the apostolate according to the Spirit of God. Even the desire inspired by grace must be purified by blind obedience, "pure" obedience, we might say, which goes beyond every other motive to cling to the mysterious purpose of God, Who does not yield up the Spirit except through the "will of him who commands."

With this in mind, we cannot restrict the practice of blind obedience to extreme and exceptional instances. To begin with, far from explaining obedience of judgment according to norms apparently less rigorous in order to leave certain deeper immolations to the unfathomable mystery of the cross, it is the reverse process that is imperative. Completely blind obedience serves as a standard for all acts of obedience, even those that are humanly reasonable and easy, provided that they are performed with the desire of the perfection of faith. It enfolds the whole mystery of obedience.

St. Ignatius knew how to shade the applications of this ideal in a pedagogical view that was unerring. Never, however, does he compromise with his teaching. This fact is particularly remarkable when it comes to "representations," which he recommends to his sons in order to make known to their superior the reactions they experience when confronted with a given command. We might be tempted to see here a concession to human nature, a kind of "return serve" permitted to the "captive" judgment. St. Ignatius views these "representations" against the background of blind obedience:

"It seems to me that obedience ought to be blind. I call it blind in two ways. In the first, the inferior (when there is no question of sin) holds his understanding captive and fulfills the command he received. In the second, if the inferior clearly sees the reasons or objections against the command received, he should humbly represent them to the superior, without moving him to one side or the other, so that later he may be able peacefully to follow the road pointed out to him, or which he is commanded to follow."[8]

Representing to the superior reasons which seem to militate against the prudence of his command is, therefore, another way of practicing blind obedience. Indeed, St. Ignatius then wishes the inferior to place himself in a state of "indifference," a spiritual attitude which strips him of every selfish or personal preference and disposes him to fulfill the divine will. By means of this indifference, the inferior wishes himself to be blind to all that does not bear the divine character in the command which will be transmitted to him in God's name by the superior.

Obedience thus understood is, therefore, a ceaseless purification of one's own motives whereby one can cling to nothing but God's will, make known by him who alone has the power to reveal it to us spiritually and authentically. In this process of purification of one's own motives, he who refuses "to allow himself to be led by his own judgment" makes of himself "a total immolation." He enters into the night of the soul, where he accepts the "void" and the "nothingness." His sacrifice is comparable to death by martyrdom or is even higher than it.

"Obedience is like martyrdom in which one's own judgment and will are continually beheaded, to put in their place the will of Christ our Lord made known to us by His minister; an act which not only suppresses the will to live, as in martyrdom, but also every will taken together."[9]

Martyrdom is the supreme offering of self for the liberation from all that is not fidelity to God's plan.

Night, Source of Light

Mystery of night by the martyrdom of one's own judgment is blindness, which is the progressive search of God's will with no other justification but itself. The search and the night open, however, into the light, the light of faith, which springs from blind obedience and gives it a new character.

In his commentary on the text where St. Ignatius, after St. Francis of Assisi, asks that the obedient man offer no more resistance to his superior than a "dead body which allows itself to be handled anyway at all,"[10] or like "a staff in the hands of an old man," Nadal clearly expresses this positive aspect of obedience.

"The comparisons with the corpse and the staff would have us clearly understand that we ought to rid ourselves of anything that is opposed to the perfection of obedience. They explain, therefore, what in obedience is concerned with its aspect of abnegation. They do not throw a light on its positive aspect, but they suppose it, just as mystical theology understands very prominent positive truths under negative forms. We must, therefore, so tend to the perfection of obedience that we offer no opposition whatever, just as the corpse and the staff do not resist those who handle them. But it remains no less necessary that even in this abnegation we exercise our will and liberty of soul in the grace and light of obedience, receiving this grace and co-operating with it in Christ, and that we see in some way in this light that what obedience proposes to us is right, good and holy."[11]

This is not getting away from blind obedience as though we wished to avoid its demands. On the contrary, it is to live it so fully that it then reveals its effects to us and succeeds in making known to us the goal towards which it is leading us.

To understand it, we must recall both the conditions in which St. Ignatius supposes obedience is practiced and, as a consequence, authority. Once again, we choose, among so many others, a few significant texts:

"There are three ways of obeying: the first, when one commands me in virtue of obedience: it is good. The second, when I am commanded to do this or that: this is better. The third, when I do this or that, on having perceived a mere sign from the superior, even though he does not command or order: this is much more perfect."[12]

The least perfect situation, therefore, is that in which one receives an order "in virtue of holy obedience," that is, by a formal precept which involves fidelity to the vow.

"He did not think that in the Society this manner of commanding in *virtute sanctae obedientiae* should be used, except in very serious circumstances, because he wished that superiors should deal gently and lovingly, like fathers, and not through fear or dread."[13]

It is not, then, to the proper power of the precept that St. Ignatius attaches the value of obedience. On the contrary, the less the command tends to constrain, as coming from without, the more perfect will be the obedience.

"Our Father was not in the habit of having recourse to obedience for anything that could be done gently without it; but rather when he could succeed in having someone do something without knowing the wish of his Reverence, but did it on his own account [*movido de sí mismo*], he was much more pleased. And when he did it because he saw the wish of his Reverence, but before receiving a command, he was more pleased than if he had given the command. It was the same when he gave the order but without giving it in virtue of obedience."[14]

The goal of the spiritual progress of the obedient man is attained in this final point, where the "sign" given by the superior is itself no longer to be seen and where the bond of obedience consists in a spontaneity which brings the superior and the inferior to act as one.

The ideal of obedience, therefore, is not to be sought in the strictness of the material bond which the order given and received constitutes, but in the spiritual spontaneity which brings the inferior to act more and more unfailingly in the direction towards which the superior is inclined. In his absence and therefore apart from all apparent sign of his will, it often happens, Nadal tells us, "that under the influence of God he who obeys wishes unhesitatingly what the superior would wish if he were present."[15]

Obedience thus tends to become a collaboration between the superior and the inferior by means of a common submission to the Spirit. But this supposes that the inferior has fully entered the realm of blind obedience, which alone is capable, as we have said, of bringing him to comply with the providential plan in which the power of the Holy Spirit is revealed through a human intermediary. Stripped of all selfishness and all personal judgment, the inferior lives ordinarily in "indifference," which disposes him to perceive the least call from God and to answer it. The blindness of his judgment has become the source of light.

The impossibility of attaining this high level in any lasting manner is evident. But it is good to know the goal, the better to know the road. It is only in proportion that the motive of faith is burdened with motives that are impure that blindness of judgment remains a night and that the command must still be exercised under form of precepts, or at least of expressions of the will of the superior that are formal and compelling: Is this not what St. Ignatius says: "that the interior law of love and charity" ought, under ideal circumstances, to take the place of every rule and of every command? Is it not also why, after having given an order or expressed a wish, he left the inferior to "the discretion of the Spirit?"

We are permitted to recall a simple anecdote that is pleasant and enlightening. When they were building the cloister wall of a garden along one of the well-frequented streets of Rome, Father Ignatius had told Father Olivier, minister of the house, to call all the fathers and brothers present, without exception, to help in the work. While they were at work, he himself came to pay them a visit. He noticed a novice in the group whose attitude and expression gave evidence of serious trouble. The novice belonged to a noble family, and he was ashamed of this servile work, carried on in the full gaze of the passers-by. Ignatius saw that he was tempted in his vocation and calling Father Olivier, he said: "Don't you see that this novice is being tempted to go home when you put him at this work? Why have you called him?" "Because you bade me call everybody in the house without exception," explained the minister. "But," rejoined Ignatius, "although I did say that, isn't it you who are minister, and shouldn't you use some discretion?" And, calling the novice, he told him to drop the work, which was not for him.[16]

It is in the light of this "discretion" that the inferior succeeds in interpreting, in order to fulfill the command which is given him and "to make his own," the judgment of the superior. To make his own is, according to Ignatian formulas, to judge that the order received is *better,* very good, more profitable, or, according to the text of Nadal, which we have just now quoted, that it is "right," good, and holy.

It is not a question of doing violence to ourselves for us to imagine that in the proper area of its exercise, our intellect is impotent or weak; the intellect does not deny itself, its evidence is without obscurity, and its laws of detection or of reasoning lead it to certainties of which it can be legitimately proud. Doubtless, it is proper to remain humble and to know that our limited intellect cannot decide everything. But this is humility and wisdom in every part human. They can, for the moment, help us to enter into the view of the superior without, however, bestowing on his thought anything absolute, which of itself it does not imply since it is itself the outcome of a fallible knowledge of situations and of psychologies. The effort by which one would be persuaded that this or that erroneous or narrow judgment has become a just and broad judgment for the sole reason that a superior has made it the matter of a command would be dishonesty and fraud. Dishonesty because we should be repudiating ourselves in the exercise of our intelligence. Fraud because the obedience would not be at all justified. Under pretext of blind obedience, we should not be entering into an obedience of faith, and we should end with an obedience that is doltish!

The attitude of faith is something altogether different. To make one's own the judgment of the superior is, to begin with, to place oneself with him at the very point where the spiritual desire which animates him arises. Without allowing ourselves to be bewildered by the complexity of motives and influences which have given to his command the concrete form in which he expresses it, true obedience attains in the thought of the superior the aim which is that of his faith.

When, in fact, St. Ignatius prescribed the duty of obedience, he placed it in close correlation with the duty of the superior, himself obliged also to conceive, mature, and decide in God's presence on the command he issues. Even if human or selfish views have been able to distort this command, we must make every effort to grasp its supernatural bearings. The inferior, therefore, trains himself to understand and love this fundamental intention and to set it back in the wealth of a tradition of which the superior is the servant and guardian.

In their sharing of this twofold movement of faith, obedience then inclines one towards the other, the inferior and the superior. It inclines the inferior to judge as "right, good and holy" the judgment of the superior, in that he here and now communicates a decision to which is attached the action of the Spirit. It inclines the superior to accept the aspiration of him who is entrusted to him and to fashion after it, as far as possible, the concrete command to be issued. St. Ignatius, we know, liked to take into account the inclinations of each of his sons, at least in the measure in which "they showed themselves to be his true sons, perfectly obedient and intirely resigned to the judgment and the will of their superiors." One of his biographers has preserved a sentence which he is once supposed to have uttered:

"I very much desire a universal indifference in all; and so, taking obedience and abnegation for granted on the part of the inferior, I would find it very easy to follow the inclinations of each."[17]

We know how attentive he was to question each one about his preferences and how far he felt himself disposed to make the total sacrifice of them. In the inclination of those who are under his authority, does not the superior receive suggestions from the Spirit? If he happens, unfortunately, to refuse them or to make himself deaf to them, he would transform his authority into the worst of tyrannies and would himself be responsible before God should one of his inferiors succumb under the burden he had laid upon him.

True communion in the faith is a common sensitivity to the Spirit. Obedience can then be transformed into an intimate collaboration, in the center of which a spiritual dialogue is established, firm, frank, free, which comes more and more to bear the seal of love. Even, and especially in the case where the superior is inspired only too plainly by human or ill-adapted views, the inferior, moved by blind obedience, that is to say, careful to give his submission only to God through him who commands, will "represent" to the superior the difficulties he feels. The more indifferent he is, the freer will be his daring. But in no case will he consent to break off this dialogue of obedience by an attitude of refusal or reserve, for that would be to withdraw from the source by which God's will is made known. Obliged to obey, he will incline towards the thought of the superior, not to justify it humanly, if it is unjustifiable according to human norms, but to wish by this effort of humility to receive the light of the Spirit. After the superior has created a certain bond between God's power and a determined form of action, the inferior will make every effort to wish nothing else and to bring about the success of the command he has received by applying to it all the enthusiasm of his human strength, always giving his faith to the transcendence of the mysterious design he seeks to serve.

Light, The Driving Power of Action

Obedience therefore makes its appearance under the twofold aspect of darkness and light, like a new birth through the Holy Spirit. To its eye of faith, the world has become a "symbol" of God.

Earlier we quoted the reflections made by Nadal in connection with the dead body and the old man's staff. Explaining the Ignatian teaching on obedience, Nadal returned again and again to the necessity of recognizing, under negative images, the positive truth they contained:

"Through its blindness ... our judgement obtains the true light and clearness of view, so as to be able without dimness to unite itself with God, by following Him in all things, growing strong in Him, so as the better to carry out what is commanded in His name."[18]

To grow strong in God, the better to carry out the order received—such indeed is the goal which obedience of faith reaches. But Nadal particularizes on the carrying out he is speaking of:

"By this blindness ... it happens that the shadows of falsehood are dispelled, and that the understanding grasps the truth with the greatest consolation, *as though by a genuine contemplation* of God our Lord, a contemplation which dispels any falsehood it might encounter, so as to arrive at the truth and make the discovery of many other things which help us to love God and to serve Him with all our will.

"Let us have, then, this blindness which is so suitable for obtaining us this sovereign light and to help us understand that all that is commanded us is good. . . . God is known 'in the darkness,' as the Blessed Denis expresses it, when he says that God is neither this nor that, nor anything else. Thus, to deny one's own judgment in the matter of obedience is to succeed in acquiring true light and true knowledge for understanding that all that the superior may command should be done with promptness of execution, resignation of judgment and purity of will."[19]

Just as we do not attain to God except through the Darkness, so does obedience cause us to contemplate God in the heart of the darkness which, in the faith, blinds our judgment. This, then, is to assert, on the one hand, that obedience is assimilated to true contemplation and, on the other, that it is such a contemplation only in that it submits to being blind.

Perhaps we are here close to the ultimate secret of our obedience. To obey, we have said, is first of all, through the purifying movement of blind obedience, to disengage the command received from every consideration foreign to faith. Then, in the light of the Spirit, it is to accept it as good and holy. But it must go even further. To obey is to contemplate God in the execution of the command that is given.

Of course, there is no question here of a contemplation of God such as He might reveal Himself to be in Himself, but as He works in the world. On this point, Nadal's comparison with the mysticism of the pseudo-Denis must be understood. The God Whom we perceive through the superior is always He Who accomplishes His work in history. The superior is himself subject to error or imprudence in his government. But the authority that he wields makes known at a given moment of time both the everlasting will by which God has bound His activity to the necessary mediation of a Church and His salvation to the dispensing of His grace by means of men.

To carry out an order received is to submit oneself to this mysterious law. In the initiation of action, in the intelligent use of the means employed, in the desire of bringing success to the task for which we have become responsible, it is to be certain that we carry with us the power of the Spirit. On this point no failure can unsettle him who obeys. It is even certain that this power of the Spirit may manifest itself by miracles, for nothing is impossible to God. And these miracles will truly be "miracles of obedience," that is, they will crown the faith of him who by obedience clings solely to the divine plan. When the will strains only to obey, when the judgment seeks only to be united with that of the superior, the impossibility of the action commanded cannot be an obstacle, even if it carries the night of the spirit to its extreme intensity:

"If you are commanded to do something that cannot be carried out, you ought to undertake it in all purity and simplicity of obedience to the point just short of actual impossibility. If, for example, the superior commands you to walk upon the water, you should, without any thought of the impossibility, take at least one step on the water, and as soon as you see that you cannot advance, go back to the superior and tell him that you wanted to walk upon the water, but could not."[20]

Such submission to a given order may seem strange and ridiculous. But if we place it within the perspective of obedience, which is an act of adoration of God's plan in His will, concretely expressed by a human superior, it rises to true greatness.

To be sure, it cannot be lived "in its purity and simplicity" unless faith is sustained by an exceptional grace. But for all its being exceptional, this grace is no different from that which is given to every obedient man. It is the grace of contemplating God through the "symbol" of human wills.

Texts from St. Alphonsus Rodriguez show how far this grace can lead in a privileged soul. For St. Alphonsus, in fact, the first degree of perfection to be attained in blind obedience consists in the soul's exercising itself in it "without further search or reasoning, by a general apprehension which brings it to believe that the command of the superior is the voice of God." It is what he calls "living faith." But in a second degree, "the soul is all on fire with love of its God, Whom it obeys, and this love which comes from heaven enlightens its judgment to such a point with a divine light that it comes to know and to see how obedience to the superior proceeds from God. . . . The soul has its gaze fixed on God from Whom it sees that obedience comes."[21] This was his own experience, which he thus summarized: "God communicated so great a light to him . . . by which he clearly saw in God Himself how the command of the superior proceeds from God."[22] A mystical experience, to be sure, but one that makes clear what every obedient man is called to live daily through grace.

Thus we find verified once again in the case of obedience what we already said of the usual attitude of St. Ignatius.[23] Finding God in activity is not to rise from creatures to God by an ascent which purifies the senses, but to descend from God to creatures in a movement of love which, beginning from the Father, bears us on in Christ towards the realization of this love in every created being. Finding God in obedience is not rising from the superior, who speaks to God, Who inspires (this would run the risk of conferring on the superior a dignity and an infallibility which he has not), but "seeing" how the command that is given "proceeds" from God. Obeying, then, is submitting oneself to an action willed by God and manifested through the contingency of human symbols.

That is why obedience is the surest guarantee of finding God in activity. The texts in which St. Ignatius invites us to find God no less in works of charity than in prayer often indicate that this will be all the easier if these works are commanded by obedience. Through obedience, in fact, the apostle is assured that the activity undertaken proceeds from the will of God. Working for its development and its success, he contemplates through the concrete forms imposed by human circumstances the realization of God's glory.

His prayer ceaselessly brings him back to the work willed by God. It not only disposes him to obey by clarifying his faith, but also causes him to discover in his doings of the day the mystery of God working for the salvation of the world. Concerning this direction of prayer, Nadal bears us a temperate but clear witness:

"A man begs for the gift of prayer. At once he feels that he is referred to obedience, and hears these words: *Obedite praepositis vestris.* (Heb. 13:17)

"*Ipsum audite*. The end of every spiritual visitation, however sublime, is obedience.

"If in prayer you find spirit and grace, they will refer you at once to obedience."[24]

To be referred to obedience does not mean to leave prayer, but to enjoy the prayer that St. Ignatius wishes to be continuous, in submission to the action of God.

We should not be surprised, therefore, that, speaking of obedience, St. Ignatius relentlessly insists on the interior cheerfulness which should accompany the execution of the command.

"They who are perfectly obedient are already so dead to themselves that they do not in any way wish to feel within themselves an opinion or an inclination that is their own, but desire only to accomplish God's will, which is made known to them through the superior. Humbly, they are ready for anything that will be told them. Thus indifferent and without personal inclination, they receive with equal joy the decision the superior makes for them, whether it be for their life or their death, because it is God's will, the fulfilling of which is their desire and their consolation."[25]

Such a consolation is made of "relaxation," of "repose," of "exultation." It is like a song of triumph and freedom, which is encountered more than once in the letters of St. Ignatius when he recalls the blessings of obedience lived in its perfection. He even ventures to write that the obedient man already experiences "the relish of the repose of heaven."[26]

At any rate, promptness and ease of execution grow in proportion to the depth of faith, that is, in the last analysis, of one's clinging to the divine economy. The obedient man places himself at the very point where the Spirit of God becomes power of salvation and sanctification while passing through the mediation of a man to whom has been assigned this formidable role of "binding another man and leading him wither he would not." It makes him draw close to the contemplation of God's plan. It permits him to associate himself with it in an action which then reveals a prodigious efficacy, for it bears the Spirit Who gives life to the world.

To arrive at this plenitude, where sacrifice becomes joy and spiritual fecundity, the road will doubtless have been long. But the apostle can, in all truth, then take up the word which St. Ignatius applies to the perfectly obedient man: "It is no longer I who live; it is Christ Who lives in me." His sole nourishment is the progressive realization of God's plan, which he contemplates with a purified gaze in each of the blossomings of the Spirit, of which obedience is at once the means and the promise.

Conclusion

"The foolishness of God is wiser than men." (1 Cor. 1:25) Shall we have words other than the "foolishness of the message" announced by St. Paul to the Corinthians? Shall we have strength other than the "weakness of God?"

Foolishness and weakness are united in Jesus Christ. Instead of taking possession of His Kingdom by the means that the crowds would have wished and which Satan suggested, He became the Servant, obedient unto death, to the men of His nation and His race: to Caiphas, the heir of the Prophets; to Pilate, to whom "the power had been given from on high." For it was thus that He accomplished the will of His Father. Breathing forth His last sigh, He gave up, by an act of supreme obedience, the Spirit which would be the source of the world's regeneration.

United to this mystery of sacrifice and of fruitfulness, the obedient man tries, according to the measure of his grace, from fresh submismions, to enter each day into the plan of the Father for fresh outpourings of the Spirit.

Christus, No. 9, January 1956

Continual Mortification

ANTOINE DELCHARD, S.J.

"Speaking one day to Father Ignatius of a good religious whom he knew, I said: 'He is a man of great prayer.' Our Father corrected me: 'He is a man of great mortification.'"[1]

Beginning with this anecdote, we could, undoubtedly, draw the portrait of a St. Ignatius who is hard, austere, and insensible to the progress the soul makes in the discoveries of the mysteries of God. But he who recounts the story is one of those who lived in daily intimacy with him and who is aware that he is passing on to us, without betraying it, a decisive light on the mysticism of the founder.

As a matter of fact, there can be no doubt St. Ignatius has marked the teaching of abnegation with an accent that is quite his own. To show at once its demands and its true depth, we shall limit ourselves in this article to analyzing one of the fullest texts, and doubtless one of the most beautiful, that St. Ignatius ever wrote. A sober text, as was his wont, dry in outline, the controlled fervor of which equals and perhaps surpasses all less restrained utterances.

We here surprise Ignatius in one of the attitudes in which he expresses himself with greater truth. A man presents himself to him, still young, or perhaps matured by experience, whom a call from God, as yet ill discerned, has led to the doors of his Order. Between the Superior General and the Jesuit candidate, a dialogue ensues. St. Ignatius wishes to be frank and not to conceal any of the conditions that are required. He wishes, on the other hand, to get deeply enough into the soul of him whom grace has stamped with its seal in order to purify the motive of his step from every natural design and bring it into agreement with the highest demands of his vocation. He thinks, finally, of the future of his "little Company," in which he dreams of gathering free and vigorous apostles who, far from being a dead weight, will help in its spiritual expansion. It is all these desires together that give their true scope to the pages of the *General Examen,* which is to be given to all those asking to be admitted into the Society of Jesus,[2] a document in which in a few chapters are set down the essential questions to be discussed in this dialogue which we are presenting.

"Examen." The word seems strange. It is indeed, however, a matter of "examining" the candidate, of setting him face to face with the ideal he shall have to strive for. One after the other are explained the religious Institute and its apostolic end in the service of the Church, its idea of poverty and obedience, the kind of life led by those who make profession in it, and so forth. Juridical aspects are mingled with those that are properly spiritual. One whole chapter, the fourth, draws a portrait of the perfect "companion of Jesus," not merely in his outward behavior in the midst of a community, but in the thoughts which ought to animate him. In full fidelity to the religious tradition (in that alone would the plan followed make sense), St. Ignatius first of all asks the candidate to renounce the world and to give himself over entirely to the service of God: surrender of his property, separation from his friends and his family, renouncing of a certain esteem on the part of others by accepting in advance and for good the manifestation and correction of his faults. He then outlines the main "experiments" which the novice must undergo to free himself from the spirit of the world and to place all his confidence in his Creator and Lord.

At the end of this chapter it would seem that St. Ignatius had definitely drawn the image of the Jesuit, such as he ought to be at his entering the religious life, such as he ought to remain until death, tending to the perfection of charity. But his thought takes a rebound, and in three paragraphs it assumes an unexpected breadth and accent. We feel that this conclusion is the expression of the very heart of Ignatius. In a final "trial" he wishes to prove his son and at the same time reveal to him what beyond all motive and all rule will constitute his strength and his joy. Doubtless he had by this time clearly defined the ideal of religious abnegation. One could become aware of it by our too brief summary; but now he causes him to enter into the very mystery of love which absorbs all the feelings of the heart which has surrendered to God alone.

"Those who are being examined must attentively consider, and, in the presence of our Creator and Lord, hold it to be of the utmost importance as a help to progress in the spiritual life, to abhor completely and without exception all that the world loves and embraces, and to accept and desire with all their strength whatever Christ our Lord loved and embraced. For, as men of the world who follow the world love and very ardently seek honors, distinctions and the reputation of a great name among men, as the world teaches them; so they who are making progress in the spiritual life and are serious about following Christ our Lord love and warmly desire the very opposite—to be clothed, in fact, in the same garments and wear the same attire as their Lord, out of love and reverence for Him: and this to such an extent, that if it could be done without offence to His Divine Majesty, or sin on the part of their neighbor, they should wish to suffer abuse, injustice, false accusations, and to be considered and treated as fools (without however giving occasion for such treatment), their whole desire being to resemble and in some way imitate our Creator and Lord Jesus Christ, by being clothed in His garments and raiment, since He so first clothed Himself for our greater spiritual benefit, and gave us an example to lead us to seek, as far as possible with God's grace, to imitate and follow Him, seeing He is the true Way which leads men to life.

"The candidate will be asked whether he feels such desires, so salutary and fruitful for the perfection of his soul. Should he not, because of the weakness of human misery, feel these enflamed desires in our Lord, he should be asked whether he has some desire to experience them. And if he answers that he does have such holy desires, he should be asked, for the better realization of this desire, whether he is determined and ready to suffer patiently, with God's grace, all the insults, scoffs and derision which this raiment of Christ our Lord supposes, or other treatment of the kind, whether it be on the part of anyone in the house, or in the Society (in which he wishes to obey, to be humbled and to gain eternal life), or on the part of anyone from without, not returning evil for evil, but good for evil.

"And the better to reach so precious a degree of perfection in the spiritual life, it will be his first and foremost duty to seek in our Lord his greater abnegation and continuous mortification in all things possible. It will be our duty to help him in this as far as our Lord gives us His grace for His greater praise and glory."[3]

It is this text that we wish to comment on by following its three paragraphs: the participation in the mystery of Jesus, Who, by His death, leads to life; the purification of the desire to be faithful to Him; the concrete means to insure against failure on the way.

Participation in the Mystery of Jesus

To the young man who questioned Him on the conditions of "everlasting life," Jesus hid none of its demands: "Go, sell what you have, give to the poor; and you shall have treasure in heaven; then come, follow Me." (Mark 10:21) To the candidate for the religious life, St. Ignatius speaks with the same clearness. He proposes the same renunciation, the same hope, the same engagement: follow Christ, that is, take up one's own cross and walk in His footsteps.

A period of silence, a long look, indicates the seriousness of what he is going to say. The language of the cross, which the Founder is going to use with a passion that betrays his love, should not be listened to distractedly: "Those who are being examined must attentively consider and in the presence of our Creator and Lord hold it to be of the utmost importance . . . " This introduction awakens attention, a prayerful attention. It is "in the presence" of Christ "our Creator and Lord" that the candidate should take cognizance of what is being proposed to him. The step which he has taken to the threshold of the religious life may be hasty, inspired by a thoughtless burst of enthusiasm. Let him recollect himself, have recourse to prayer, and consider at length all that this implies. To become a companion of Jesus is to follow Christ in the way of humility and renouncement which He has chosen. "The foundation of this Society," said Father Nadal, "is Jesus Christ crucified."[4]

" . . . hold it to be of the utmost importance as a help to progress in the spiritual life, to abhor completely and without exception all that the world loves and embraces, and to accept and desire with all their strength whatever Christ our Lord loved and embraced."

A choice is imperative: God or mammon, for no one can serve two masters. As in the meditation on the Two Standards [136–148],* St. Ignatius marks the vivid contrast. The demands of our Lord, which the Examen has already emphasized—surrender of material goods, giving of the heart to poverty, loss of self in obedience—are here formed into a knot and made inescapable. The alternative leaves no loophole for escape, and it is placed in the most interior part of the will. A choice must be made between two dispositions of heart; to love Christ is to hate the world. To bargain with the world, not to renounce by a total refusal what is pleasing to it, is to refuse Christ. "Love not the world, nor the things which are in the world. If any man love the world, the charity of the Father is not in him. For all that is on the world is the concupiscence of the flesh and the con-cupiscence of the eyes and the pride of life which is not of the Father, but is of the world. And the world passeth away and the concuspi-scence thereof: but he that doth the will of God abideth forever." (1 John, 2:15-17)

To do the will of God is to follow Him Whose food it was to do the will of Him Who sent Him. In renouncing the world we choose Christ. Not by halves, but completely. We shall then obtain "com-munion of life with the Son." But to receive "eternal life," they must "accept and desire with all their strength whatever Christ our Lord loved and embraced."

There is no proud pretention in this choice, for if Jesus loved and embraced the cross, if He engaged in battle against the world and sin, it is because He is strong in His obedience and that He remains in the love of the Father. The grace of loving and desiring with all our strength what Christ loved and embraced is communion with the love and obedience of Jesus.

This demand prepares us to understand the precise call of Christ to every Christian, particularized here in view of an engagement to the religious life. Ignatius sets the requests out in detail. The sentence

*Spiritual Exercises of St. Ignatius, Westminster: Newman Press, 1951.

develops slowly and, little by little, causes us to enter into the mystery of the Son obeying Him Who has delivered Him over to death for us. An ample parellelism is going to oppose, point by point, the demands of the world and those of Jesus. The candidate, after having meditated, will better understand in what resemblance to Jesus consists.

"For as men of the world who follow the world love and earnestly seek honors, distinctions, and the reputation of a great name among men, as the world teaches them."

In writing these lines, Ignatius undoubtedly recalled the feelings of his youth. Youngest son of a noble family, he had grounds and right to make much of his quarterings. This "hidalgo" was without fortune, but he could not suffer the slightest besmirching of his honor. A courageous soldier, he resisted to the end at the citadel of Pamplona. Man of action and firm believer, he was a mediocre Christian. During the night of March 24–25, 1522 he made his nobleman's last watch of arms, in truth, his first watch of arms as a soldier of Jesus Christ. In the morning, he went off, "not by the direct road to Barcelona, where he ran the risk of meeting people who would recognize him, but by a detour to a place called Manresa."[5] On the evening of the twenty-fourth, as secretly as possible, he divested himself of his fine clothes to put on the sack which brought upon him the mockery of children. In truth, he had then put aside "honors, distinctions and the reputation of a great name."

The influence of Ignatius' experience is probable here, but the inspiration of this text is to be sought, especially in the lights he acquired at Manresa on the false attractions which the demon employs to keep back those whom God is calling to His service. In the triple colloquy of the first week, St. Ignatius has us implore the grace to "feel the disorder of our actions and to hold it in horror ... for a knowledge of the world, so that having it in horror we may remove from us all that is worldly and vain." [63] In the meditation of the Two Standards he gives the meaning of true values and the degrees by which we renounce the world—poverty and humiliation—to attain to humility; for, he says, "insult and contempt are opposed to worldly honor, and

humility to pride." [146] The candidate to whom St. Ignatius is talking has already resolved on poverty. But has he also understood that
he ought to renounce honors and the reputation which his situation in
the world promises him? Hence the insistence on effective attitudes,
on the renouncing of this worldly honor, from which grace releases,
not without a wrench of pain, the heart of the young hidalgo from
Loyola.

Ignatius knew that this temptation to seek the esteem of men remained possible to apostolic religious in the world. According to the
Constitutions, was not knowing how to deal with men one of the
natural qualities which should be found in the Jesuit? This, he notes,
is one of the possible obstacles to the union of religious among themselves and with their superiors; for, "for the most part, they are men
of broad culture, and will be able to obtain a great deal of influence
with princes, with the great and with people at large."[6] Perfect
obedience, which requires the abnegation of one's own will and judgment, should remedy this drawback. But in order to bear these fruits
and to be possible should not the Jesuit be a man determined to refuse
"all that the world loves and embraces?" Not only in fact, but in intention. For since obedience is, in the will and the understanding,
the undertaking of faith, and since an ardent love of God's will is
needed to execute that which is commanded, so also to guard against
the many occasions of coming to terms with the world in which the
Jesuit must labor, he will need a love of Christ crucified, which will
make him abhor, by a sort of instinct, the preferences and tastes of
those who are, according to the word of St. Paul, "enemies of the cross
of Christ."

Opposite Babylon, Jerusalem; opposite the "evil chieftain," the Lord,
meek and humble. Their ways are opposed, their preferences contrary.
"So, those who are making progress in the spiritual life and are seriously following Christ our Lord love, intensely desire the very
opposite."

The adverbs give this sentence all its relief. It is not a question of
following Christ in any way whatsoever, but of truly following Him
or, as the Latin has translated it (and so many generations of Jesuits
have meditated this modifier), "seriously." One does not mock God,
and He Who has not "loved us for nothing" would not be satisfied

with a negligent service. Indeed, St. Ignatius asks an *intense* desire. It is the attitude of those in the Kingdom "who wish to give proof of greater love and to signalize themselves in every service of their King ... by engaging in the struggle against that which attaches them to the flesh and the world." [97]

If for a moment he came upon the foolish dreams of worldly honor previous to his conversion, in speaking of the teaching which the world lavishes on its clients, he now sees again in an act of thanksgiving the hour of the calls which marked his way: those of Manresa and of La Storta. This Jesus, Whom His Father asks to take Ignatius as servant, is the Master Who makes His way to Golgotha carrying His cross, poor humiliated, flouted, and bleeding. Would it be possible to follow Him cheerfully without sharing His shame? "To be clothed in the same garments and wear the same attire as their Lord, out of love and reverence for Him." What the Master chose should not the servant choose as well? "The disciples is not above the Master." These are demands of a love infinitely respectful.

"I desire and choose poverty with Christ poor, rather than riches, in order to imitate and be in reality more like Christ our Lord; I choose insults with Christ loaded with them, rather than honors; I desire to be accounted as worthless and a fool for Christ, rather than to be esteemed as wise and prudent in this world." [167] This is the third degree of humility which St. Ignatius proposes to a candidate for admission to the Society. He ought to be ready for corrections and penances, for poverty and for want, for persecution under every form, and perhaps for martyrdom, if he really wishes to become the companion of the Son of God, Who received no other treatment from men.

"And this to such an extent, that if it could be done without offence to His Divine Majesty, or sin on the part of their neighbor, they should wish to suffer abuse, injustice, false accusations, and to be considered and treated as fools, without, however, giving occasion for such treatment."

From Manresa Ignatius experienced the most painful poverty. On his return from Palestine, he lived more strictly the mystery of the humility of Christ. Every period of his studies was under the sign of the opprobrium of Jesus. From the first hour, one scene depicts it clearly. Without listening to human prudence, Ignatius took the great highway occupied by the armies at war. Arrested, stripped of his miserable clothing, taken for a fool, he is dragged along "through three main streets." He then had "the representation of Christ led along." It is He Whom he must follow, sharing in the ignominies of Good Friday.[7] It is Christ outraged, judged on false witness, insulted by the Jews, dragged through the streets, turned to derision, scoffed at, and outraged, going to His death by way of the most shameful humiliations; it is He Whom he contemplates and Whose image he here evokes. For it is He Whom he must follow to be treated like Him.

Folly of the cross which is the highest wisdom! In evoking it in all its realism, Ignatius does not forget his habitual prudence, and he does not take leave of his discretion. Without diminishing the demands of love, he recalls that obedience to God's will remains. To follow Jesus should thus not be rashness or imprudence. The humiliation we desire out of respect for God supposes that there is neither "offense to the Divine Majesty, nor fault on the part of their neighbor." And if one wishes to be taken for a fool because Christ was so treated, it is always on the condition that one gives no occasion for it. Ignatius is not unwilling that his sons be taken for "imposters," provided they be "truthful"; for, called to be "God's ministers," they should not give anyone the "slightest reason for scandal, for fear of discrediting their ministry." (2 Cor. 6:3)

" . . . their whole desire being to resemble and in some way imitate our Creator and Lord Jesus Christ, by being clothed in His garments and raiment, since He first so clothed Himself for our spiritual benefit, and gave us an example to lead us to seek, as far as possible with God's grace, to imitate and follow Him."

"Christ suffered for us, leaving you an example that you should follow in His steps." (1 Pet. 2:21) Jesus has given us the example, and He asks those who wish to follow Him to resemble Him and imitate Him. It is in prayer, enlightened by the Holy Spirit, that we discover the secret of this imitation, that we fathom the lesson of the third degree of humility. The candidate's religious life will not be too long for him to comprehend what the imitation of Christ asks of him. But his feet are already set on the royal road of the cross.

For, from the first contact, St. Ignatius teaches him that he is part of a body entirely pledged to the work of redemption, pledged to apostolic labor, pledged to the imitation of the suffering and despised Christ. The two are mutually involved, and only he who bears in his heart and in his flesh the marks of Christ can be called His apostle. Nadal, in one of his Pauline formulas, plainly says so: "We follow Jesus still bearing His Cross in the mystical body which is the Church. That is why we must fill up what is lacking to the sufferings of Christ. ... When I am crucified with Jesus Christ, I live and I do not live. I am alive by the exercise of my faculties. But this life is the life of grace. It is not human, but divine. It is not according to the flesh and the world, but from on high and according to the spirit. It is not trite, but fresh. It is the life of Christ, which by grace, by the virtues, by the gifts of the Holy Spirit has become mine, just as Christ has become wisdom, justice, sanctification, redemption for us. Rightly then do I no longer speak of my life, but of the life of Christ."[8]

The imitation of Christ poor and humbled opens to us all the dimensions of the apostolate since it causes us to enter into the mystery of redemption. Sharers in the death of Christ, we share in His resurrection. And we shall announce the Resurrection more by our life than by our words only if our life is crucified in Christ. "Our cross is sweet," Nadal says again, "because it already has the splendor and the glory of the victory of Jesus over death, of His resurrection and His ascension." The fervor which ought to animate the Jesuit in renouncing himself and in imitating Christ is like a need, a constant demand of his apostolic vocation. "Let us, therefore, brethren, imitate Christ as closely as we can with His grace, so that we shall wish nothing in this mortal life that He has not wished. It is ours to be pure, chaste, obedient, humble. It is for us to suffer insults, wrongs, outrages in His name."[9]

Thus detached from ourselves and from the world, we become capable of an unwearied charity, capable "of loving God in all creatures and all creatures in Him." "We should be especially watchful," says Nadal, "to find God in all things, according to the admonition of Father Ignatius, and we shall find in that much repose and consolation. We ought to seek to attain this end by means of the third degree of humility."[10]

Seeing He Is the True Way Which Leads Men to Life

Divine Life has appeared to men in the Crucified. To receive this Life we must go to Calvary. To have access to it, we must pass through the way which Christ has followed. He is the path, He is Himself the way. We must go along this path, and identify ourselves with the Son of God if we wish to receive the life and give it to others. We follow Him by entering on His road, through heaviness, obscurity, destitution, the abandonment of the cross and death, but to go on to life, to live always more of His own life. It is the law of "our greater spiritual progress," of religious and apostles. Sacerdotal spirituality and religious spirituality are wonderfully wedded in the ideal which St. Ignatius presents to the candidate who asks to be instructed in the spirit of his Society. Those priests and religious who, by God's mercy, are called to work in the Church in apostolic labors, can know only one thing: Jesus Christ, and Jesus Christ crucified. "It is good for us," writes Nadal again, "to train ourselves to experience with an interior relish that Jesus Christ is in us the way, by our participation in His sufferings and by our imitation; that for us He is the truth, in the true contemplation of simple, clear and unalloyed truths; that He is the life, in the union of charity which overflows upon the neighbor."[11]

The Desire of Following Christ Crucified

Honestly and candidly, St. Ignatius thus places the candidate in the presence of Christ. He has heard the call of the Gospel: "Follow Me." What shall be his reaction to the clear exposition of all the demands contained in this call?

"The candidate will then be asked whether he feels such salutary and fruitful desires for the perfection of his soul." It is possible that the candidate will answer with an unhesitating and all-embracing "yes." Such an answer ought to be weighed and examined. It might be illusion or boyish presumption. Must we not conclude that the candidate has not understood what has just been told him, that he has given only a superficial attention, that in his prayer he has not faced up to our Lord's demands? In that case a deeper meditation is imperative, which will inform the Master of Novices, through the experiment of the discernment of spirits, about the real fitness of the candidate. He will know only at the end of this repetition whether he ought to dismiss the candidate, give him to understand that he has not, at least at the moment, "enough spiritual resources to raise the building and bear the weight of his vocation,"[12] or whether the first impulse, generous but thoughtless, can be deepened by prayer.

But it is equally possible that the candidate who gave a frank answer was moved to it in a decisive fashion by the Spirit of God and that we are here in the presence of the first time of election. This may be a justified impression which the conduct of the young man in the trials and "experiments" of the novitiate will serve to prove.

A number, at any rate, will simply admit that they are not aware of feeling these desires. They undoubtedly understand the high spiritual quality of the ideal proposed to them. They would like to agree to it with all their soul. But before God, they must admit that these desires are not in their heart.

Far from drawing a pessimistic conclusion, St. Ignatius would rather rejoice at this. Such an admission reveals the quality of a soul which will not yield to illusion and knows that a hasty and not fully sincere answer should not be given to our Lord.

"Should he, because of the weakness of human misery, not feel these enflamed desires in our Lord, he should be asked whether he has some desire to experience them."

One might smile at the thought of desiring to desire and think this an ingenious solution or too clever. Is it not putting pressure on the candidate, and bringing him by a subtle detour to will what he does not will, to wish what he is opposed to? Is it not to lead him to be mistaken with regard to his own dispositions, to accept an illusion which will soon fade, or to surrender to an insistence which is unwilling to respect his liberty? Victim of suggestion or defenseless, will the young man, already upset by this inquisition, not abandon all resistance and perhaps sincerely believe what the Master of Novices wishes him to believe? But what will he think of this spiritual blackmail in a month?

Thus to interpret the formula of St. Ignatius is to misunderstand it in two ways. First of all, it is to forget that St. Ignatius relies essentially on grace and that he exacts of the director, "already invited to leave the creature with his Creator," an unconditional respect for the plans of God. It would also be to see only a feeling in the affective order, where there is an attitude of total generosity in the presence of God.

The generous soul wishes to follow Christ, not in the way it might wish it to be, but such as He in fact wishes it to be: poor, humbled, scoffed at, condemned, and put to death. This profound disposition cannot suppress the stirring of our sensitive nature or the repugnances felt in our emotions which the cross shocks and nettles. But the generous heart consents. It cannot yet say that it desires. If the higher powers of the soul acquiesce, the sensitive parts cannot follow them. Such a program is surely beautiful and true; he cannot yet, however, awaken a real desire, not even if he wishes to experience it. At most, he would like to experience the desire, without being able to recognize that the true desire is there.

Such a disposition was enough for St. Ignatius, for he recognized in it an effect of faith. It is not deceptive because it has not yet been experienced. It affirms in fact the action of a grace which, although it has not yet entirely appeased the emotional powers, is strongly at work in the intelligence and will. It is sufficient for the candidate sincerely to wish to tend to the perfection of those who follow our Lord, even if he experiences very lively repugnances. For such a will is not in the power of man; only the gift of the Father can awaken it when it is received in a heart generous enough to welcome it.

Indeed, there is no question here, in this important moment, of delaying over fruitless analyses of feeling. A program must be accepted and submission made in advance to the concrete demands of a strong and exacting love.

"And if he answers that he does have such holy desires, he should be asked for the better realization of this desire, whether he is determined and ready to suffer patiently, with God's grace, all the insults, scoffs and derision which this raiment of Christ our Lord supposes, or other treatment of the kind, whether it be on the part of anyone in the house, or in the Society (in which he wishes to obey, to be humbled and to gain eternal life), or on the part of anyone from without, not returning evil for evil, but good for evil."

Practically, will the candidate honestly accept the life of the Society and begin its apprenticeship?

What he will find will be the daily exercise of the imitation of Christ: an effective poverty, not only in the sacrifice of comfort and of dependence, but in humiliation (so painful to proud characters), in begging from door to door; obedience at every moment; reprimands and penances, "even for a fault that is not blameworthy." His faults, however slight, will be manifested to the superior, and he should keep nothing hidden from him, "not even his own conscience." St. Ignatius hides nothing from the candidate of what awaits him on the morrow if he consents to be inscribed among the novices of his Order. What he wishes on entering is "to obey and humble himself" for life eternal.

Outside, persecutions await him, the persecutions which the holy Founder asked for his sons and which have never been denied them. The candidate, clearly warned, will not be taken by surprise; henceforth they will form part of his life. And he will accept them gladly, "not returning evil for evil, but good for evil." This is a program that is truly Pauline: "For I think that God hath set forth us apostles, the last, as it were, men appointed to death. . . . We are reviled and we bless. We are persecuted, and we suffer it . We are blasphemed and we entreat. We are made the refuse of this world, the offscouring of all, even until now." (1 Cor. 4:9–13)

It is this prospect which ought to be presented to the candidate as calmly as possible, so as not to excite him. Is he disposed, with God's grace, to accept it? Will he really consent to this imitation of the persecuted Christ? In one sense, his feelings and repugnances make little difference. There is question of an attitude of will open to the influence of grace. Has he enough confidence, does he bear in his heart a strong enough hope to offer himself for this "raiment" of the Lord? If he answers yes, even though he bears in his heart that disgust, without which Blessed Claude de la Colombière did not think a vocation inspired confidence, St. Ignatius is set: This young man is called by God, and Christ has bestowed upon him His infallible regard.

Abnegation and Continual Mortification

The preceding characteristics sketch clearly the ideal of the life to which the candidate offers himself with all the lucidity of his faith. St. Ignatius does not seek to add anything, but, always the realist, he wishes to specify still more how one disposes oneself daily and concretely for the cross of Christ.

"The better to reach so precious a degree of perfection in the spiritual life, each one should make it his first and foremost endeavor to seek in our Lord his greater abnegation and continual mortification in all things possible."

Three aspects are here considered. Abnegation, the first, is realized by continual mortification, in the "discretion" of the Spirit.

Abnegation

If St. Ignatius speaks rarely of abnegation, it is because he is more inclined to describe its demands than to define the word itself.[13] It is the fruit of grace and, inseparably, the bringing into exercise of our natural forces. It reaches to the sensual and selfish love in us which dreams of being self-sufficient and of becoming the center of the universe. It implies, therefore, an ever greater renunciation, as radical a rejection as possible of all the passions. But it is also directed to the knowledge and love of God. It is not of itself the source of light, but it opens us, by freeing us, to the light and to love.

Abnegation appears from then on as the living attitude of the man who at God's call offers himself and hands himself over to serve. Attentive to the will of his Father, the man wishes thereby, generously and without reserve, to be aware of the grace of the moment, docile to the appeals of the Spirit. Thereby he orders himself more and more on God's plan, triumphing over the disorders of his soul and the solicitations of his flesh. Our will, thus "converted," turned toward Jesus, keeps us in Him. It is the way we must run to go through Him to the Father. In this work Christ is present, not only as a model to be imitated, but as He Who conforms us to His image.

Abnegation is placed by St. Ignatius in close relation with humility and obedience. What we have just said shows to what extent abnegation always places us more in the hands of the Creator. It makes of us those faithful and earnest servants who want to submit their will to God. It thus joins the obedience of Jesus to His Father and, through grace, allows us to participate in the mystery of this obedience.

St. Ignatius could not fail to insist on the relation between abnegation and obedience. It is by bringing all our attention to bear on this point that he wishes us to grasp the scope of application and the depth of obedience. It is in connection with religious obedience that he speaks of it expressly, but it is clear that what a perfect obedience to the superior, Christ's minister, imposes upon man is the duty of wishing fully to accept and perform God's will, the will of Christ, and of the Church. Abnegation makes a man free and therefore capable of obeying, for it has a tendency to reduce in man his love of self, and the thought of his own excellence.

Obedience, even in the measure in which it tends to externalize itself, cannot be satisfied with the simple execution. The perfectly obedient man knows, in the light of his faith and under the pressure of love, that he "should also make every effort to have an inward resignation and a true denial of his own will and judgment. He will, moreover, conform that will and judgment to the will and judgment of the superior in all things that are free from sin, and will then look upon the will and judgment of the superior as a norm for his own will and judgment, his purpose being a more perfect conformity with the first and highest norm for every good will and judgment, that is, the Eternal Goodness and Wisdom."[14]

By delivering us from the power of sin and the world, abnegation thereby opens us to God. By making us truly humble, it makes us completely obedient to God's will as made known by His Word or by His Spirit. It leads us to the cross. Then death is no longer only the fatal consequence of sin. It becomes in and through the obedience of faith, as in and through obedience of the will and judgment, a way of

salvation in Christ. Struggle and suffering remain our lot, for we have
to share in the death of Christ, but only that His life triumph in us,
to the glory of His Father.

Continual Mortification

This movement of self-dispossession, which is realized in time all our
lives through, involves us ever more deeply in the death and resurrection of our Lord. Abnegation finds its food in "continual mortification."

"Know you not that we who are baptized in Christ Jesus are
baptized in His death? . . . So do you reckon that you are dead to
sin, but alive unto God in Christ Jesus our Lord. Let not sin, therefore,
reign in your mortal body, so as to obey the lusts thereof. Neither yield
ye your members as instruments of iniquity unto sin; but present yourselves to God as those that are alive from the dead, and your members as instruments of justice unto God." (Rom. 6:3, 11–13)

Participation in the sacraments, notably the Sacrifice of the Lord,
causes us to enter efficaciously into this death and this life. But the
reception of grace supposes our human collaboration, and mortification should realize continually in our deeds the interior attitude of
abnegation so that we know "how to yield our members to serve
justice unto sanctification" (Rom. 6:19) and so that the old man "will
be renewed to knowledge, according to the image of Him that created
him." (Col. 3:10)

Mortification will therefore be continual. It will cause us to bear
our sinner's cross in the footsteps of Christ bearing His cross in the
Church. It will last as long as our sin and our redemption.

In patience and fidelity, the soul thus gains in pliancy and liberty.
A certain state of renouncement is built into a man who is truly mortified. He will never be able, moreover, to take leave of an active at-
tentiveness and vigilance, for in this domain everything acquired is
only relative. But we must recognize that self-abnegation, death to
the world and to oneself, is continual mortification, combined in a
single indistinguishable reality. The mortified man becomes in reality

"the grain of wheat which falls into the earth" to die and bear much fruit. He loses his life, he hates it in this world, but he keeps it for life everlasting. (John 12:24–25)

Discretion of Spirit

Rooted in the mystery of the death of Christ, which it brings to reality every hour in our flesh and our spirit, inseparable companion of our sin, but instrument as well of our redemption, "continual mortification" is first of all a work of grace in us. It is Christ Who, to introduce us to the love of the Father, frees us from our selfishness and unifies our divided will. No human effort could have done that. That is why our "mortification," in the measure in which it wishes to be continual, that is to say, in which it is identified with the radical abnegation of the sinful and corruptible being in us, demands our generous collaboration, but in submission to a work which surpasses our generosity. It ought to be "sought in the Lord," as St. Ignatius says, not by the tension of the will, but in the humility of the creature who expects his salvation. For we know that only the power of grace can cause us to take the last step, which will make of the mortified man in the succession of his actions a man of radical abnegation in the likeness of Christ.

That is why the *intransigence* of St. Ignatius is always accompanied by wisdom and prudence. To remain "spiritual," mortification will have to be discreet in order, be ruled by the hierarchy of values which control the apostolic life. On June 1, 1551, Polanco wrote to Father Urban Fernandez: "On the subject of mortification, our Father thinks more of those which touch honor and self-esteem, than those which make the flesh suffer, such as fasts, disciplines and hair-shirts."[15] Without denying anything of the value of corporal austerities, for they are "useful to overcome oneself and to obtain more graces from God," St. Ignatius, in his purpose of forming a man wholly pledged to apostolic activity, placed mortifications essentially in the abnegation of the will and judgement. He wanted his sons to reach a liberty of spirit and of heart both by having a humble opinion of themselves and by their contempt and refusal of all personal renown. "It is more difficult," he thought, "to subdue one's own spirit than to make the flesh suffer, unless it is necessary to afflict the rebellious flesh in order to subdue the spirit."[16]

He advises, then, that we keep such a measure in corporal mortifications as will not interfere with the strength of the apostle. It is for each one to use this discretion, which is a gift of the Spirit, to judge for himself what he is able to do, according to his character, his task, and his grace. "When one loses this moderation, good changes into evil, virtue into vice. By indiscreetly crucifying the old man, one crucifies the new, for weakness makes the practice of the virtues difficult." "With a healthy body you will be able to do much; I do not know what you will be able to do with one that is ill." By every abuse of penances or austerities, St. Ignatius felt "how much one was exposed to the peril of pride and of vainglory, even if it were only in preferring his judgment to that of others. . . . Discretion is necessary in the exercise of virtue, so that we may keep a middle course between tepidity and indiscreet fervor. Speak to our Lord, and take your stand on the side of obedience. You have great desires of mortification, try to break your own will, subject your judgment to the yoke of obedience rather than impair your strength by unjustified excesses."[17]

Discretion is wisdom of the Spirit. The last words of the formula of St. Ignatius—"as far as possible"—well show that if the principle of mortification is not in us, but in the life-giving power of the passion of Christ, its measure and its object are no longer to be judged according to human norms, however generous. Only the Spirit of Christ is capable of guiding our continual mortification in such wise that the apostle is constantly purified without being broken, docile to "Him Who knows our nature infinitely better than we do," and Who in a most perfect pedagogy knows how to arrange the stages towards total immolation of heart. There is no other way for "greater abnegation" than this mortification which, little by little, becomes, in the soul that is mistress of its passions, a continuous passivity under the activity of God.

We thus reach the summit of the spiritual life, which is the expansion of life through death. We know from experience that the cross is often heavy to bear, that its mystery wraps us in obscurity. But we also know from experience that the fruit of abnegation is "inner liberty," the gift of the Spirit which the immolated Heart of Christ Himself will bestow. Father Nadal sings its praises as the supreme victory of mortification.

"If one mortifies himself in everything by a well regulated exercise, and if one regulates one's love for all creatures by the love one owes our Lord, loving none of them but for His will, one succeeds in acquiring liberty of spirit, which is nothing else than a facility in all things, by the use of one means or another, whether it be prayer or anything else in keeping with circumstances. It is thus that we shall become prompt to choose what is more useful and conformed to the service of our Lord, and reject all that is opposed to it. And all this with great sweetness, without regret, or disgust, or anxiety, whether our work be with kings, princes, or other lords, or with more ordinary people; now in spiritual matters, or in others that require human prudence and which could involve the sensual nature or the will in imperfection or wrong. Through the superiority which liberty of spirit gives, there will be nothing which is not done well, by making use of the means which will more serve and glorify our Lord, and by rejecting everything that does not tend to this end, with an intelligence that is enlightened and clarified and thus made able to discern among them."[18]

It will be, then, in fact, that the apostle is finally pledged to the sole service of the Kingdom of God, because his abnegation makes of him a free intrument, one that is intelligent and passionately in love with the redeeming cross of Jesus.

Christus, No. 9, January 1956

Abnegation and Joy

PAUL AGAESSE, S.J.

Seen from without, renunciation appears to be a negative attitude. Imposed on us by the opposition of men and events, by the insistence of morality or religion, or, finally, by the limitations which each one meets with in himself, it sometimes appears to be a fear of hazard, a depreciation of values which are beyond one's reach, a servile obedience to an arbitrary command; in a word, a refusal towards life which bears in itself its own sadness and sterility. If such interpretations proclaim the possibility of ambiguity in the attitude on this point of some men, even some Christians, they do not touch the essence of evangelical renunciation because they misconstrue the mystery of God and have not been able to lay bare in man himself a positive need of renunciation.

There is, however, a privileged instance where renunciation is not a denial, a fear, or a resignation, but the result of a spontaneous impulse which leads to joy, and that is when it is born of an interior demand of love. All joy supposes love, and the the quality of joy depends on love, which is its principle. But there is no true love without forgetfulness of self, and it must pass through sacrifice to reach the depth and the stability to which it aspires. We must make this our outlook if we are to understand Christian renunciation. But there is no question here of a love limited in its source or its extension. There is question of a love which ought to invade the whole man because it is the perfection of his being and coincides with his end. Definitively, this love, because it is a participation in the divine life, overflows, in its fullness and its intensity, all description and all experience. "God is charity," writes St. Bernard, "and there is nothing which can fill the creature made in God's image, except the God Charity, Who alone is greater than it." The Gospel is, therefore, a schooling in joy because it teaches us to love. And if it demands a total renunciation, it is because this love ought to be perfect.

This necessity of renunciation, if we are to have an approach to joy, is suggested by the very fact that we are commanded to love. We can conceive of being commanded not to kill, or not to lie, but how can we be commanded to love? Love by compulsion is not love. To make it the object of a precept would be to destroy it, to misconstrue the gratuity that is essential to it, to deny the character of freedom and spontaneity that makes it precious. This apparent contradiction is disturbing, but it enlightens us at the same time that it baffles us. It is indeed true that it is essential that love be gratuitous and that it flow from the depths of the will. But if we are to pass by this stage of the law, if we are to accept this system of commandments which set forth in detail the demands of charity, it is because we do not know how to love, or at least because our love is enveloped in the matrix of a selfishness which impairs its purity. The commandment which seems to bind liberty frees it; the spontaneity of sinful nature, which seems to expand it, enslaves it. This paradox is of the very fabric of the Gospel. We must die to live. The spiritual life is not an expansion but a rebirth. It is not a growth but a resurrection. Progress is assured only by a perpetual conversion. That is why joy is inseparable from sacrifice, which reveals it in causing it to be born. To persist in the wish to find this joy apart from detachment is to confuse love with self-interest and to hope to reconcile that which is irreconcilable.

This confusion is only too easy. It is almost imposed upon us by language, for an ambiguous experience, in which the fundamental yearning of man is burdened by the the servitudes of sin underlies the words love and joy. In fact, to love, he must get out of himself, place his reason for living in another, know himself only by this aspiration, be himself only by this gift. Such was man's vocation before the Fall. Keeping nothing of his own, he was rich only in his dependence, he lived only by this adherence to God in a freedom proportioned to his worship, given to himself only by this love which caused him to live out of himself. But pride broke this aspiration because in every sin there re-echoes the *eritis sicut dii* of the first temptation. It was a movement of competition, of rivalry, of jealousy which shut man in upon himself and by that very fact made him the exile from love. His will became fixed in self; then it centered in self the aspiration which bore him to God. It retained, however, the illusion of loving. Too poor to be self-sufficing, it sought about itself that increase of being which it no longer found in itself. It is this lust which is called love because it mimics the leaving of self, which is the soul of charity. But this love is not charity, for it tends to another only to fill a void that is ceaselessly renewed, and it is this selfish self which man seeks through these raptures of desire.

It is divine pedagogy to restore man to joy by teaching him how to love again. But this step towards life supposes that one passes through death; for the will, having identified itself with egoism, cannot separate from it except by renouncing its own will. Father de Montcheuil has well developed this paradoxical aspect of sacrifice in which man finds himself by losing himself: "The peculiar nature of man in whom concupiscence reigns—and every man begins with that—is to place his end, his good, outside of God. In order to give himself to God, he must renounce what for him constitutes the prize and the value of life. He must engage himself in a life where he finds nothing of that in which he had placed his reason for living. Thanks, doubtless, to the sacrifice, that from which he withdraws is illusory and negative. But it is just the peculiar nature of his first state for the negative to appear to him as the positive, the only positive, while the true Good seems to him the total absence of good. We cannot, therefore, ignore the aspect of death which every sacrifice presents, and it is this aspect which shows itself first. The other is only felt in the sacrifice itself." It is this progressive experience of a joy discovered in sacrifice and through sacrifice whose stages we should like to point out.

The first stage of this purification is that of the Law. It was given to the Jews, but the Gospel, far from suppressing it, made it more interior and more exacting. The "And I, I tell you ..." of the Sermon on the Mount goes further than the Mosaic commandment, denounces the hypocrisy of an observance, correct perhaps in appearance, suppresses the toleration which the weakness of a people still in its childhood justified. The "do not" became "desire not," and God's demands are expressed in negative formulas which seem to be opposed to the inclinations of man. Under the diversity of precepts, there is this negation, this denial of what man seeks spontaneously. And yet at the heart of this negation there lives an essential affirmation, lacking which all the precepts would be without meaning. It is that God loves man and that His demands are not the bullying of a master who likes to rule his slaves but the demands of a Father Who wishes to bring his children to a higher life, a more delightful life, a more beatifying life. In a word, even under its primitive form, the attitude which the Decalogue supposes is truly religious only because it affirms a positive value and is supported by a confidence which is the source of joy. Obedience is not the servility of the weak, who bend under the yoke of the strong, but the recognizing of the holiness, the goodness, the justice of God. It is thus that we must understand the fear of God of which the Scripture speaks. Man awakens to the love of God by recognizing that God loves him. Avoiding idolatry is not merely refusing to prostrate before the golden calf or uplifted stones. It is treating God as God, perceiving His sanctity and His justice even in His threats and punishments.

There is, then, from this moment, a relation between abnegation and joy. It is a relation as yet ill perceived because it is not grasped by direct experience, but a relation, nevertheless, of which we have a confused presentiment through the mediation of God's will. Man implicitly recognizes that he does not know where his true happiness lies and that it is hidden from him, but God knows for him. He perceives it through the signs which reveal it to him: the escape from Egypt, the land of slavery, the crossing of the desert under God's guidance, the hope which dwelt in the heart of the wandering host making its way to the Promised Land. The desert is the apprenticeship of an austere joy which is like a dawn on the horizon of conscience.

It would be wrong to see in this hope only a selfishness which postpones its fulfillment and which, for being more subtle, is only more dangerous. It is possible that love is not perfectly pure. But is it not essential that man rediscover the meaning of the divine will and recognize its holiness? We have here, obviously, a transfer which is a first renunciation of self and the foreseeing of an unknown joy. Israel's hope was concerned, undoubtedly, with the earthly goods promised to its fidelity. Nevertheless, it submitted to God and awaited from Him the time and manner of its realization; it followed the line of march drawn up for it; in surrendering to the mystery, it submitted to being balked. It is not a bargain, but a respect for an Alliance, the initiative of which belongs to God. Is it not a characteristic quality of prayer, such as we know prayer in the Psalms, which the Church places upon our lips, to be, at the beginning at least, a request for material goods, an effort to turn the divine will? It is enough that the prayer perseveres for the initial attitude to be reversed and for the suppliant to enter into the will of God, Who hears him, by postponing, or even by refusing the good sought.

But there is another benefit to the Law to which St. Paul has called our attention. It awakens love by the knowledge which it gives of sin. It is characteristic of sin to make what it touches obscure and to hide in its own darkness. It presents its requests as though they were the demands of nature; it disguises lust as love and selfishness as the lawful seeking of honor. It is then inevitable that the Law appear first as an intolerable yoke. Nevertheless, because it is the projection of the divine holiness on a world of sin, it is a light which cures the sight. Its absolute character, which is at first perceived only through the threat of punishment, becomes an appeal to inner sincerity. Man understands that that which he used to call health and balance is, in fact, corruption; that it is not the commandment that is arbitrary, but his will that is diseased. This will ceaselessly undergoes the attraction of lust, but it already judges it to be an enslavement. A conflict which divides the will within itself, a call to a liberation which one desires and fears at the same time, such is the experience which St. Paul describes in his letter to the Romans: "For I am delighted with the law of God according to the inner man, but I see another law in my members warring against the law of my mind and making me prisoner to the law of sin that is in my members." (Rom. 7:22–23) The hesitation of Augustine on the brink of his conversion betrays the same inner division. He wishes and he does not wish. He tears himself painfully from the domination of his vanities, his friends of old, which gently hold him back by his vesture of flesh. He does not venture "to die to death and to live to life." There is a long and painful debate, the end of which is the "contrite and humbled heart," a true sacrifice, where the joy of love regained comes from the disavowal of sin still desired. Sin is sad because it is a sufficiency, a shutting up of self. Contrition is joyous because it opens the soul to God. It is not a barren regret or a depressing confession. It is already the experience of the gratuity of love because in renouncing what it holds to be evident and in despising its lusts, the soul begins to know itself by going beyond itself. It goes through the experience of the goodness of God and holds itself as the term of the creative and sanctifying love of God. It is by this death to itself that it enters into joy.

But this life looks to developing itself further and can do so only by remaining faithful to the initial law of conversion, that is, by keeping sin in a state of death. Now selfishness is still too hardy for us not to have to fear its return offensives and its play of illusions. Its redoubtable magic is to bring us to desire even divine things carnally and to take complacency in our own will even when we think we are obeying God's will. Hence the need of a fresh renunciation and the beginning of a new stage of purification, the mainspring of which is faith.

The turning back of the soul which this purification supposes is described in Psalms 72 and 73, which present us with the confusion of a man who has been deprived of the signs through which he read God's benevolence. The Psalmist, troubled by the prosperity of the wicked and the distress of the just, is on the point of yielding. The temptation is violent—regret for having kept his heart pure, a feeling of having sacrificed the real for the illusory. But the feeling of his belonging to God is stronger. He enters into the sanctuary, into the great night of faith. All his errant desires are concentrated in one only, his Good, that is, God Himself, and joy comes of the gratuity of this love: "For what have I in heaven? And besides Thee what do I desire upon earth?" A decisive separation of love from lust. It is not the object of desire which changes, but the appetite for happiness which is transformed.

The Psalm sets before us the outline of a "conversion" which, in the Christian life, is the fruit of the long working of grace. For it concentrates on a single act, an experience which is spread over and divided into successive acts. It is this concentrated quality that makes it illuminating. It gives perceptibility to the two sides of sacrifice as they mutually penetrate each other: the recoil before an absolute renunciation which seems to be without counterpart and the liberty of a purified love which rises from the agony of the will itself. Faith and faith alone permits the transition. For sacrifice first presents itself under an aspect that is abrupt, the negation of that which seems to give delight and value to life. This purification undoubtedly leads to joy; this joy, since it is inseparable from the experience which brings it to birth, offers no footing to the imagination, or even to the intelligence, so that no base is given from which to seek this joy, none except faith, a fearless confidence in God's fidelity to His promises. Faith anticipates the joy which must be born of sacrifice. It survives the trial before which nature recoils. It makes a passageway of the obstacle and in the one prospect sees both the cross and the Resurrection.

The history of the Apostles, from the day on which they met our Lord until Pentecost, covers the same path, reveals the same transformation of the soul under the influence of grace. Whatever the break which the first engagement supposed, it was the beginning of successive renunciations which were not yet visible at the beginning. The Apostles thought that they had left all to follow the Master, but they imagined the Kingdom under colors which flattered their imaginations. As they advanced, these colors blurred, but the knowledge they had of the Master deepened. The hostility of the Pharisees, the desertion by the crowds, the scandal of the discourse on the Bread of Life, the prediction of the cross, the anguish of the last return to Jerusalem, the Passion, finally, marked the crumbling of their dreams and at the same time the rooting of their fidelity. If we wish to find the source of their joy, we must look for it in the purification of their love, in the growth of their faith, in their march forward, in the movement which carried them beyond their repugnances, in their insistence on following Christ wherever He went, even when He led them where they did not care to go.

Without doubt, the cures, the resurrections, the Transfiguration, and the triumphal entry into Jerusalem were occasions of genuine joy, born of the love they had for Christ. But they are signs which must be left behind; they are halting places at which we are not permitted to linger. True joy, that which remains because love also remains, does not depend upon either persons or events or changes of feeling. In its essence, this love is the spiritual act by which the soul allows itself to be seized by God and by which it submits to being transformed. That is why it sometimes, like joy which results from it, takes on the look of necessity. The compulsion of the event only signifies the brunt of an interior demand. We do not desert God, no matter what. We cannot fail to follow Christ, even when we are engaged in a kind of life that we would not have chosen. Joy dwells even in repugnances. It is the interior strength which permits us to surmount them. It is in this way that we must understand St. Ignatius' third degree of humility, St. Francis Asissi's perfect joy, and the thirst for poverty and abasement of Father de Foucauld. It is love which begets joy, but love is not the attraction of sentiment. It does not exclude, at least at certain periods of the spiritual life, the instinctive recoil before sacrifice, and it does not operate after the manner of a narcotic which lulls suffering to sleep. It is, as St. Ignatius said, *humility,* an enduring preference for the divine will, an acquiescence in God's plan, an unconditioned esteem for the way the Father has chosen for His well-beloved Son.

And thus it goes with the joys of the saints and through the stages of their purification. It is to be found, of course, in spiritual consolations. But we cannot shut it up in privileged moments, imprison it in disconnected instants, for this joy is something permanent. It springs from the continuity of sacrifice, from the interior transformation which it effects, from the approach of a purer love. It excludes neither dryness nor weariness (the *taedet vivere*) nor the feeling of emptiness and the absence of God. It is perceptible only in its movements, for it originates in the weight of love which draws the will, and if sometimes it looks like the negation of human joys, it is because it is incompatible with the forms of selfishness which worm their way into our idea of happiness. Attachment to self can be found even in the feeling of love we have for God; not that this feeling is bad, but it is good only if the soul finds in it a footing for going further, if it dreads to appropriate grace to itself or to close itself up with this gift. That is why St. John of the Cross was so mistrustful of mystical consolations. More than in visions or favors, it is in humble fidelity to the grace of the present moment that he finds the genuineness of a love which, through purifying suffering, frees itself of the selfishness in which it is steeped.

Thus we should not be surprised if the joy of the saints overflows the classifications within which we try to enclose it because it is the wake which the transforming action of God leaves in their life, the mystery of which is revealed to us only in the measure that we ourselves are transformed. It is reconcilable with an experience of suffering which apparently ought to exclude it. Our Lord, foreseeing the persecutions of which the Apostles would be the object, said, "No one will take your joy from you." It is understandable, however, if instead of judging the experience of the saints by our own, we place ourselves in the interior of their testimony, to judge according to them, the direction and the movement of the Christian life. It will then be impossible for us to dissociate joy from the renunciation which prepares the way for it, or suffering from the resurrection on which it opens. "The saints made the Gospel sing," said St. Francis de Sales. By their whole lives they comment on and make actual the dreadful "must" of our Lord on the road to Emmaus: "Must not Christ have suffered all these things and so enter into His glory?"

It is on this aspect of resurrection that we must now insist, for it is, as it were, the third stage and the consummation of this long purification. In truth, the joy of the Resurrection is already present in the most humble sacrifice, for it is one of its constituent elements. There is no death to sin which is not an approach to life, more intimate union with God. Nevertheless, as long as love remains mingled with selfishness, man comes up against the scandal of the cross, and life seems like an eternity of trial to be borne. A moment arrives, however, in which it is the life-force which causes one to yearn for death: "Live all of life, die all of death, love all of love," said St. Teresa. Joy coincides with liberty of soul, which is under complete dependence on the Holy Spirit. Not only is there no longer an external law dominating the will, but the submission of the human will to the divine Will has no longer the character of a tiresome effort. It is the stage defined by St. Augustine in his *ama et fac quod vis*. This liberty should not be understood as a return to the spontaneity of a selfish instinct, but as the movement of a will completely given over to the rule of charity.

Is this to say that there is no longer place for suffering or abnegation? Of course not, for in this life there will always remain some traces of selfishness to be purified. We cannot see God without dying. But this selfishness, instead of betraying itself by a repugnance in the present trial, serves as the fuel for charity, and joy is all the purer as the renunciation proceeds from a demand anterior to love. The great suffering, then, is not to love enough, not to be united to God closely enough. Love no longer seeks any other reward than its own transformation: "The soul seized by love," writes St. John of the Cross, "cannot fail to desire the recompense and the reward of its love. It is even for this recompense that it loves the well-Beloved. Otherwise, its love would not be true. This recompense and this reward are nothing else (and the soul cannot wish for anything else) than always more love, until it succeeds in establishing itself in the perfection of love. Love has only one recompense, itself." The effort of love, then, is not to enjoy itself, but to renounce itself in order to be purer and to love the better. It is in this effort that it discovers its true nature, the intimate law that constitutes it. It becomes itself only by leaving itself, it exists only by dispossessing itself, it perfects itself only by renouncing itself, it is free only when its initiative comes from a total dependence on God. An explanation is offered by saying that joy obeys the same law of ecstasy which constitutes love. "Perfect joy," writes Simone Weil, "excludes the feeling itself of joy." Not that joy sinks into the unconscious, but it no longer reflects on itself to enjoy itself. Consciousness no longer turns back upon itself. Joy is born of this transport of charity which fixes the soul in God and becomes inseparable from it. *In lumine tuo videbimus lumen.* The Blessed Virgin is incapable of knowing herself otherwise than in this act of love which surrenders her to God.

The life of the Christian is, therefore, very close to that of the Word Incarnate. It becomes by grace, and according to the measure of the gift which is given it, a created image of the life of Christ. In the Trinity, the Son receives continuously from the Father all that He is, and therefore Himself—His eternal generation. This dependence is

His very Person. By becoming incarnate, He only showed forth in His human nature this twofold movement of receiving and recognizing, which is His mode of existence in the Trintiy. Commenting on the word of Christ, "My teaching is not from Me," St. Augustine shows his surprise: "There is here apparently a contradiction. How is it My doctrine, how is it not from Me?" But the reading of the Prologue of St. John gives him the answer: "What then is the teaching of the Father, if not the Word of the Father? Christ is, therefore, the teaching of the Father, if He is the Word of the Father. But because the Word cannot be without being the Word of some one, He says that it is His teaching, that is, Himself, and that it is not His teaching, because He is the Word of the Father. What is there, in fact, more thine than thyself, and what is there less thine than thyself, if thou holdest from another that thou art what thou art?" When there is in him no longer any appropriation, man imitates the dependence of the Incarnate Word, and he finds the principle of his love and his joy. He is doubly dispossessed because he receives all and because he returns all. Love is the scene of this transmutation, for man receives from God this love itself and this liberty by which he gives it.

And yet this life, which is the life of heaven, we possess only by expectation and faith. It is only fully revealed to us by the Resurrection of Christ, which is the model of ours, and by the interior transformation, which is accomplished in us by the Holy Spirit to conform us to Christ. Under the appearances of a total death, this transformation brings us to joy. Of ourselves, because of our sin, we should not be able to wish it. But God wishes for us. He goes to seek in the depth of our soul—since He Himself has placed it there—this capacity for love and joy which man does not know.

NOTES

Notes

FINDING GOD IN ALL THINGS

1. *Const.* P. IV, c. 4, n. 2.
2. *Fontes Narrativi*, I, 167–70.
3. *Ibid.*, II, 76.
4. *Ibid.*, II, 309. The first biographers of St. Ignatius have all insisted on this point. Cf. Laynez: "He felt much repugnance to study . . . because they were human and stale in comparison with heavenly things." (*Ibid.*, I, 90–92) Nadal: "From the days of his novitiate, the student had kept so great a habit of prayer that he was bound to have difficulty in applying himself to study, and for that reason had to do violence to himself; I think that he took a vow to overcome himself in that matter." (Quoted in Calveras, *Los tres modos de orar*, 274, and in J. Nicolau, *J. Nadal*, 235)
5. *St. Ignatius' Own Story* (English translation, Henry Regnery Company, 1956), n. 95.
6. *Ibid.*, n. 99.
7. *Fontes Narrativi*, I ,140.
8. Cf. *ibid.*, I, 635; *ibid.*, II, 123, 158; *Scripta*, I, 523. See also Nicolau, *Pláticas del P. Nadal en Coimbra*, 66, 71, 195–96.
9. *Epist. Ignat.*, III, 502.
10. *Ibid.*, III, 510.
11. *Ibid.*, VII, 270.
12. *Ibid.*, IV, 127.
13 *Ibid.*, IX, 125.
14. MHSI, *Const.*, II, 178, 408.
15. *Epist. Ignat.*, VI, 91.
16. *Fontes Narrativi*, II, 419.
17. MHSI, *Nadal*, IV, 691. In his journal, Nadal frequently expresses himself in the impersonal form of the word "someone."
18. *Fontes Narrativi*, II, 315–16.
19. *Ibid.*, II, 122. The "points" refer to the preparation of the meditation of the preceding evening.
20. It is not possible in the space of this article for us to insist on the delicate pedagogy which has the "beginner" pass to the state of "spiritual adult."
21. *Fontes Narrativi*, II, 123.

22. *Epist. Ignat.,* II, 234.

23. *Const.* P. IV, c. 4 B.

24. *Ibid.,* VI, c. 3, n. 1.

25. *Epist. Ignat.,* XII, 652.

26. *Ibid.,* I, 687–88.

27. *Ibid.,* I, 255.

28. It is in this sense that we can speak of a "practical" prayer which orientates us towards the future, that is, to the Kingdom to be raised, and therefore disposes us to activity.

29. *Epist. Ignat.,* I, 124.

30. *Ibid.,* I, 339.

31. *Ibid.,* I, 340.

32. *Ibid.,* I, 514.

33. *Const.* P. X, n. 3.

34. *Epist. Ignat.,* I, 96–97, *et passim.*

35. *Spiritual Exercises,* n. 23.

36. *Epist. Ignat.,* I, 339; *ibid.,* II, 236, 234.

37. *Ibid.,* I, 340.

38. *Spiritual Exercises,* n. 237.

39. *Epist. Ignat.,* XII, 222; *ibid.,* I, 100, *et passim.*

40. *Spiritual Exercises,* n. 39.

41. *General Examen,* c. 4, n. 46: "to seek in the Lord their greater abnegation and continual mortification *in all things possible."*

42. *Spiritual Exercises,* n. 351, sixth rule for scruples.

43. *Const.* P. III, c. 1, n. 22.

44. *Fontes Narrativi,* I, 677: "The Father added that out of a hundred persons who give themselves to long prayers and to long mortifications, the greater number usually fall into great embarrassment, and especially, he insisted, into stubbornness of judgment. Thus he placed the whole foundation (of the spiritual life) in mortification and abnegation of the will."

45. *Epist. Ignat.,* I, 627.

46. *Ibid.,* I, 514.

47. *Fontes Narrativi,* I, 138.

48. *Ibid.,* II, 315–16.

49. MHSI, *Const.,* I, 282.

50. *Fontes Narrativi,* II, 240. "For he often contemplated the Divine Persons and the whole of the Trinity and the Divine Essence by means of a brilliant light and a spiritual representation. That is why his prayer or contemplation was not multiple."

51. MHSI, *Nadal,* IV, 651–52.

52. This last sentence does not appear in MHSI following the preceding text, where it belonged. It is found in M. Nicolau, *J. Nadal,* 256. Not knowing it, Father Verny, in his study *In Actione Contem-*

plativus (Revue d'Ascétique et de Mystique, 1950, 60–61), is led to interpret Nadal's text as though he wished to speak of two distinct privileges, that of being elevated to the contemplation of the Trinity and that of finding God in all things, the first being particular to St. Ignatius and the second extending to the whole Society. Father Verny therefore translates the rather vague formula of Nadal, *tum illud praeterea ut,* as "but he had knowledge of another [privilege] as well." I have kept the ambiguity (and the heaviness) of Nadal by saying merely, "to this was added that." At any rate, the *quod privilegium* can only refer to the *magno privilegio* designating precisely the contemplation of the Trinity; the formula of conclusion, *haec cum ita sint,* would remove, if necessary, the final doubts. The text being important, these explanations are not altogether useless. What we must retain of the distinction made by Father Verny is that St. Ignatius lived *mystically* that which could and should be lived, even without mystical favors, by every soul who prays and acts in the faith.

ST. IGNATIUS AND THE GREATER GLORY OF GOD

1. If it is true that no Ignatian text gives us a carefully worded definition of the "glory of God," it is not less true that every work of St. Ignatius speaks of it and that it will be difficult to find a single page in which there is not a call to work for it. Because we must limit ourselves, we have chosen to follow the theme of the *glory* through the development of the Exercises, being satisfied with illustrating it as we go with commentaries taken from other works of Ignatius. Some of these works would, however, merit a special study. This is especially true of the Constitutions, an unexcelled monument of the mysticism of the glory of God. The few passages which we quote as examples in the third part of this article evidently will not suffice to give us a complete idea of it.

2. *Génesis de los Ejercicios,* AHSI, 1941, 32.

3. MHSI, *Epist. Ignat.,* II, 84; *ibid.,* I, 659.

4. *St. Ignatius' Own Story,* n. 28.

5. *Ibid.,* n. 29

6. *Ibid.,* n. 11.

7. Ribadeneira, *Vida de San Ignacio,* V, Part 1, 325.

8. It appears only once, in the entry for March 8: "Making an effort to be satisfied with all, praying that, if it be equal glory to God, He do not visit me with tears." (MHSI, *Journal,* 121) The word "service" is found only twice, a surprising rarity when we think of the frequent occurrence of these words in all other writings of the saint. On the other hand, it is interesting to note that the word "love," which St.

Ignatius used in other respects with such discretion constantly recurs in these pages, which were written strictly for his own personal use.

9. MHSI, *Journal,* 120.

10. *Ibid.,* 112–13.

11. *Ibid.,* 127.

12. *Epist. Ignat.,* I, 496.

13. *Ibid.,* I, 503. Cf. *Constitutions* P. V., c. 1, n. 4: "Thus considering one another they will grow in devotion and praise God our Lord, Whom each one should try to recognize in another, as in His image."

14. *Epist. Ignat.,* I, 508.

15. For convenience in the exposition, as well as to follow the actual order of the Exercises, we have begun with the *Foundation* (following the theme of creation to its conclusion in the *contemplation for obtaining love*). We should not forget, however, that the Kingdom is first, both in the order of publication and in the spiritual experience of St. Ignatius. It is the fruit of his first meetings with Christ, at the time of his conversion at Loyola and at Manresa. On this point, see O. Manare, *Exhortations sur l'insitut de la Compagnie de Jesus.* (The work was first published at Brussels in 1912, but Manare is one of the fathers of the early years and well acquainted with St. Ignatius.) We read on page 344: "From the first days of his conversion, during his retreat at Montserrat and in the solitude [of Manresa], he gave himself to two exercises especially: the *Two Standards* and the *Kingdom,* which prepared him for the war against the infernal enemy and against the world." See also the testimony of Nadal: "Exhortation in Spain, 1554," in *Fontes Narrativi,* I, 305–306.

16. In fact, the word has already appeared three times [16] and [78], but in marginal notes which were intended especially for the director to guide the retreatant and which belong to a later redaction than the contemplation of the Kingdom itself.

17. *St. Ignatius' Own Story,* nn. 51–52. This kind of imaginative "representation" of the Passion is relatively rare in the spiritual experience of St. Ignatius. He himself remarks that "it was not a vision like the others." In fact, it is usually the glorious Christ, or what comes to the same thing, the Eucharistic Christ, Whom St. Ignatius is called to contemplate, the Christ "like a sun." A significant detail—the memory which he is anxious to carry away from the Mount of Olives is not that of the agony of our Lord, but that of His ascension. See *Ibid.,* n. 48.

18. *Epist. Ignat.,* I, 124.

19. Cf. P. Tacchi Venturi, *Storia della Compagnia di Gesù in Italia,* I, Part 2, 1950, 43–44.

20. MHSI, *Const.* P. I, 5. Quite another article would be needed to explain this clause of the Deliberation of 1539 and of the Third

Degree of Humility in the Exercises: "with equal glory to the Divine Majesty." What is essential here is not a theoretical distinction between *equal glory* and *greater glory*. What the Exercises ask, above all, is that the soul desire poverty with Christ poor "if the service and praise of His Divine Majesty should be equal or greater. [168] Neither is there here a question of a rule for choosing a way of acting or of living, but of a preparation of the soul, which is trying to conform itself, its tastes, and its desires to God's will. The choice will come only later, in the election, and it will be less the result of a rational reflection than an adherence to the divine will made known by the Spirit. Then the soul will be able to hesitate no longer; it will know to what the greater glory of God is calling it. The movement is the same in the Deliberation on obedience of 1539, which is a commentary in act of the Third Degree of Humility and the Election as they are presented in the Exercises.

21. *St. Ignatius' Own Story*, n. 96.

22. MHSI, *Fontes Narrativi*, I, 8–10.

23. MHSI, *Nadal*, IV, 678.

24. L. Richeome, S. J., *La Sacrée Vierge Marie au pied de la Croix*, quoted in *Christus*, No. 3, 110.

25. This, even in the Exercises, is one of the rare instances where we find the precise formula for "God's greater glory." It is quite characteristic of St. Ignatius, for he never gives an exposition on the whole of what he understands by "God's glory." He is satisfied when occasion offers, to give examples and practical applications. Here the expression does not deal with the duty of almsgiving in general, but with the "manner" of distributing alms.

In this, St. Ignatius has an illustrious predecessor. The motto in which we often see a résumé of Benedictine spirituality is also encountered in connection with a detail that is as secondary and as prosaic as possible. In Chapter 57 of his Rule, St. Benedict asks that all merchandise manufactured by the monks always be sold at a little less than that produced by seculars, *ut in omnibus glorificetur Deus.*" (Cf. 1 Pet. 4:11)

26. *Const.* P. X, n. 2

27. MHSI, *Fontes Narrativi*, I, 356.

28. *Const.* P. VIII, c. 7, n. 1.

29. *Ibid.*, P. IV, c. 17, n. 8. Similar examples are to be found in *Const.* P. III, c. 1, n. 9; *ibid.*, c. 2, n. 7; *ibid.*, P. IV, c. 4, n. 6.

30. *Fontes Narrativi*, II, 187 (Exhortation at Alcalá, 1561).

31. There is not the same difficulty in translating these comparatives, *magis, major gloria*, into English as in French.

32. *Epist. Ignat.*, I, 101.

33. *Epist. Ignat.*, I, 172, Cf. *Const.* P. III, c. 1, n. 22.

34. MHSI, *Fontes Narrativi*, II, 203.
35. *Ibid.*, II, 137.
36. *Ibid.*, II, 5 (Exhortation at the Roman College in 1557).
37. *Ibid.*, II, 188 (Exhortation at Alcalá, 1561).
38. *Ibid.*, II, 157 (Exhortation at Coimbra, 1561).
39. Nadal, *Scholia in Const.*, 279.
40. *Const.* P. VII, c. 2, n. 1, D.

THE SERVICE AND LOVE OF GOD

1. The formula is untranslatable: The Creator envelops the creature with His love to incite him to praise and love his Creator; He thus draws it to himself. The formula of Jeremias quoted above, equally untranslatable, ought to have the same meaning: By My everlasting love for you I have drawn you to serve Me through love. (Jer. 31:3)

CHRIST IN THE SPIRITUAL EXERCISES OF
ST. IGNATIUS

1. The notes refer to several series of Ignatian texts:
   (1) The *Autobiography*, or recollections recounted by St. Ignatius in the last years of his life and reported by Father Gonzales de Cámara. The text is known under the title *Récit du Pelerin*, which Father Thibaut gave it in his French translation (Louvain, 1922). [An English version has appeared under the title *St. Ignatius' Own Story*, by William J. Young, S.J. published by the Henry Regnery Company (Chicago, 1956)—Translator] We will note the reference by a number in brackets, the number of the paragraph quoted, since all the edition—Spanish, French, and English—follow the same numbering. Quotations will be from the English version cited, which is based on the original Spanish.
   (2) The Spiritual Exercises are quoted according to the numeration adopted in 1928 by Father Codina and followed later in all editions and translations.
   (3) For the *Spiritual Journal*, the *Letters*, and the *Constitutions*, which have not yet been translated, we refer to the Spanish manual edition of the *Obras Completas de San Ignacio* (Madrid, 1952), which is more accessible than the collection of the *Monumenta Historica Societatis Iesu* (MHSI).
2. *Exercises*, 315.
3. P. de Leturia, *Génesis de los Ejercicios*, AHSI (1941), 14.
4. P. Rouquette, *Saint Ignace de Loyola et les origines des Jésuites* (ed. by Albin Michel, Paris, 1944), 14.
5. MHSI, *Chron. Pol.*, I, 20.

6. *Exercises,* 23.

7. H. Rahner, *Saint Ignace de Loyola et la genèse des Exercices* (ed. by de l'Apostolat de la Prière, Toulouse, 1948), 69. The author gives "things concerning learning" an interpretation different from ours. For him it is a question of speculative theology.

8. F. Sacchini, in the *Proemium* de *l'Historia Societatis Jesu de Nicholas Orlandini* (Cologne, 1721) 2.

9. P. de Leturia, *loc. cit.,* 56.

10. *Ibid.*

11. Ignatius also said "the eyes of his spirit." [30]

12. P. Rouquette, *op. cit.,* 16.

13. J. Brodrick, *Origin of the Jesuits* (1947) 26.

14. The Syrian Christians who served in the convent of Mont Sion were called "belted Christians" because of the belt they wore.

15. *Exercises,* 142–46.

16. H. Rahner. Cf. *infra,* 50.

17. *Obras Completas,* 667.

18. MHSI, *Fontes Narrativi,* II, 595 ff.

19. *Spiritual Journal, Obras Completas,* 299.

20. MHSI, *Fontes Narrativi,* II, 133.

21. MHSI, *Scripta,* I, 715.

22. H. Rahner. Cf. *infra,* 56.

23. *Exercises,* 116.

24. *OC* 669.

25. *OC* 725.

26. *OC* 725.

27. *OC* 653.

28. *OC* 748.

29. *OC* 847.

30. *OC* 669.

31. *Constitutiones,* Proemium, 2; *ibid.,* Part IV, c. 3, n. 2 D. *OC* 400, 447, 511.

32. *Exercises,* 353–55. Cf. *OC* 778.

33. *OC* 847.

34. *Exercises,* 136, 138, 143.

35. *OC* 747 ff.

36. *Exercises,* 145. Cf. *OC* 658.

37. *OC* 703. In the original text, it seems sufficiently clear from the context that the expression quoted here is attributed to Christ.

38. *Exercises,* 71.

39 *Exercises,* 98. Cf. *OC* 689.

40. *OC* 704. See preceding passage and the remark in Note 37.

41. *Exercises,* 95.

42. *Const.* P. V, c. 3, n. 3, 6.

43. *OC* 731.

44. *Ibid.*

45. *OC* 681 ff.

46. *OC* 751.

47. *OC* 748.

48. *OC* 681.

49. *Exercises,* 15.

50. *OC* 725, Cf. *OC* 681.

51. *Exercises,* 95.

52. *OC* 710.

53. *Exercises,* 365. Cf. *OC* 758.

54. *OC* 729.

55. *OC* 755 ff.

56. *OC* 703.

57. *Ibid.*

58. *OC* 747.

59. *OC* 772.

60. *Const.* P. IX, c. 2, n. 1; *ibid.,* P. X, c. 2 *et passim.* Cf. *OC* 725, 729, 948. D. 139; 146, *et passim.*

61. *Spiritual Journal, OC* 301.

62. *Exercises,* 365. Cf. *OC* 756.

63. We should perhaps complete the assertion of Père de Guibert, who notes "the absence [in the *Spiritual Journal* of St. Ignatious] of what we might call the nuptial aspect of the mystical union. Nowhere does God or Christ appear as the Spouse of the soul. . . . There is no spiritual marriage, no transforming union, founding the life of the soul on that of God, causing our own life to disappear in that of Christ living in us," but "a mysticism of service and of religion, completely bathed in love." (J. de Guibert, *Mystique ignatienne,* in *Revue d'Ascétique et de Mystique* [1938], 120, a study published separately under the title *Saint Ignace Mystique* by the Apostolat de la Prière [Toulouse, 1950]. All that is quite correct if we add that at the basis of this mysticism of service, explaining it and supporting it, there is the mystery of the union of Christ with His Church.

64. *Spiritual Journal, OC* 285, 286, 287, 290 *et passim,* 291, 299, 300, 301, 302, 308.

65. J. de Guibert, *loc. cit.,* 125.

66. *Spiritual Journal, OC* 304.

67. J. de Guibert, *loc. cit.,* 113.

68. *Spiritual Journal, OC* 303. St. Ignatius here speaks as he usually does: "Jesus," meaning Christ in that He is man.

69. *Ibid.,* 298, 299, 300, 303, 305, 321 (Cf. 319: he sees the divine essence under the form of a sphere), 291, 299.

70. *Exercises,* 109.

71. *OC* 270.

72. *Exercises*, 196.

73. *OC* 681.

74. MHSI, *Exercitia*, 562.

75. From the point of view of mystical experience, Father Brodrick makes a comparable remark: "Put beside St. John of the Cross or St. Teresa or Mother Mary of the Incarnation, he seems at first sight like a sparrow among nightingales; but deeper understanding reveals him as belonging to their company." (J. Brodrick, *Origin of the Jesuits*, 17)

CONTEMPLATION OF THE MYSTERIES OF CHRIST

1. *St. Ignatius' Own Story*, n. 11.

2. The editors of the *Obras Completas* think that the idea of transcribing the words of the Gospel in inks of different colors came to St. Ignatius from *The Life of Christ*, by Ludolph the Carthusian, which had been done in the vernacular by Fray Ambrosio Montesino and which could have been put into Ignatius' hands at Loyola.

3. In 1551, St. Ignatius confided to Father Baldwin Delange that at the time of his conversion, he used an illustrated Book of Hours. In it was a picture of our Lady which reminded him of one of his relatives and interfered with his prayer. MHSI, *Scripta*, II, 434–35.

4. *St. Ignatius' Own Story*, n. 20.

5. *Ibid.*, n. 29.

6. *Ibid.*

7. MHSI, *Exercitia spiritualia et directoria*, 1048–49. This interpretation is not imperative, and a number of annotators of the *Directory* do not accept it, thinking that it contradicts the "form" given by St. Ignatius. Cf. the remarks of Father Quadrantini on p. 1084.

8. *Comentario y explanación de los Ejercicios espirituales de S. Ignacio de Loyola* (Barcelona, 1945), 178.

9. MHSI, Nadal, *Epistolae*, IV, 682.

10. *Adnotationes et meditationes in Evangelia* (Antwerp, 1594), 436–37.

11. *Op. cit.*, 178.

12. Cf. Directory of Polanco, n. 68, MHSI, *Exercitia spiritualia et directoria*, 812–13.

13. *Op. cit.*, 179.

14. Directory of Polanco, n. 68, in *op. cit.*, 812.

15. *Ibid.*, n. 19, 802.

16. *Adnotationes et meditationes in Evangelia.*

17 *El Evangelio meditado* ed. by Cervos, Madrid, 1912 [meditations on the Gospel selections for the proper of the season] *Meditaciones*

sobre los Evangelios de las fiestas de los santos (ed. by J. March, Barcelona, 1925).

18. J. Nadal, *Adnotationes,* 224.

TRUE LOVE FOR OUR LADY

1. *Problèmes de vie spirituelle,* c. vii, 121.
2. Italics ours.
3. One might question the religious and pedagogic value of a story such as this, quoted as an "example" in a Marian manual for the use of children:

"A few years ago a young man of 17, rosary in hand, climbed the slope which ascends from the town of Honfleur to the shrine of Notre Dame de Grâce, and entered the church on his knees.

He thus advanced to the foot of the statue, where he remained a long time prostrate. Questioned by a priest who found him there, he answered: "You have certainly heard of the accident which happened at sea the day before yesterday. Out of three young men, two were lost; only one was saved. I am the survivor. My two friends had taken the examination for the bachelor's degree together with me the day before. Together we were celebrating our success, and to end the day we decided, in spite of the rolling sea, on a boat party. We sang and joked. One of my friends tossed out a few light words, and soon jokes about the Blessed Virgin were mixed in the conversation. I protested. "My friends," I said, "let us laugh and joke, but let us respect the Blessed Virgin!" My words had little effect. But two or three stronger waves soon came to terrify us, and soon our little boat capsized. None of us could swim. My two friends were lost. I alone was saved, and I attribute my life to Mary, whom I had just defended. I am coming on my knees to thank her, for death would have found me very ill prepared."

4. *Le Christ, Marie et l'Eglise* (1952), 83.
5. Sermon for Sunday within the Octave of the Assumption, 1–2, PL, 183, 429–430, quoted by Congar, *op. cit.,* 83–84.
6. Congar, *op. cit.,* 84.
7. *Actes de Pie X* (ed. by B. P.), I, 79–81.
8. *La Mère virginale du Sauveur* (Desclée de Brouwer, 1954), 204.

BORN OF THE VIRGIN MARY

1. We shall speak henceforth of "chastity" rather than virginity. Virginity designates a fact. We are thinking here of chastity outside

marriage, which consists in the voluntary abstention from sexual relations and from sexual pleasure both in fact and desire. It goes without saying that there is a chastity in marriage which consists not in abstention from sexual relations, but in their disciplined use.

2. By divine vocation and free human choice. The two movements, that of the divine will and that of human liberty, are not incompatible. Liberty attains its perfection when it meets and loves God's preventing grace. This does not imply that this active love of a vocation, which God proposes without imposing, is not difficult or even painful. This difficulty and pain are loved. We should mistrust a vocation to chastity which would be a simple absence of difficulties and more still, a pseudo vocation which betrays a repugnance more or less pathological to sexual realities. Even from the simply human point of view, voluntary chastity has an undeniable grandeur and beauty because it is a victory over self and because it is an effort at spiritualization. We should not, however, make of it a sport or an aestheticism. This would be the place to recall that playing the role of the angel might risk playing that of the beast. Christian chastity is not a pelagian victory, nor is it a human performance. It is an imitation of Christ, an adherence to His state of virginity, an active adoration of the creative act of the Eternal Word "by Whom all was made and without Whom nothing was made that was made."

SOME THOUGHTS ON PRAYER AND ACTION

1. *Apostolat et vie intérieur,* I, col. 784–86.

2. *Revue d'Ascétique et de Mystique* (January-March, 1948), *l'Oraison diffuse.*

3. *The Soul of the Apostolate.*

4. *La doctrine spirituelle* (ed. by Pattier), V, Principe, Arat. 3, c. ii, 308.

5. Cf. Garrigou-Lagrange, O. P., *Perfection chrétienne et contemplation,* I, c. iii; II, c. vi, Art. 5, 662; Appendix IV.

6. *La spiritualité de la Compagnie de Jésus,* pp. 559–60. Quoted especially are St. Robert Bellarmine, Lallemand, Baiole, Surin, and nearer our times, Fathers de la Taille and Peeters.

7. The teaching explained by M. Lochet recalls that of Père Surin. Cf. *Catéchisme spirituel,* VII *partie,* c. viii.

8. Cf. the article by Mme. Daniélou in Number 6 of *Christus.* This "virtual prayer" is called upon in *La religion personelle:* "Many are eager to please Jesus Christ, to imitate Him, to work for Him, to conform themselves to His suffering life and His redemption. . . . An anxious fear of not serving well, of not doing enough; a cruel and dear compunction, bitterness at the sight of one's own wretchedness,

interior humiliation which abases without discouraging, which mortifies self-esteem, without suggesting either desertion or despair. Such
prayer feels itself heard, such movement is distinctly perceived as
desirable, as a sacrifice even before it is accomplished; such reproach
is related without illuminism, but without fear of error, to the voice
of the inner Master, a voice which resembles no other." (p. 171)

9. *Catéchisme spirituel,* VII *partie,* c. viii.

10. We have undertaken to write a book on this subject: *La doctrine
spirituelle des hommes d'action* (Spes).

11. We assume that the reader has a theological knowledge of the
Gifts of the Holy Spirit; we cannot here repeat an explanation.

12. Cf. J. de Guibert, S.J., *Theologia spiritualis* (1938), n. 137, 128;
n. 427, 377.

13. We think that the passive purifications take place as much in
action as in prayer.

14. *Mélanges théologiques (La loi d'amour),* 360. The question of
passive purifications is treated at length by St. John of the Cross in his
Ascent of Mount Carmel. We assume that the reader has read this
book.

15. St. John of the Cross, *Oeuvres* (ed. by de Seuil), 484–510; "The
Night of the Senses"; 550–55, "The Dark Night of the Soul."

16. R. Garrigou-Lagrange, O.P., *Perfection chrétienne et contemplation,* I, 186.

THE CYCLE OF ACTIVITY AND PRAYER

1. Nadal was named visitor by Ignatius, Laynez, and Borgia in succession, with full power to promulgate the *Constitutions* and to bring
the customs of the various provinces into uniformity. From 1553
until 1568, he traveled through Spain, Portugal, Germany, Austria,
northern Italy, France, Belgium, and Bohemia.

2. This folio volume of more than 600 pages contains commentaries and meditations on all the gospels of the season. The work was
composed by Nadal during the last years of his life, and appeared at
Antwerp in 1594, fourteen years after his death.

3. All numbers in parenthesis, except those in the last section of
this essay, refer to pages of *Annotationes et Meditationes in Evangelia.*

4. Nadal said of the holy women, for example: "Their hearts were
surrounded with the light of the resurrection" (p. 423); and of the
Blessed Virgin: "She was aware that she was entirely surrounded
by the immense love of the Holy Spirit" (p. 419); and of all of us:
"The infinite goodness of God penetrates and fills our hearts, if we
co-operate with the movement and the illumination of the Holy
Spirit" (p. 323).

5. The following is a more theoretical description of this first key word: *"Spiritu:* that is to say, as a thing the source of which is God. It is He who directs and governs the Society, I do not say by direct revelations, but by the Holy Spirit and His Grace. By Him He moves, governs and vivifies the whole body of the Church by communicating to it His gifts and various graces according to the diverse needs of its members. And He does so sweetly, in accord with natural light and concrete experience by His gifts and His virtue. By these means God communicates Himself to us, and is the source of everything." (Quoted according to M. Nicolau, *Jerónimo Nadal, Obras y Doctrinas espirituales* (Madrid, 1949), 307.

6. "Outwardly Jesus spoke to her with His lips and at the same time inwardly in her heart spiritually." (p 213)

7. *"Corde:* that is, He does not learn to act in a purely speculative way. It is not enough to understand what the Lord commands us and counsels us to do. We ought to set our wills to carrying it into action." "When I say *heart,* I do not mean merely the natural organ, but that which actually proceeds from it—charity and the affective love of God. There is the true heart. I desire that you all have it in order to draw from it many acts of love for the Lord, so that we shall be attached to Him and united to Him. And this union ought to extend to all our occupations, whether it be study, work in the kitchen, preaching, hearing confessions. . . ." Quoted in Nicolau, *op. cit.,* 306, and Nicolau, *Pláticas espirituales del P. J. Nadal en Coimbra* (Granada, 1945), 44.

8. A few texts chosen from a thousand will help us to catch the thought of Nadal: "The parable of the sower teaches us first of all not to turn a deaf ear to divine inspiration, which is the word of God and the divine seed. Otherwise, we do not understand with the heart *(corde non intelligant)*. . . . But, on the other hand, it is not enough to understand with the heart, as long as one does not give himself eagerly to obedience." (pp. 69–70) "Take care that your faith is not merely speculative, without any repercussion in your heart. Try hard to make it practical, to inflame your heart with love for God and your neighbor." (p. 98) "I [Christ] am the peace of your heart. And you will find Me—that is, I Myself will be the strength in your heart that will carry you on to action—if you direct all your actions towards perfection through Me." (p. 514)

9. *"Practice:* that is, the desire of the will *(affectus)* which is expressed in our actions, although it is and ought to be practical in itself, should not be dealt with in a speculative way. Contemplatives who do not devote themselves to the active life *(ad praxim)* are content with the good desire. They leave to others the care of putting the desire to work while helping them with the intercession of their

prayers to God. But we must add to it the effective desire *(inclinatio efficax)* of going forward ourselves to the practical execution of the desire. . . . And besides, we ought to try to make practical all the activities of the intelligence and the will, even when they do not seem to be so." (Nicolau, *J. Nadal,* 307)

10. "We must note," says Nadal, "that the Society has received the grace of a special form of prayer, which is not common to all. It should, therefore, give itself up to prayer and the drawing of the Spirit, so as to conceive in this prayer an unquenchable thirst of helping the neighbor. No matter how good prayer is in itself, if it lacks this desire, it will be a danger for the Society." (MHSI, *Fontes Narrativi,* II, 8) Let us never lose sight of the fact that Nadal begins with the concrete experience of a man to whom God confided a "special" *(specialis, peculiaris)* grace. An unswerving fidelity to the divine call permitted Ignatius to discern the exact scope of the grace of *his* vocation. Nadal is not seeking to establish what is the most perfect prayer, absolutely speaking, but rather what is the perfect prayer for the followers of Ignatius. Other Orders have received other graces as their portion, for which we can and should praise the Lord, Who distributes His gifts with unequaled liberality. But only the graces proper to the vocation of Ignatius can and should orientate the life of his sons. If the prayer of the Jesuit does not lead to zeal for souls and to the direct apostolate, it is foreign to his Institute and a danger, even when it is good in itself.

11. Nicolau, *Pláticas,* 190–92.

12. Nicolau, *J. Nadal,* 476 ff., 513 ff.; *Pláticas,* 180; MHSI, *Nadal,* IV, 673, 676.

13. The following passage from Nadal is decisive on this point: "The beginning and end of prayer is love. That is, it tends towards the greater glory of God when it proceeds from the fullness of charity. The result is that I wish through prayer what I ask and seek to obtain for the purpose of serving God more according to the vocation and Institute of the Society. It is thus that the prayer of the Society favors activity." (Nicolau, *J. Nadal,* 477)

14. Nicolau, *J. Nadal,* 479; *Pláticas,* 121, 188, 190; *J. Nadal,* 517.

15. "We must bear in mind that the spirit is weakened by labor. It is necessary, therefore, frequently to return to prayer, and to complete a circular movement which moves from prayer to activity and from activity to prayer." (Nicolau, *J. Nadal,* 511)

16. In *Examen Annotationes,* published in MHSI, *Nadal,* IV, 650.

17. Two passages will illustrate Nadal's position: (1) "This was the practice of the Blessed Father Ignatius: Do you wish to help yourselves, do you wish to make progress? Help the neighbor. How? In this way: suppose you are going to preach; pray first, call upon

God, study, assimilate all that, and go to your duty. You will advance and receive new graces. When you return to prayer, you will feel an even greater drawing to prayer, and so on. In this way the circle is closed. Again you will be drawn with greater attraction to preaching." (2) "This is what I usually call the circle of occupations in the Society. If you are busy with the neighbor and God's service in your ministry, or in any other duty at all, God will help you later more efficaciously in your prayer. And this more efficacious help from God will in its turn assist you in busying yourself with the neighbor with greater courage and spiritual profit." (Nicolau, *J. Nadal*, 324–25)

18. Nicolau, *J. Nadal*, 145.

19. The numbers in parentheses in this last section of the essay refer to pages of *Orationis Observationes*, or *Spiritual Journal*, of Nadal, in MHSI, *Nadal*, IV.

20. The following are Nadal's expressions: *"Est spiritus Societatis claritas quaedam occupans ac dirigens." "In Incarnatione, claritas de caelo descendens atque occupans, ac virtus hominibus indita." "Nativitas Christi, egressus gratiae ad operationem. Unde oratio Societatis, ex qua extensio ad ministeria."*

21. In Nadal's text, the word is *sacrificio*.

APOSTOLIC PRAYER

1. Luke 18:10.
2. 1 Thes. 5:17–18.
3. Cf. Matt. 26:41; Jam. 5:13.
4. Matt. 6:7.
5. Rom. 8:26.
6. Ps. 118:55; 26:7; 118:62; 133:2.
7. Luke 6:12.
8. Luke 22:39.
9. Matt. 25:6.
10. Eph. 5:14.
11. Heb. 10:7.

DISCERNMENT OF SPIRITS AND SPIRITUAL DIRECTION

1. Our readers know that the first visions which St. Ignatius had at the hospital were deceits of the demon. (Cf. *Christus*, No. 4, *passim*) For his part, St. John of the Cross asserts in several places that it is very difficult to unmask the demon. "It is often necessary," he writes, "that the person be very spiritual to recognize him [the demon]. The devil does that the better to cover his tracks, knowing very well at times, how to draw tears, touching the feelings which he gives, in

order to pour into the soul the affections he wishes. But he always incites the will to *esteem* these interior communications, and to make much of them, so that the soul will give itself to and to be busy with what is not virtue, but rather the occasion of losing what it has." (*Ascent,* II, 29)

2. Péguy, *Le Mystère de la Charité de Jeanne d'Arc* (ed. by de la Pléiade), 149. Péguy calls this intervention of the demon "a wonderful canalization . . . an incredible turning aside, a return, a winding canalization, a prodigious diversion."

MOVEMENTS OF THE SPIRIT

1. Certain texts in the *Exercises* lead us to distinguish clearly between two aspects of our spiritual experience: "If the exercitant is not affected by any spiritual experiences, such as consolations or desolations, *or* if he is not moved by different spirits . . . ." [6]; "when enough light and understanding are derived through experience of desolations and consolations *and* discernment of diverse spirits . . . ." [176].

2. *St. Ignatius' Own Story,* nn. 6–10.

3. We insist here on the reality of the feelings experienced and not on their nature or their diversity. This latter point belongs to the experience of the discernment of spirits, which was treated in the preceding articles.

4. The text reads: *se le confirmaron.*

5. The *Autograph Directory* of St. Ignatius speaks of "consolation in its different elements, such as interior peace, joy, hope, faith, love, tears and elevation of soul, which are all gifts of the Holy Spirit." (MHSI, *Exercitia,* 780)

6. In the course of the working out of the *Directories,* the verb *persentiscere,* adopted by the Vulgate to translate the verb *sentir* used in No. 184, deserves this word of appreciation from Father Gonzalez Davila, one of the revisors who was most sensitive to the excesses of the *Alumbrados:* "Many find fault with this word. If it is explained in accordance with sound doctrine, it offers no danger. But since the *Illuminati* and the *Derelecti* of Spain abuse this expression, I would explain the thought of Father Ignatius rather than make use of this word without some distinction." (MHSI, *Exercitia,* 901) We know, moreover, how Nadal had to contend with certain adversaries of the *Exercises,* who thought they found in them dangerous traces of Illuminism.

7. Letter of June 18, 1536, to Teresa Rejadell. (MHSI, *Epist. Ignat.,* I, 105)

8. MHSI, *Const.* I, 282.

9. Letter quoted in *ibid.*

10. We have no wish to discuss here the relations between the written law and the inner inspirations of the Spirit. We quote only this sentence, in which St. Ignatius summarizes all his thought on this point: "It often happens that the Lord moves us. . . . And this thought which is His cannot but have us conform to the commandments of God, to the precepts of the Church, to obedience to our superiors, filling us with a complete humility, because in all things there is the same Divine Spirit." (MHSI, *Epist. Ignat.,* I, 105)

11. MHSI, *Exercitia,* 781.

12. Bérulle, *Opuscules de piété* (Aubier, 1944), 558.

13. MHSI, *Exercitia,* 781.

14. MHSI, *Mon. Nadal,* IV, 845.

15. It is clear that these two cases are not opposed. More frequently, the "second time" in the experience of inner movements and the third, in the use of the natural faculties enlightened by grace, call for each other and complement each other. St. Ignatius himself gives us a luminous example in his *Journal.* But we have the right, according to the *Exercises,* to distinguish them, the better to understand them.

16. J. de Guibert, *Histoire de la Spiritualité de la Compagnie de Jésus* (Rome, 1953), 115–16.

17. It is possible that certain minimizing interpretations of the word *confirmar,* used in Number 183 of the *Exercises,* are due to the influence of the *Vulgate,* which translates it by the word *stabilire.* But the meaning of Ignatius seems to us to be attested by too many other uses to permit us to reduce this *confirmation* to the strengthening of the will or the facility of execution, although these last elements constitute a part of the grace asked by St. Ignatius.

18. *St. Ignatius' Own Story,* n. 99. The original of this last part of the *Story* is written in Italian, but it keeps the Latin for the final formula of this sentence, which gives it a very significant stress.

19. "It is even such a supplication, ardent, sometimes anguished, almost impatient to obtain this divine confirmation which takes up the larger part of the notes of these forty days." (J. de Guibert, *op. cit.,* 40) It will suffice to transcribe here this astonishing prayer in which St. Ignatius expresses his desire: "Thereupon, while preparing the altar and vesting, this prayer came to me: 'Eternal Father, confirm me; Eternal Son, confirm me; Eternal Holy Spirit, confirm me; Holy Trinity, confirm me; my God, Who art one only God, confirm me.' With so great an outburst of devotion, of tears, repeating it so often, and feeling it so interiorly, and with the words, 'Eternal Father, will You not confirm me?' the impression was that He answered yes. And the same to the Son and the Holy Spirit." (*Spiritual Journal,* February 18)

20. MHSI, *Mon. Nadal,* IV, 669.
21. MHSI, *Epist. Ignat.,* II, 236.
22. *St. Ignatius' Own Story,* n. 34, n. 37, *et passim.*
23. MHSI, *Fontes Narrativi,* II, 327–28.
24. MHSI, *Const.* I, 53–54. There is question here of the first "experiment" imposed on the candidate for admission. Other experiments come later—service of the sick, begging, and so on—the purpose of which is always the same: to study how the soul is led by God, its leanings, its temptations, its inner struggles. It is on the movement of the Spirit in his soul that the candidate will be finally judged to be suitable to share the spiritual life of the Order he wishes to enter.
25. *Ibid.,* 12.
26. *Ibid.,* 10.

THE NIGHT AND THE LIGHT OF OBEDIENCE

1. MHSI, *Epist. Ignat.,* XII, 662.
2. In the first sketch of the important text of the *Constitutions* on obedience (Part VI, c. I, n. 1), it is said: "This holy obedience should *always and in all things be blind* in the will and in the judgment." (MHSI, *Const.* I, 217) The second redaction is more precise: Obedience, taking it in its three degrees (execution, will, and judgment), should be *"always and in everything perfect"*; only obedience of the judgment is blind. (*Ibid.,* II, 207–208, 522–53) It is this formula which appears in the definitive edition. In place of *con obediencia ciega,* the Latin translation has it *caeca quadam obedientia.* We know that this does not imply any attenuation in meaning. The preciseness which attaches blind obedience to obedience of the intellect alone is important. But it is not a matter of indifference to discover that the first and spontaneous expression of St. Ignatius asserts that all obedience is blind, even obedience of the will. It clearly indicates his tendency to consider only the attitude of him who obeys, in its ultimate perfection, to the point where one's own judgment "denies itself."
3. MHSI, *Epist. Ignat.,* III, 513.
4. The fact that, in his *Letter on Obedience,* St. Ignatius places blind obedience among the three means "which will greatly help to attain to the perfection of obedience of the judgment" should not make us think only of a method of exercise quickly felt as exceptional. If it is true that blind obedience is presented as a *means,* it is in the same way true that the eye of faith discerns behind the superior the Christ Whom we obey. The means, therefore, is not a mere discipline which we can afterwards disregard. It assures us of the reality to which it leads, and as such, it is also the end. Besides, in this same *Letter,* St.

Ignatius speaks of "the simplicity, so highly praised, of blind obedience," which clearly excludes the idea that this blind obedience is only a kind of school exercise.

5. MHSI, *Epist. Ignat.*, IV, 677.

6. Because the inferior is blind to the content of the command in the sense we indicate, the superior would in no way be justified for failing in his duty by not putting himself in the spiritual attitude which he requires of those who obey him and playing, so to speak, with their consciences. We are taking the point of view, exclusively, of the inferior who wishes to enter into the religious mystery of perfect obedience.

7. MHSI, *Mon. Fabri*, 284–86.

8. MHSI, *Epist. Ignat.*, I, 228.

9. MHSI, *Epist. Ignat.*, I, 556.

10. We know that St. Ignatius owes this comparison, *perinde ac cadaver*, to Franciscan tradition: "Take up this lifeless body," said St. Francis of Assisi, "and place it where you like. You will see that it will not resist you, that it will not murmur against the place where you have put it, and it will not object if someone places it elsewhere. If it is placed in a chair, it will not look aloft or below, and if it is clothed in purple, it will be only twice as livid. Such is the truly obedient man." (Thomas de Celano, *Vie de saint François d'Assise,* Ch. XII) Francis remains a poet, even in this macabre description. Ignatius, more temperate, retains only the "dead body which allows itself to be borne and to be handled in any way at all." This temperance is not without its value.

11. Nadal, *Schol. in Const.,* 120.

12. MHSI, *Epist. Ignat.,* XII, 660.

13. MHSI, *Fontes Narrativi,* II, 487.

14. *Ibid.,* I, 681.

15. Nadal, *Exhortation on Obedience,* quoted in Nicoleau, *J. Nadal,* 484.

16. MHSI, *Fontes Narrativi,* II, 482.

17. *Ibid.,* I, 596.

18. Nadal, *Pláticas en Coimbra,* 178.

19. *Ibid.,* 170.

20. Nadal, *Schol. in Const.,* 59.

21. *Obras espirituales,* III, 388–94.

22. *Ibid.,* 405.

23. Cf. *Christus,* No. 6, 172–94.

24. Nadal, quoted in Nicolau, *J. Nadal,* 402.

25. MHSI, *Epist. Ignat.,* XII, 664.

26. *Ibid.,* I, 557.

CONTINUAL MORTIFICATION

1. MHSI, *Fontes Narrativi*, I, 644. Gonzales de Cámara also reports this word of the saint to Nadal: "A quarter of an hour is enough for a man truly mortified to unite himself with God in prayer." (*Ibid.*, I, 676–77) The relation abnegation-prayer-union with God is worthy of a longer pause. However, the answer given to Nadal would of itself demand a place at the beginning of every study of the time of prayer in the Society, a study which evidently goes beyond the limits of this article. Cf. M. Giuliani, "Finding God in all Things," *Christus*, No. 6, 172 ff.

2. The *Examen*, although it constitutes a real part of the *Constitutions* of the Society of Jesus, is a whole sufficiently distinct, having a *raison d'être* of its own and its own particular form.

3. *Examen*, IV, nn. 44–46.

4. *Fontes Narrativi*, II, 10.

5. *St. Ignatius' Own Story*, n. 18.

6. *Constitutiones* P. VIII, c. 1, A.

7. *St. Ignatius' Own Story*, n. 52 Cf. D. Mollat, "Christ in the Spiritual Experience of St. Ignatius," *Christus*, No. 1, 32–34.

8. J. Nadal, quoted in *Christus*, No. 1, 92–94.

9. *Ibid.*

10. J. Nadal, quoted in M. Nicolau, *J. Nadal*, 480.

11. J. Nadal, quoted in *Christus*, No. 1, 93.

12. *Formula Instituti*, n. 4.

13. Cf. *Const. P. III*, c. 1, nn. 23, 27; P. IV, Proemium; P. V, c. 2, nn. 1, 2.

14. *Const.* P. III, c. 1, n. 23. Cf. M. Giuliani, "Night and Light of Obedience," *Christus*, No. 7, 349 ff.

15. MHSI, *Epist. Ignat.*, III, 501.

16. P. Ribadeneira, *Vida de S. Ignacio de Loyola*, V, 1.

17. MHSI, *Epist. Ignat.*, I, 506–507. Cf. *ibid.*, II, 234 ff.

18. J. Nadal, *Pláticas en Coimbra*, 209.